Rooted in Love

A Testimony of God's Faithfulness

Elizabeth Wilson

Grace Reigns Publishing

Copyright © 2025 Elizabeth Wilson

All rights reserved. This book or parts thereof may not be reproduced in any form, stored in any retrieval system, or transmitted in any form by any means—electronic, mechanical, photocopy, recording, or otherwise—without prior written permission of the publisher, except as provided by United States of America copyright law and fair use. For permission requests, write to the publisher at the address below.

Grace Reigns Publishing
Rochester, New York
GraceReignsPublishing@gmail.com

Some of the content has been previously published as devotionals on the author's social media accounts.

Scripture quotations are taken from the King James Bible, public domain.

Cover by Elizabeth Wilson
Photo of the author in "Letter from the Author" by Daniel Pawley
Interior design and layout by Rachel L. Hall, WritelyDivided Editing and More

ISBN: 979-8-9853269-2-5 Softcover

Rooted in Love: A Testimony of God's Faithfulness / Elizabeth Wilson, 1st ed.

For my grandparents,

Marjorie, Randy, Ann and Fred,

and for anyone who has walked through

God's creation

and marveled at the works of His hand.

Contents

Letter from the Author	v
The Journey We Don't Expect	1
What to Do When We Don't Understand	17
What We Do While We Wait	37
What Our Disappointment Can Teach Us	63
When Our Faith Is Tested	79
Reluctant to Obey	101
Returning to Our Fortress	121
Redemption Over Resolution	137
A Light That Won't Go Out	157
Who We Are Now	169
Straightening Our Heart Posture	187
Redefining Beauty	201
God Sustains Us	217
When We Delight in God	225
A Time and a Season	237
The Comfort of Fellowship	255
The Joy We Don't Expect	269
Leaving a Legacy	295
Acknowledgments	317
Works Cited	319

Letter from the Author

Hello, friend,

I am honored to speak to you from these pages. I pray that you would experience God's presence and goodness in your life right now. Whatever the current condition of your faith may be, I pray the Lord would help you become rooted and grounded in His great love for you (Eph. 3:17-19).

This book was first inspired by a difficult season that I experienced in which God's enduring faithfulness brought healing and redemption. I started drawing trees in the Summer of 2022, and began writing this in 2023 because God compelled me to keep processing through writing. It began as a devotional which slowly morphed into a long personal testimony of God's work in my heart during that time. It contains truth that He strengthened for me in various stages of healing, because God was still teaching me while I worked on it.

The season which inspired this work has changed. Much has healed in my heart but I'll never be perfect and I will always need God. There is now a lot of peace and joy in areas of my life that didn't seem to contain any, but I still run to God daily and He wants me to.

God has been here with me, holding me, teaching me, and growing me. I will not be sharing all the details of this season with you, friend. I could never share them all or explain them properly. I'll share what God prompts me to share. If any of this sounds familiar to your situation, I encourage you to run to God.

"I will speak of the glorious honour of thy majesty, and of thy wondrous works" (Psalm 145:5). In these pages I am not saying anything new or different about Him, but I pray He uses it to speak to you and bless you.

Any and all glory for this project goes to God. He was and is the one directing me. I have written about the Lord, and such a task carries a weight of responsibility. With God's help and direction I have done my best to accurately communicate in these pages, but I encourage you to seek the truth, and seek God for yourself (1 Cor. 2:5, John 4:42).

We will talk about the gospel often because regardless of how long someone has believed, God's great love for us is perfectly demonstrated in the salvation which Jesus' death and resurrection brings. When we truly believe, we are planted in His care, and He grounds our roots in His love throughout our life.

I want to point out that no analogy I come up with can perfectly represent God. Furthermore, my own words may not reflect what you personally have been through in your life, nor can I hope to address every situation specifically. Please refer to the word of God for tried and tested truth to apply to your own circumstances.

Creating is part of me. He made me to see the beauty in His creation and praise Him for it. What a joy to scamper over hills and through mud, investigating all manner of greenery, decaying stumps, tufts of grass, moss and wildflowers. Standing still in the sunshine and breathing fresh air bathed in warm rays is like wrapping myself in the familiar song of all God's creation worshipping Him.

Having the chance to draw all these trees and meet with God out in His creation is something I'll always be thankful for. I'm not sure what the drawing season will look like in the future, but the trees are not going anywhere. My kids on the other hand are spinning tops of beautiful chaos that I adore and must shape and care for.

Each illustration varies due to inconsistent drawing sessions. Some were finished at home later. All of them reflect the imperfections of an artist who is gratefully forever learning and growing.

There are many more references to trees in the Bible and what they mean, but I don't have the capacity to research it all right now. I am centering this book more on what God specifically taught me through trees in this season of my life.

LETTER FROM THE AUTHOR

I'm not sure why I went through all that I experienced in the last couple years (only God knows) but I do feel called to write this and share it. It is a joy to do so and I pray God would do something good with the story.

Whatever you are going through, please know God loves you dearly and is ready to help. God bless you, friend.

Sincerely,
E.W.

~ o ~

Rooted in Love

Blessed is the man that trusteth in the Lord, and whose hope the Lord is. For he shall be as a tree planted by the waters, and that spreadeth out her roots by the river, and shall not see when heat cometh, but her leaf shall be green; and shall not be careful in the year of drought, neither shall cease from yielding fruit.

~Jeremiah 17:7-8

That Christ may dwell in your hearts by faith; that ye, being rooted and grounded in love, May be able to comprehend with all saints what is the breadth, and length, and depth, and height; And to know the love of Christ, which passeth knowledge, that ye might be filled with all the fulness of God.

~Ephesians 3:17-19

The Journey We Don't Expect

Sowing in Tears

> *"...Weeping may endure for a night, but joy cometh in the morning." (Psalm 30:5)*

> *"They that sow in tears shall reap in joy." (Psalm 126:5)*

Midway through the Summer of 2022 I was on a walk with my husband and daughter. While admiring a huge tree we often pass on our neighborhood route, God spoke to me the idea of drawing trees. I'd always wanted to try plein-air work (art that is done outdoors), but my fear of failure held me back. I was worried my attempts would be laughable. But I wanted to be brave.

This art adventure (which felt wildly brave) was driven by the consuming sadness I endured that season. A rending and tearing in my very soul. Sometimes we get to choose the journey and sometimes we don't. God works either way.

During this season it frequently felt like I was dying. I didn't recognize myself anymore. All the different parts of my identity were jumbling together and my faith was in disrepair. I wrestled with pride, sin (mine and others'), and an inability to surrender to the Lord. All of these things left me feeling abandoned and alone.

I ended up in a very dark place with regrets, shame, confusion, and a bitter sense of loss and sadness. Had I mistaken God's character entirely? I was plagued with anxiety, overwhelmed by emotion, and had little (if any) joy. My heart was a mess because I was not rooted and grounded in God's love (Eph. 3:17-19).

But God

"Come and hear, all ye that fear God, and I will declare what he hath done for my soul" (Psalm 66:16). In that dark place, God did miraculous work in my heart. He gets all the glory. I crawled into His hands wounded and broken and He began to heal my heart and bind my wounds (Psalm 147:3). He grounded my roots as they reached down into His deep love.

I had to learn to trust the Lord again and die to myself. I began to read my Bible again and gave all of this heart mess to the Lord. He kept drawing me in to approach the throne of grace for help and remember His goodness and mercy.

His sacrifice had already paid for all my sin. I have been redeemed. He reminded me that Heaven is real and Jesus Christ is my portion, hope and joy. God is the only one who opens His hand and satisfies "the desire of every living thing" (Psalm 145:16).

Can we just take a minute to thank God for how patient He is with us? He takes the time to *teach* us. God taught me as He refined my prayers and transformed me by renewing my mind with His truth (Rom. 12:2). If I had given up, if His Spirit hadn't restored me, then I would have missed everything He's done since then.

I knew God was good before…but now I've lived it. Now I know He is good TO ME. He loves everyone, but He also loves ME. Our relationship with the Lord can be more intimate than we realize. We are fully known and loved by Him.

I drew many trees that Summer. It was a glorious escape to skip through the woods and giggle over moss and tree-bark, cool mushrooms and sunrises. Waking up before the sun and driving to the beach or some park to capture the next tree. It felt like a gift from God to remind me how He designed me at a time when I'd forgotten.

When our roots are grounded in His love we experience Him in a whole new way. We are filled with the fullness of God.

The Willow Tree

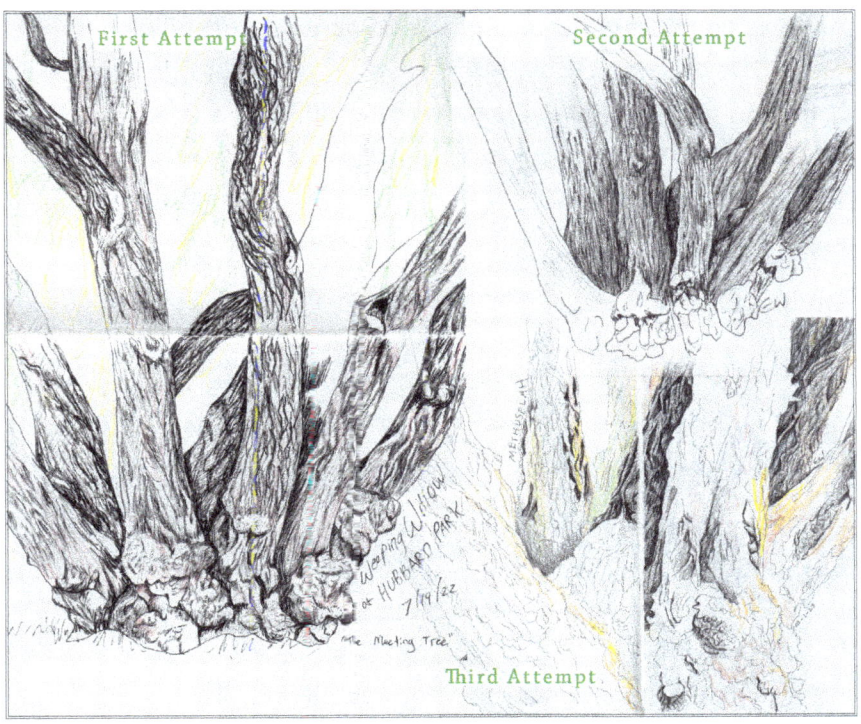

THIS WAS MY VERY FIRST TREE of the series. I woke up before the sun and birds, grabbed coffee on my way, and set up my chair in a parking lot to draw this Willow tree. The pen felt foreign in my hands. I still remember drawing the Willow that morning and feeling like I didn't know what I was doing.

Around this time God brought me to Psalm 126:5, which says, "They that sow in tears shall reap in joy." That verse spoke hope into my soul that my sadness wasn't wasted. It seems significant that this very tree is named for its long, drooping structure. At a time when my eyes were often leaking, I found some solace in a tree that's weeping. Perhaps those tears were watering the ground for a future harvest of joy.

When God is our joy, we can rejoice amidst our sorrow. In Psalm 116, David recounts a time when he found trouble and sorrow. He called upon the name of the Lord to deliver His soul and God did (vs. 3-4). "For thou hast delivered my soul from death, mine eyes from tears, and my feet from falling" (vs. 8).

God has been faithful to deliver me from that difficult season. But amidst that sadness and despair I felt His bountiful goodness and grace.

Living Unfinished

> *"Being confident of this very thing, that he which hath begun a good work in you will perform it until the day of Jesus Christ..." (Phil. 1:6)*

I returned to that Willow tree twice more and finished neither of those drawings. I was frustrated by how fast the time went by. I wasn't done adding the details and what good was a half-finished drawing?

The marks show intention, not completion. There's something interesting about seeing the middle of it, unfinished. We do a lot of our life right there.

I'm learning to let go of expectations for myself, the need to finish a drawing, and the limitations of time. I'm learning to trust the Lord and surrender my own will in favor of His.

How do we let go of the need to finish something? That desire for closure and resolution is so enticing. But so much in life may feel unresolved, ongoing and indefinite. With God we can learn to move forward even if things aren't settled around us. We can find contentment through trusting Him to continue His work even if it seems undone to us.

Is there something in your life that God is asking you to set down, even if it doesn't feel 'done?' If it is His will, do you trust Him enough to leave it unfinished and let Him work?

The Finisher

We ourselves are unfinished; we are still here. The breath in our lungs is confirmation that God must still have a purpose and plan for us. It's not time to go Home yet. Just as His work in us is ongoing, so is His plan for us.

Jeremiah 29:10-14 explains God's promise to deliver Israel out of captivity in Babylon. The prophet Jeremiah relays God's plan: He will allow their captivity for a duration before visiting them to perform good, and when they call upon Him, seeking Him with their whole heart, they will find Him. Then He will deliver them, restoring them to the place they belong.

Have you ever felt like you were in captivity to a situation you had no power over? A heart issue you couldn't rectify? Were you waiting for a deliverance only God could perform? Perhaps, in His good plan and good thoughts toward you, it is not yet time for deliverance. Continue seeking Him with your whole heart. Keep calling out for Him.

"For I know the thoughts that I think toward you, saith the Lord, thoughts of peace, and not of evil, to give you an expected end. Then shall ye call upon me, and ye shall go and pray unto me, and I will hearken unto you" (vs. 11-12). God's plan is filled with His thoughts of hope and peace for us.

What we see here in this life is just a glimpse of an unfinished story. We are still in the middle of His good plan. His plan is unfinished because it is still playing out in our lives. He knows it; we don't. But we trust He has a good plan because He is a good God. He is for us, not against us.

A Work in Progress

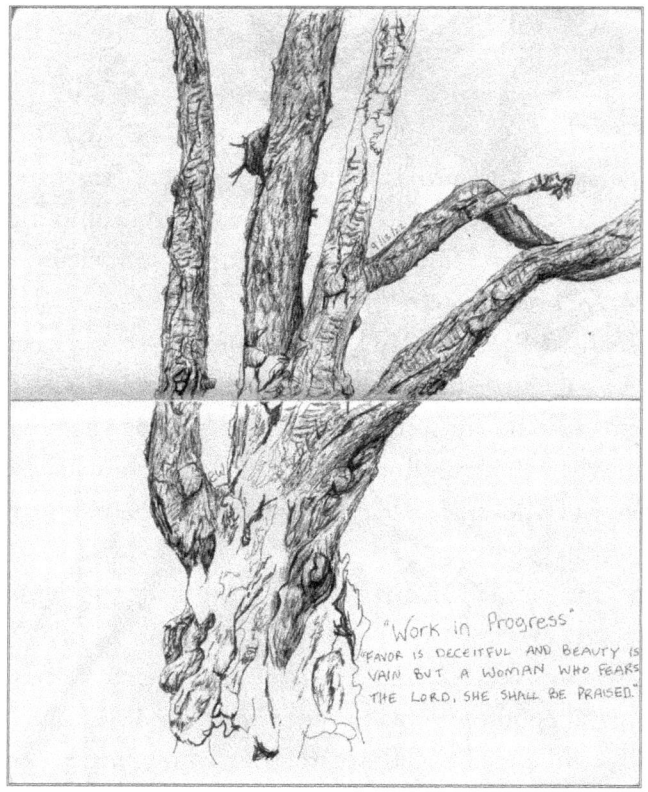

THIS DILAPIDATED TREE stands in my friend's neighbor's yard. It's striking for its disfigurement. Just like our sin before God, this tree could be described as ugly. That's what makes God's holy and redemptive work in us so amazing; He died to save us while we were sinners (Rom. 5:8)!

Do you remember the moment when you first accepted God? God has always known the condition of your heart, regardless of how long you've believed. If you think your sin wasn't as bad as someone else's, or that you met God in a more 'holy' state than others, it's just not true. Sin is sin, and God hates it.

In our sin we are all as ugly as this tree, but we do not stay this way. Praise the Lord! "For as the heaven is high above the earth, so great is his mercy toward them that fear him. As far as the east is from the west, so far hath he removed our transgressions from us" (Psalm 103:11-12). We are now counted holy and righteous before the living God.

Salvation changes our status from 'condemned' to 'in-progress.' God is the finisher of our faith, through His plan of redemption and everlasting life in Jesus (John 3:16). From the moment we say yes to Jesus He lives in our heart forever, our living hope. What a joy and comfort that God will continue His good work in us our whole life (Phil. 1:6)!

Holding Pieces

> *"…I am like a broken vessel." (Psalm 31:12)*

> *"The Lord is nigh unto them that are of a broken heart; and saveth such as be of a contrite spirit." (Psalm 34:18)*

Sometimes all we have are pieces. All we can offer God are the shredded pieces of our plans, our hopes, our sense of life as we know it. We desperately want to be whole again, forgetting we are already whole through the indwelling Holy Spirit.

Sometimes you have to first be broken to realize that you are broken.

When Jesus healed sinners and sufferers, my Bible translation uses the term "made whole" to describe His healing. Through faith, not our own actions or strength, are we made whole. He holds the power to heal and restore.

Even when we feel broken, God can use our perceived brokenness for His glory. You don't need to have it all together to be used by God. When all you have to offer God are your pieces, ask yourself how tightly you are holding onto them. Will you lay them at His feet and accept His restoration? Even if the process is uncomfortable? Even if it takes longer than you want?

Splintered

THE TREE I IMAGINED DRAWING that day did not look like this tree. Surely a unique and majestic tree was just up ahead. Definitely around the next corner. Any time now. Finally I saw this broken tree off to the corner, and stood in a pricker bush to draw it. I did not wear the right shoes and I forgot my bug spray, but it was worth it.

This tree was splintered in the same way I was: broken and vulnerable. Sometimes we go through seasons where no one sees the best version of us. Our faults spill out instead of any favorable attributes. It forces us to face the reality that there is no best version of us. We ourselves are not righteous (Rom. 3:10). Everyone is in need of the Lord's redeeming grace.

The same is true of everyone around us. When we look at others it's easy to think we're getting the whole story. That what we see in another person is the entirety of their being. Their life; signed, sealed, condemned. We feel their splinters and can't wait to get them out.

Be compassionate. Be forgiving. We don't know another person's heart and we can't possibly ever see them or love them the way God does. Maybe we're only seeing a really bad day in their life. One part of their journey. What a shame that we could be so quick to judge, act, or dismiss when we know so little.

Jesus interacted with sinners (Matt. 9:10) and often with people who were generally disliked. Why? Because He saw who they could be with the love and healing of God. He saw their need of Him, the great physician, and He answered (Mark 2:17).

Wood Stacks

THIS STACK OF WOOD sat in our driveway at the time I drew it. The tree removal company had to disassemble the tree and relocate the pieces. There was no way to move it whole.

Don't be fooled when all you see are pieces, like that wood stacked in the driveway. Brokenness is not forever. God is still working. We don't see the entirety of His plan, or understand it, but He is reminding us He is good along the way and worthy of our trust.

We are like these broken pieces that God puts back together. He arranges the circumstances and events in our life to draw us to Him, and then sanctifies us, making us holy and more like Jesus. Jesus' own body was broken for our restoration.

In 1 Corinthians 11:23-25, Jesus breaks bread, saying, "Take, eat: this is my body, which is broken for you: this do in remembrance of me" (vs. 24). Jesus was about to die on the cross, and He asks His disciples to remember that sacrifice by breaking bread and taking wine in the future.

Just as the bread was passed to the apostles and they each received a piece, God is our portion (Lam. 3:24). We have access to that portion through faith and acceptance of Jesus Christ as our Savior.

The apostles would in future days and months also partake in the suffering Jesus endured through their own trials. As followers of Christ, we suffer because He suffered but we also share His glory (1 Pet. 4:13-14). While the world would have us avoid any and all pain if possible, the Bible speaks of suffering in God's will as a thing to rejoice over with eternal reward.

During a practice drawing of another wood stack in our backyard, I saw the green of the grass beyond it framed in little pockets between the rounds. There are greener pastures coming in Heaven. Even if we just see glimpses now of His green goodness, we know there is a well-laid and perfect plan underway orchestrated by God.

When the broken pieces of us are shifting around, being rearranged by the Lord, we get the ultimate privilege of watching Him work and experiencing the progress inside us. Oh, it can be uncomfortable at times, but it is glorious work!

Impatient for Progress

"Wait on the Lord: be of good courage, and he shall strengthen thine heart: wait, I say, on the Lord" (Psalm 27:14).

My Dad used to tell me, "Where you are at is not as important as where you are going." When we look at our lives, what direction are we going? Is it toward the Lord?

Trees are always growing toward the light, though it's not always evident. Young saplings, if growing at the foot of a larger tree, have to wait for their chance to thrive. The light there is limited and much of the rainfall is absorbed by the larger tree on its way down. For years the saplings can slow their growth, conserving resources. During this time you might write them off; their days are numbered.

However, once a spot in the canopy opens up, they soar upward toward the sunlight. Now their progress is evident and they are growing strong.

Progress can be slow. Like those saplings we too might feel doomed to stagnate in life as our trials take all our energy and attention. But God is growing us and sustaining us during that time. We must be patient and wait on Him.

I remember being so desperate for progress, for distance from that Summer (and myself), for being over the trial and beyond it. But progress was slower than I wanted. It felt non-existent. Now I see it was measurable, and that God was working the whole time.

He has a plan for the pace of progress. He is a God of intent, and always follows through. He fulfills every promise in His timing. He is a God of impossible things (Jer. 32:27). So why do we feel the need to rush Him?

Still Floating Here

I think of Noah sometimes, and how he was on the ark with his family floating on the water (Gen. 7-8) with no landmarks in sight. Only water from horizon to horizon, covering even the tallest trees and mountains.

They did not sail in a specific direction. God did not tell them to go somewhere once they got in the ark, nor how long they would wait. They got in and waited on the Lord for *His* direction. They were patient and trusted Him. They were safe.

During our trials we might feel like we are in a boat too. We're trying to get ahead of the wave, but we just get pushed along with it.

We don't have a sail. All we have are our flimsy intentions and they make lousy oars.

Are you impatient for progress, or waiting for direction?

That is when we are at His mercy, in his hands, and very much not in control. It is a beautiful place to be.

When His disciples woke Him, pleading for help in their tempest-tossed boat, Jesus spoke to the storm and calmed the wind and waves. "But the men marvelled, saying, What manner of man is this, that even the winds and the sea obey him!" (Matt 8:27). God has control over nature (He made it). He has control in our lives as well.

No one's hands are more capable. No one else's voice can calm the wind and waves in our hearts.

The Jellyfish

We went to Florida on a family vacation and the only wildlife we saw were jellyfish. We went to the beach almost every day (that's what happens when a bunch of rainy, gray New Englanders travel south) and there they were: Jellyfish in the water around us. Jellyfish washed up on the beach.

I remember how lifeless they looked in the water, simply floating there. It was easy to see them as creatures of no intention; everything happened to them. They barely had substance to their form.

Do you ever feel this way?

I watched the waves beat back the jellyfish near me over and over, waiting for it to end up on the beach. But it made progress. Every time it was swept back by another wave, it was also somehow a little farther from the shore than last time. It was very slowly heading back out to deeper waters.

Are we beaten down by our circumstances in life, or are we moved by the Lord for His good purpose? Are we moving toward Him, or away?

The Journey We Don't Expect

Trees Watching Waves

UP THE SHORELINE were the trees planted by the water. I straddled the shoreline as I drew, caught between intentions that first Summer. I kept wavering between what I knew I needed to do, and what I wanted to do.

James 1:2-8 says that when we waver we are like waves driven and tossed by the wind. We end up double-minded, and therefore "unstable in all our ways" (James 1:8). My prayers at the time differed wildly and sometimes contradicted each other depending on my mood.

Did you know that at low tide you can see a history of where the waves meet the sand? It looks like irregular, overlapping impressions. God compares His rebellious people to waves that try to push past the sand. "…though the waves thereof toss themselves, yet can they not prevail; though they roar, yet can they not pass over it?" (Jer. 5:22).

Just like those wave lines on the sand, we too have a history of where we met God over and over again. We might wrestle with God over His will and not getting what we want, but for all our rebellion we make little progress.

His will drives our life like the wind and currents drive the waves. Progress is smoother when we yield. When it feels like God is pushing you, letting you rest, and pushing you again…are you yielding? Or are you braced against Him?

God has a plan for the waves in our life. I sat there with my chair literally in the back wash of waiting and certainty (the waves that came, the waves that left), and I had this sense of necessity. It was as if God was telling me that sometimes we need to find the shore. All those waves will drive us there one way or another.

We find the shore, we rest, we go back out to sea and it starts all over again. We journey until we are called Home. He teaches us until we are in His presence.

As we mature in our faith we learn the value of waiting on the Lord and seeking Him. We become more stable-minded instead of tossed around by whatever circumstances come. Asking in faith, nothing wavering, means we don't fear God's answer.

Those trees by the water were a reminder of how I too could be firmly rooted and blessed as I trust in the Lord (Psalm 1:3). Their roots draw up water as needed because the source is right there. We too have access to God's love and grace, which never runs out, when we are planted at the Source.

There was so much God was going to teach me, and it was only just beginning. I watched the smooth, dark boulders at the shoreline glisten in reflected sunrise hues, and felt the mist on my face that morning at the beach when I drew the shore.

Color Escape

WHEN I ARRIVED AT THE PARK that day I turned my car off and looked through the windshield. My car was pointed directly at the tree I would draw. Mostly I remember the color flying out of its bark.

During this season the color was flying out of me too. I was bursting open, hemorrhaging emotions from old and new wounds. God allowed me to see them all, and eventually understand them.

At the time, I thought I was making definitive progress through healing and change. Instead, I would learn that the work God does in our hearts can feel more like a mysterious forest. But it is a forest we can navigate when we trust and cling to Him.

I explored the park after completing the drawing. All the color and sunshine made me grin and giggle like the child I am. It was a grand adventure, bounding down the path and wandering around. Any cool trees that I found I allowed myself to investigate, touch and climb.

Just as I explored that park, we have the privilege of exploring what God is teaching us. We might prefer a straight path with the end in sight. With God, whatever direction He takes us will move us in

His ultimate plan for our life, even if it seems circuitous to us. We might even feel lost sometimes, but He has not left us.

When We Can't See the Forest

There is a saying that goes something like, "I couldn't see the forest for the trees." When all we focus on are our adversaries or trials, we lose sight of God and don't trust His greater plan. Each obstacle becomes a looming distraction stopping us like a giant tree appearing in our path.

In the beginning of Deuteronomy 31, Moses is telling the people of Israel how God is going to help them conquer their enemies so they can possess the land promised to them. He tells them not to be afraid of them, because God will be with His people. He will not fail them or forsake them (vs. 6).

If Israel was too focused on the presence of their enemy or the impossibility of defeating them, they would not move into the land God was giving them. They would miss the blessing, distracted by fears.

We live in this incredible landscape of all that God is doing, with its hills and valleys. It is possible to go from an unwilling participant with a front row view, to stepping courageously forward in His will and experiencing His work.

God compassionately changes the way we view trials by remaining with us and helping us overcome them. We walk by faith. Each 'tree' becomes part of the forest again; a forest of His goodness, where He orders our steps and leads us with capable hands.

> *Whether we choose the journey or God chooses it for us, we experience God's great goodness and blessings. Each journey with Him grows our understanding of His love for us and grounds our roots.*

What To Do When We Don't Understand

Trusting God

> *"Trust in the Lord with all thine heart; and lean not unto thine own understanding. In all thy ways acknowledge him, and he shall direct thy paths." (Pro. 3:5-6)*

Jeremiah 17:7-8 compares the one who trusts the Lord to a tree planted by the water. The tree spreads out its roots by the river. It does not merely dip one toe in and 'sample trust.' It is fully rooted and searching for that water, thirsty and ready to suck it up. It knows there is life there. In Christ our life is found.

Notice that the tree planted by the water is not spared trials. Jeremiah 17 assures that the heat and drought will come. The difference is that the tree doesn't see it (vs. 8). When we are saved we are so full of God's love, mercy and grace that the heat of those trials does not wither our leaves (Psalm 1:3).

We must trust the Lord through each trial, regardless of whether we understand it.

In this trying season the enemy consistently tempted me to doubt God's goodness. There were a few prayers that, in my limited understanding, it felt like God wasn't answering. The lie was this: 'If God doesn't do this then He isn't good, and can't be trusted.'

It took me too long to identify the lies. Our false ideas about God can make it difficult to trust Him. But God was patient with me.

Trusting His Will

> *"O the depth of the riches both of the wisdom and knowledge of God! how unsearchable are his judgments, and his ways past finding out! For who hath known the mind of the Lord? or who hath been his counsellor?" (Rom. 11:33-34)*

We may not understand God's plans, but can we know God's will? "And be not conformed to this world: but be ye transformed by the renewing of your mind, that ye may prove what is that good, and acceptable, and perfect, will of God" (Rom. 12:2).

As we read His word, our minds are healed of the world's wisdom and renewed by His scripture. We begin to know what pleases Him. It becomes clear what would not be in His will for us.

We must still pray over anything in our life that is not explicitly addressed in the Bible and apply our knowledge of God to it, seeking His direction and wisdom. We must wait for His answer too. Our understanding of His plan will influence our actions in response to it.

God is bigger than all the things we can't control. He can even work in our misunderstandings, unmet expectations, and mistakes. God made the heavens and the earth. All the vast and complex systems out there in nature, each star, every planet in its orbit in every galaxy in space – God formed them all. He did it without our help. Rest assured that when the God who made everything does not do exactly what we asked, it is not because He *can't*.

Trust means letting go of every possible outcome. All the outcomes we hope for, dream of, and fear. We let them go and do life knowing God is good and His will is perfect.

When We Can't See

If your backyard has trees, you can imagine how it looks after a bad windstorm: sticks and twigs everywhere littering the ground. It is daunting to consider picking up every single stick when you look at the entire yard.

Not knowing His plan calls for trust and faith in the Lord. I'm learning that not knowing can be a huge advantage.

Maybe God knows we would be so overwhelmed by the entirety of His plan (even a great plan) that He chooses not to show us the whole thing. We would faint in our hearts thinking about everything He will ask of us in our entire life. Instead, He just asks that we pick up the next stick. He'll take care of the details.

Can we learn to accept that if God has not chosen to reveal something to us, He must have a good reason? Ecclesiastes 1:18 says, "… he that increaseth knowledge increaseth sorrow." Perhaps it is just not time for us to know. Or He has a plan for how we will respond to not knowing.

Not knowing why something is happening is different than the confusion the enemy creates. Satan leaves us spinning and uncertain. Within our faith, our 'not knowing' has a solution. We trade it for the One who knows: God.

My brain tells me that the only way to truly know if God heard my prayer is if I see Him answer it. See it, then believe it. The Holy Spirit reminds me that God's word says He hears the prayers of the righteous and answers them (Psalm 34:6,15,17, 1 Pet. 3:12).

Our minds were not designed to understand the complexities of God's great plan and workings. Why trust our own understanding, our own eyesight, at all? We have One worthy of our trust who is above all and in control of all. What if learning to see actually means letting God see for us?

When we try to understand God's plan in a season where He has not chosen to reveal it, we are like uncertain tree roots meandering in the ground. Let's let God direct our way in the soil when we cannot see. We walk by faith, not by sight (2 Cor. 5:7).

Letting Him direct us means we are re-rooted back into His love.

When We Don't Agree

Jeremiah 29:11 tells us that God has a plan for us. Proverbs 16:9 tells us that we have our own plan.

In our faith there may be times when we are tempted to carve our own entrances and exits when we are not satisfied with the Lord's plan. We saw out a little door to our new plan, or we chisel away a hidden exit in case we want to escape the place God has us.

Every door leads you toward something, and away from something else. So many doors opening and closing in our life, and so many choices to make. There will be less confusion over which to enter and exit through when we surrender control to the Lord.

Over and over in this season I asked the Lord, 'Why aren't You doing it? Why aren't you answering this prayer?' Because He wasn't doing it my way I assumed He wasn't doing anything. Who are we to instruct God?

"Rejoicing in hope; patient in tribulation; continuing instant in prayer;" (Rom. 12:12). Continue forward trusting the Lord. His good plan allows for the growing years where we are reshaped by His teaching.

When He Doesn't Tell Us Why

We seem to think it will be easier to follow God's plan if we know God's plan. He is the only one who truly knows how knowledge will affect us. Psalm 139:1-3 says He knows our thoughts afar off and is acquainted with all our ways. He knows what we can or can't handle, and His timing and procedure shine His glory, grace, and mercy.

Letting go of that need to know is what it means to trust Him. If God were to show us the plan, we would try to prepare for it instead of allowing Him to equip us in far better ways that glorify Him.

Perhaps God, in all His infinite wisdom, knows we would reject the reason that He allowed our pain if we knew it. We finite Christians cannot truly understand its purpose.

Perhaps He withholds information from us as a mercy and kindness. He invites us to trust and rest in Him through our trials instead. He knows there is some good He will work from it even when we doubt it.

Would I exchange all the sanctification and teaching God gave me, in order to escape this challenging season? Absolutely not. What He gave me is far more precious. But would I have answered that question the same way before going through it?

When you don't understand His plan, recommit your faith. Exchange your will for His.

With Our Whole Heart

There was a day recently that I went to draw and the drawing looked nothing like the stump in front of me. I was disappointed. But I was alone with God, asking Him my questions. He is a safe place for our questions.

During this season there was a period of time when I couldn't stop asking the same questions. They consumed me. But overtime as I prayed for help, God released me from the need to ask those questions. It was easier not to. He wasn't going to answer them and He finally gave me peace in accepting that I wouldn't know and it was okay.

I admitted defeat in my drawing that day and put my sketchbook away. As I explored I was telling God how I just didn't understand. He spoke to me that I didn't have to. He also asked me whether I was trusting Him with my whole heart. Because His word says, *"Trust in the Lord with all thine heart;"* and I wasn't doing that.

Trusting in the Lord with our whole hearts means we hold nothing back for ourselves to worry about. God promises to keep us in "perfect peace" when we trust in Him (Isa. 26:3). Only with the Holy Spirit's help can we truly trust God with our whole heart. Only with His help can we accept anything He wants to do.

Surrendering to the Process

> *"The Lord will perfect that which concerneth me: thy mercy, O Lord, endureth for ever: forsake not the works of thine own hands." (Psalm 138:8)*
>
> *"...Even so now yield your members servants to righteousness unto holiness." (Rom. 6:19)*

There was one night in particular that God had me on my knees surrendering a spent heart. I had gone through a day of worrying and spiraling and then I hit a pivotal point. That's when the fight went out of me completely.

I realized I had been wrong about everything. I had nothing left. I didn't want to fight anymore.

I would go through this. I would surrender now.

Surrendering is not the same as giving up. In any trial we will naturally reach the point where we just want to be done. Surrender means a heart committed and compliant to the process. You're still moving forward but you're letting God lead it now.

It means laying aside ourselves, along with our own desires and comfort, in favor of what God chooses for us. My uncle once said that during trials, God is not doing it *to* us, but *in* us. We surrender to God's holy heart work.

Surrendering to the process means we yield to whatever He wants to do in our hearts. We stop fighting and start listening. We're ready to learn what He wants to teach us.

"But the wisdom that is from above is first pure, then peaceable, gentle, and easy to be intreated, full of mercy and good fruits..." (Jam. 3:17). God's wisdom is a truth that first stuns us, before becoming peaceful and gentle. A kind wisdom that God helps us accept.

Obtaining a better understanding from the Lord can preserve us, shield us, lift the blinders, and be a mercy to us. God's good understanding contains both mercy and truth (Pro. 3:3-4). Thank You, Lord! Oh, may that be the wisdom we crave!

What To Do When We Don't Understand

God's wisdom is one we can rest with instead of wrestle with.

Rest Over Wrestle

What is the cost when we don't trust God? We sacrifice peace of mind, time, contentment, joy, security, and the list goes on.

Sometimes worrying feels productive. It's a false sense of capability, control, and taking action when there's none to take. God asks us to trust Him and wait. He directs our steps (Prov. 16:9) He promises peace that passes understanding when we pray and give our worries to Him (Phil. 4:6-7).

The enemy wants us to believe that in order to rest we must be free from the trial itself. Only when we surrender our worries and stop resisting God's will can we actually rest. Do you believe God is capable of bringing us rest while we endure?

A Wreck at Rest

TREE DRAWINGS AT THIS TIME were scarce as life was winding toward other priorities. Even as I prayed that He would allow the time to explore and draw, God was whispering that He was giving me a chance to rest.

'Rest' in this season meant continuing forward with more of God and less of myself. When we set the Lord before us, drawing near to Him and seeking Him, we shall not be moved from the path of righteousness. Our hearts will be glad and even our flesh will rest in hope (Psalm 16:8-9).

I wandered around that shady respite looking at knobby moss-covered rocks, flowers, hidey-holes for critters, bark patterns and breakage. Farther ahead I came to this decaying wood in the mud: a wreck at rest.

I felt like a former wreck too. When God is still healing and helping us overcome, we should be careful how we look back. Depending on the day, my heart investigations during this season varied greatly. Some days it felt like nothing had changed.

Sometimes we remember the wreck so strongly that when we look at our healing heart we still see the old wreck instead. Lord, help us lay that wreck to rest!

In this season I couldn't stop picking up the pieces of my wreck. My hopes, intentions and plans were all scattered around me. My joy was shattered everywhere. This wreckage…where was God in it? I couldn't understand what God was doing and what He had done with my prayers. Why was I still here?

I realized one day that I can't pick through the wreckage anymore. It takes tremendous courage to walk away from something that feels so unresolved. He helps us move forward from the wreckage trusting Him. Trusting that He is good.

I have this hope that I will look back someday and see that this dark season of struggle is no longer a wreck. That God had been working and making it into something new in His good plan. That

He will allow me to look back with fresh eyes and all I will see is God's redemption, love, and goodness.

When we pray and surrender to God, miraculous peace pours in where we couldn't imagine it before. We find strength where our heart had none. Our story is moving forward again and it is all because of God's goodness and faithfulness.

Learning to Love God's Plan

In Acts 16:23 we find Paul and Silas in prison. After they called the demon out of a lucrative soothsayer, her employers became angry and these two righteous men ended up in jail for doing God's will. "Blessed are they which are persecuted for righteousness' sake: for theirs is the kingdom of heaven" (Matt. 5:10).

Did Paul and Silas hang their heads and worry that God had abandoned them? If faced with the same circumstances – what seems like punishment where reward is due - how many of us would respond likewise?

If they had been imprisoned for doing wrong, that would be cause to bow their knees and repent. But they did nothing wrong and still submitted to God's plan.

"And at midnight Paul and Silas prayed, and sang praises unto God: and the prisoners heard them" (Acts 16:25). They were worshipping right there in that prison! It was a testimony to the other prisoners. Furthermore, it impacted the prison guard in a profound way.

An earthquake frees the prisoners, and the prison guard and his family accept Jesus as their Savior! He accepted Jesus into his heart because God ordained Paul and Silas to be in that prison. This is just one example of God having a very good reason for all that He does.

The prison guard is about to end his life, thinking this is the end; all his prisoners have escaped and he will be killed anyways for failing in his job. But Paul cries out to stop him. Later, he washes Paul and Silas' stripes from being beaten, and then they baptize him. Together in the water.

Whose plan will we learn to love better: ours, or Gods? Do we ever, in our flesh, think God's plan is bad? Or maybe it's just 'not as good' as our own. But God has infinite understanding, compassion, mercy, and lovingkindness. He is holy in all His ways. Why wouldn't we submit to His good plan, even if it doesn't seem good at the time?

When God answers Job out of the whirlwind He asks, "Where wast thou when I laid the foundations of the earth?" (Job 38:4). He asks Job, "Wilt thou condemn me, that thou mayest be righteous?" (Job 40:8). In these chapters where God responds to Job He is making the case of His sovereignty over all the earth. He alone is mighty, not to be instructed. Job answers the Lord, "…I uttered that I understood not; things too wonderful for me, which I knew not" (Job 42:3).

Friend, I understand how frustrating it can be to not understand God's plan. I have been angry at Him over His plan, sorrowful over His plan, broken over His plan, remade and sanctified by His plan. Pray through all of it. Bring every emotion to Him. Ask for forgiveness over any anger, pride, and regret. His plan is so good, and He asks us to trust Him.

If God hasn't made a way for something then maybe it's not in His plan. His plan is good but not everything we want may be part of it.

Even when we strive to love and follow God's plan, it can be tempting to abandon it when we don't understand it. God's good plan is better than any dream of mine. This is something I wrestle with at times but it remains true. God has a good, loving plan to sanctify us for His glory.

What He Did Before

THIS MAGNIFICENT OAK TREE rises from a hill, towering over me. Strong, mighty, immovable. It took significantly longer than a few days to grow. After dropping one tiny acorn it would take decades to reach this size again. We might look at that unassuming acorn and think, 'No way you can grow a giant.'

What To Do When We Don't Understand

God grew that tree. It reminds me of His incredible plan, so vast and of unknown duration. We are down at the foot of it with our heads craned back trying to see the whole thing.

Have you ever found yourself thinking that God is 'less good' in your life now than He was before? Sometimes we are tempted toward disappointment in God's plan when we compare the good God is doing now with the good He was doing back then.

In Ezra 3:10-13 the temple of the Lord is being rebuilt. We see the completion of the new foundation. While many are worshipping

God, "because he is good, for his mercy endureth for ever toward Israel" (vs. 11) there are those who weep instead.

The men lamenting this wonderful thing, "who were ancient," had seen the first house in all its astounding glory. They were now beholding the new foundation which was very different. Instead of rejoicing over what God had done this time, they "wept with a loud voice" while others "shouted aloud for joy" (vs. 12).

Some generations celebrated while others mourned what had been lost. The builders praised God with trumpets and cymbals, singing and giving thanks (vs. 10-11). God gave them this mission to rebuild the temple and was with them as they did.

Verse 13 is beautiful: "…the people could not discern the noise of the shout of joy from the noise of the weeping of the people: for the people shouted with a loud shout, and the noise was heard afar off." The sound of joy was louder.

Many years after the temple is rebuilt, Jesus tells the Pharisees, "Destroy this temple, and in three days I will raise it up" (John 2:19). They scoffed at Him, saying it took forty-six years to build. Who was this man boasting impossible speed?

Jesus was referring to the temple of His body which would be crucified. Three days later He would raise from the dead. It is God who builds, by providing, giving skill to the builders, laying the foundation, and blessing the effort. That temple was rebuilt in the way God wanted it to be. And it is God who has the power to raise up life. God is still good to you now regardless of how you perceive His goodness in your present season of life. We cannot measure the value of His works with our own hands. God is always good and always worthy of praise.

May we learn to say, 'Yes, God, this is different than what You did before, but I will praise You because You were good then and You are still so good to me.'

Keep Singing

> *"But I have trusted in thy mercy; my heart shall rejoice in thy salvation. I will sing unto the Lord, because he hath dealt bountifully with me".* (Psalm 13:5-6)

I was sitting at the playground once with my daughters when God sent an older woman to walk by me. Her shirt said the word "abundance." God is abundantly good to us, and His blessings are everywhere.

In seasons of waiting, wanting and confusion, don't focus on what you feel God didn't do for you. Don't dwell on his 'no.' Trust that He has a good plan and praise Him. Act like you are living in His abundance. Lift up His name in worship.

We are called to worship the Lord in any circumstance. Psalm 95:6 says, "O come, let us worship and bow down: let us kneel before the Lord our maker." It does not say, 'Let us worship and bow down, unless we have a really bad day.'

"The Lord is my strength and song, and is become my salvation" (Psalm 118:14). If God is our song we always have a reason to sing. His lovingkindness is compared to a song we can hear in the morning and a song with us in the night (Psalm 143:8, Psalm 42:8). What if we could learn to hear His lovingkindness over our day like a song? Let it forever be a song in your ears and on your lips.

There are a variety of God-given talents we can use to praise the Lord. God has also given believers different spiritual gifts according to the measures of grace He has given each of us (Rom. 12:6). May we use our gifts for His kingdom and glory.

When we don't understand what God is asking us to go through, continue to worship Him. If you are walking through a trial right now, how might you glorify the Lord in it? How may you worship Him through it?

He is Worthy of Our Song

There was a time when I opened my beat-up, borrowed hymnal every single day to pour out melodies for God. My heart was broken and every time I felt the darkness descending I had to sing. The familiar melodies were a lullaby to my soul in remembering my Father loved me.

I was fractured into a melody I couldn't help but sing. God did something beautiful with that song. "And he hath put a new song in my mouth, even praise unto our God: many shall see it, and fear, and shall trust in the Lord" (Psalms 40:3)

Why do we sing? Because He is worthy of our song. In this season I strongly felt Satan's attack as he did everything he could to stop me from singing the Lord's praise. I knew I had to keep singing. It felt like the only thing I could offer up to the Lord. I would keep opening my mouth to sing whatever song He put there. He gave me so many songs to sing…from that hymnal and in my life.

Singing through the trial was a way to resist the enemy. God was helping me rise, keeping me on my feet to worship, and on my knees to pray.

Sunday mornings in church I would show up and sing. Sometimes we're bursting to praise God, and sometimes we can barely get a sound out. I am thankful for the music ministry at our church that kept the songs going.

Musical worship is hearts unified to praise the Lord during finite displays of skill shared by those listening and those creating. "O magnify the Lord with me, and let us exalt his name together" (Psalm 34:3). May our songs be for His glory.

Worship sets our eyes on Him instead of everything else.

God's very creation brings Him glory. Psalm 148 says the heavens, sun, moon and stars praise Him. Psalm 19:1 describes how the skies show His handiwork and heavens declare his glory. We get to join in the song.

What To Do When We Don't Understand

In Revelation 4, the Lord shows John a vision of what "must be hereafter" (vs. 1). Verses 10-11 show the 24 elders falling to their knees before the throne to worship Jesus. They cast their crowns at Him, telling Him how worthy He is of all glory and honor. He is worthy because He "created all things," and they were created for His good pleasure (vs. 11).

Keep worshipping the Lord. He alone deserves it. Whether your song is a beautiful reflection of God's peace and prosperity over you, or your afflictions are becoming songs of deliverance with which to praise the Lord, may the steadfast praise of the Lord be on your lips always. Keep singing.

Busker Tree

I WAS WALKING WITH A FRIEND late in the tree-drawing season, discussing life and all we were learning. When we were closing back in on her home I saw this huge tree with golden leaves. I grinned at it, knowing it would go in my sketchbook.

As I was drawing it a few days later it began to look like a busker tree. In my mind it was playing saxophone on the street corner. Fun fact: I used to play the saxophone.

When someone busks, or plays music in public, they are usually looking for money of some kind. Maybe you've seen a guitar player jamming with his case open nearby. I once listened to an accordion player on a subway in France who moments later rousted the obligatory audience with his donation cup. Years later I listened to a bagpiper on a street in Scotland, and was then informed by a passerby that filming them costs money.

1 Chronicles 16:29 says to bring an offering, come before God, and worship. God calls us to worship even if we get nothing back from the world; no accolades, money etc. Even if no one shows up for our song. God is our witness and it pleases Him. Like offering money to a musician or street artist, our worship is an offering to the Lord because He deserves it.

"Wood fibers conduct sound particularly well, which is why they are used to make musical instruments such as violins and guitars" (Wohlleben 127). Trees can praise their Creator by existing, and further be crafted to play songs of worship. May we too yield our "members as instruments of righteousness unto God" (Rom. 6:13).

Flute Tree

THIS TREE CAUGHT MY EYE because it was full of woodpecker holes and looked very different from the trees around it. Woodpeckers might save a tree from infestation but they can also significantly damage the tree in the process (Wohlleben 54).

Sometimes we might feel like we're walking around damaged too. We have injuries that can't be seen. If that's true for you now, let those wounds be holes where the music pours out of you. Keep singing even when it would be easier not to.

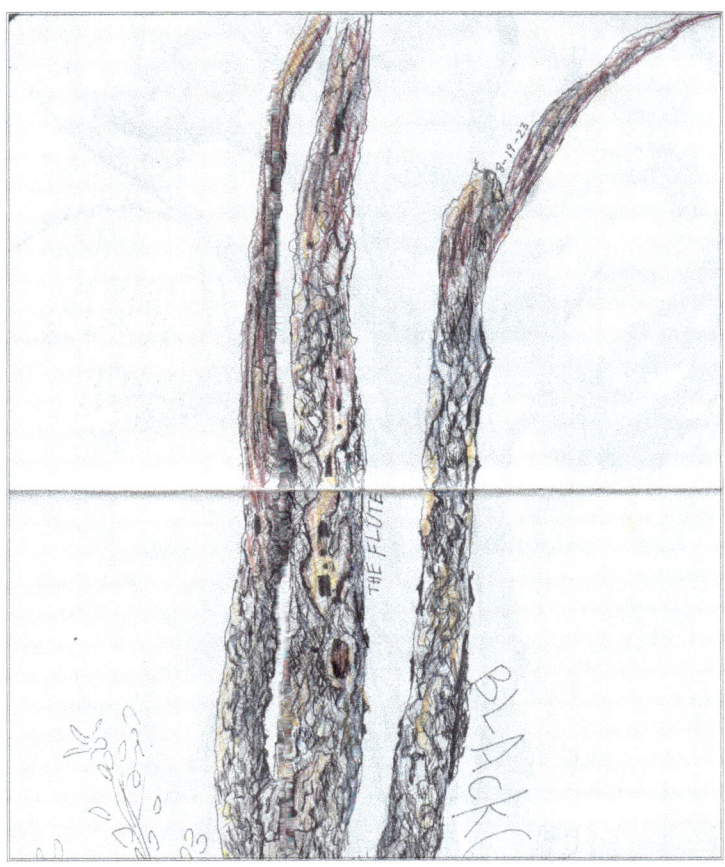

The woodpecker holes made the tree look like a flute. Wind instruments, like the flute, produce sound when our breath is blown through them. When you play you have to time your breaths so you can continue to blow 'wind' into it and produce notes.

God asks that everything that has breath praise Him (Psalm 150:6). God breathed life into mankind, and Jesus breathed the Holy Spirit on His apostles after rising from the dead. If the Holy Spirit inside us is like God's breath, then may it move through us and exude praise for God above!

Instruments create a melody, or a "distinction in the sounds" (1 Cor. 14:7). These melodies communicate a message so the hearer may understand what is played. The sounds have meaning.

For instance, trumpets were used in biblical times as a call to get ready for battle. An "uncertain sound" would cause confusion about whether to prepare to fight (vs. 8). It is important to make the sounds understandable so that others may glorify God as well (1 Cor. 14:9). How can we worship in spirit and in truth (John 4:24) without understanding what is played, or what we are singing?

1 Corinthians 14:14 says, "For if I pray in an unknown tongue, my spirit prayeth, but my understanding is unfruitful." And onward in verse 15, that we ought to sing with spirit and understanding. Otherwise what is played will not instruct us spiritually or stir us to righteousness. Our words will be spoken "into the air" (vs 9) instead of into the ears and hearts of others.

When you don't understand what is happening around you or in you, keep worshipping and orient your heart toward the One who understands it all.

Worship through the Sorrow

Have you ever tried to sing while crying? It's not easy, and it doesn't sound pretty. When we sing in sorrow, brokenness, or shame, those trial songs sound like a wail, or cry. It's too sharp or flat or out of tune. Sing anyways. Your true song is for the Lord (Col. 3:23-24) and He is not concerned with how eloquently you worship Him. He just asks you to.

"Speaking to yourselves in psalms and hymns and spiritual songs, singing and making melody in your heart to the Lord; Giving thanks always for all things unto God and the Father in the name of our Lord Jesus Christ;" (Eph. 5:19-20). The melody didn't come from me, nor did the desire to sing. His Holy Spirit was helping me offer praise.

Music can be heard and felt in the soul of anyone listening. What testimony might it share with the world when we sing praise to our God in the midst of song-stealing trials?

Is His praise continually in your mouth? If not, what can you do to praise Him more often in your day? "From the end of the earth will I cry unto thee, when my heart is overwhelmed: lead me to the rock that is higher than I" (Psalm 61:2). God can turn our sorrow cries into songs of joy.

> *It is possible to stay rooted and grounded in His love even when we don't understand His plan. We surrender to stay rooted where we are. We worship to remember why we are rooted with Him. He continually reminds us who He is, how much He loves us, and how good He is!*

WHAT WE DO WHILE WE WAIT

Committing Prayers to God

"For this cause I bow my knees unto the Father of our Lord Jesus Christ." (Eph. 3:14)

"Pray without ceasing." (1 Thes. 5:17)

What do we do when it feels like God is not answering any of our prayers? There are many encouraging verses to remind us God hears our prayers and will answer them (Psalm 34:4,15,17, Matt. 7:7-8, 21:22, John 16:23-24). And yet, because we may not understand the way He answers, we begin to doubt.

Psalm 37:5 asks us to commit our way unto the Lord. As I prayed all my prayers His Spirit convicted me: what else was I looking for God to do? I seemed to have some idea of what His answer should look like.

When we can't accept His answer to our prayers then the problem is in our own heart, not His.

God does what He knows is best according to His will even if we have trouble accepting it. He is healing and fixing my heart in spite of my false ideas about what He owed me (Does God *owe* us anything? We deserve *death* as sinners, yet Jesus gave us His life).

The Holy Spirit reminded me that God doesn't answer our prayers with yes when we are praying for something that isn't good for us (Psalm 84:11). Nor when our motives for praying are not pleasing to Him and would lead to sin (James 4:3). If He hasn't answered a prayer in the exact way you wanted, He may have a different plan (Isa. 55:8-9) or timeline.

God will refine your prayers while you wait. His Holy Spirit is at work in our hearts revealing hidden motives as we wait on Him. God is holy and righteous in all His ways (Psalm 145:17) and cannot be bargained into doing something out of His character.

Commit your unanswered prayers to the Lord, trusting He has a good plan for you.

Keep Praying

If you stand still long enough in the woods you might hear trees groan and creak in the wind. The Holy Spirit makes intercession for us according to the will of God with "groanings which cannot be uttered" and God understands it. The Holy Spirit Himself can pray in our stead when we don't know how to pray as we ought to (Rom. 8:26).

If we received everything we wanted immediately, if every problem were solved without delay, then we would know no miracles, never learn patience, build no hope or faith, and end up rejecting the power, sovereignty, and goodness of God altogether. We would end up denying His very existence because we would never see His hand at work.

Having faith can also be described in terms of Abraham's belief; "And being fully persuaded that, what he had promised, he was able also to perform" (Rom. 4:21). Abraham did not experience the fruition of God's promise for many years, but He had faith God was able to do it. God grew his patience by having him faithfully wait for the promise.

God knows how to speak to each one of us. His word is unchanging, but our walk with Him is personal. The ways He speaks to me may be different than the ways He speaks to you. When God speaks it will be in recognizable ways for us, and we must listen.

First John 5:13-15 calls us to believe on His name, and that if we ask anything in His will, He hears us. Matthew 7:7-8 is very clear about the relationship between asking the Lord and receiving from Him. "Ask, and it shall be given you" (vs. 7), and "every one that asketh receiveth" (vs. 8).

Do you believe that God hears your prayers? God answers prayer, but our prayer and our own heart need to be weighed. My pastor reminded us that a 'no' from God can be as good as a 'yes.' You will have an answer and a direction, and that's a wonderful thing! Will you trust God enough to accept that His answer is good, even if you don't like it?

When you are God's child, you have not been screaming into the wind. You have not been whispering into the black void of space. Your prayers have been heard, and God has a good plan for you. I don't know what it is, but I know He loves you and will be with you.

Before We Are Driftwood

RIGHT BEFORE THE SEASON OF DRAWING TREES I went on a family trip to the lake. My heart and spirit were pretty torn up. One of my favorite things to do, there at the end of myself, was float in the lake where we were staying. I would put on my life jacket, put my head back, close my eyes and float.

There, in that moment, I was weightless. That is what it feels like to be held in God's hands. Even though nothing felt normal, and I knew it wouldn't for a long time, I was still in good hands. I was a floating prayer: a state of need. I was driftwood.

Driftwood is dead and water-logged. As believers, we too are called to die to ourselves. We are like this driftwood; our own will surrendered, and dead to sin. But we do not drift aimlessly. God's will is not aimless. He carries us forward in the direction He wants us to go.

As believers we are not weighed down by an overabsorption of water. We are filled up by His living water. 1 Peter 5:7 tells us to cast our cares upon the Lord, who cares for us. One by one our prayers become cares cast on that water as our burdens shift onto the Lord. The peace of God that replaces our cares (Phil. 4:7) makes us weightless.

When we pray, we are giving God our hopes, dreams, desires and deepest longings. They enter the current of His will like driftwood.

Just as the Lord answers our prayers in His sovereign knowledge and timing, driftwood will wash ashore. It does not float forever. Pieces of wood washing up on the shore indicate a driving force in that direction. When our prayers our answered, the Holy Spirit gives us insight into the will of God. If we see a lot of 'driftwood' at the shore, or many answered prayers in one area, we know God is moving in that direction.

Before we are driftwood we are like this felled tree laying in the river, holding onto our heart's desires. Keeping our issues to ourselves while God stands present and ready to receive them. His ears are ready to hear our prayers; His hands are capable to carry our cares.

All those branches are about to be driftwood.

He held me weightless for a season, and now I am planted by the water, alive in His wonderful will and abiding in His presence and love. "Return unto thy rest, O my soul; for the Lord hath dealt bountifully with thee" (Psalm 116:7).

A Heart Over Her Home

THIS IS THE TREE that my family and I were walking by when God gave me the idea to draw trees. This tree is massive compared to the others around it. I really wanted to draw it but kept putting it off because I was too nervous to knock on the door and ask the people inside if I could draw their tree. If I was supposed to draw it then God would have to help me.

On one of my walks that Summer, I was pushing my daughter in the stroller and praying over different things. Ten minutes later I rounded the corner and saw the owner of the aforementioned house at her mailbox. I'd never seen her outside before. Before I could talk myself out of it I approached her and ineloquently spilled my desire to draw her tree. "Oh, and nice to meet you."

Instead of answering she asked me to take a walk with her. Across the street she stopped us and had me look back at the tree.

"What do you see?" she asked. I told her it looked like a heart.

Then she told me a story of how the Lord answered a very specific prayer on her heart. Her father had passed away almost a decade earlier and in the depth of her mourning she prayed that if God loved her, He would make that tree shine for her. She asked Him to show her His love through it.

We had a great talk about how sometimes we pray the prayers that seem silly. God cares about those things too. He chose to answer her prayer. It didn't used to look the way it does now, she said. It gradually took on the shape of a large heart over her home.

It is a blessing after a trial when God opens our eyes to see His heart toward us all along.

Matthew 21:22 calls us to pray with faith, knowing He will give us what we seek. Especially when we seek His help, peace, and healing. "When you come to Christ for mercy and love and help in your anguish and perplexity and sinfulness, you are going with the flow of his own deepest wishes, not against them" (Ortlund 38).

He is able to perform all we ask of Him. In fact, Ephesians 3:20 reminds us He can do "exceeding abundantly above all that we ask or think." He can and does answer our prayers. It is not always in the way we expect but He is faithful to answer.

I'm still learning to surrender my prayers to Him. My prayers have changed to please Him as He helps me understand. As Christians we are forever learning and growing.

Remembering Who He Is

> *"The Lord is gracious, and full of compassion; slow to anger, and of great mercy." (Psalm 145:8)*

During this season in my life, Satan used the trial of my faith to make me question the very goodness of God. God, however, used the trial to build my faith and show me His overwhelming goodness.

"When our perception of God has been damaged or compromised, everything around us falls into confusion and turmoil" (Tozer 89). In that season, my perception of God was compromised. God allowed this trial to compromise my perception of Him because He wanted to grow my faith. He wanted me to better understand who He is.

Jesus gives God glory as the One who is good (Matt. 19:17). It is the very goodness of God that leads us to repentance (Rom. 2:4). We experience His love and mercy toward us and it transforms our heart.

How it must have grieved the Lord for me to question His love for me simply because he didn't answer a prayer the way I wanted! He already gave His Son Jesus to die for my sins – that is proof of His great love for me.

When you are in a season of waiting, open your Bible and let the Holy Spirit remind you who God is. Read actual truth about Him from His word. Commit some verses to memory for any time when lies try to warp His character.

There are many ways God can speak to us. He has written His word as the guide in all we do on this side of Heaven. It is His love letter to us. In it He communicates who He is, who we are, and records the history of many generations of believers. He outlines salvation, introduces us to Jesus, reveals and rectifies our fallen sin nature, reconciles us to God, and restores us to righteousness with the promise of a heavenly inheritance.

I have to return to His word often to remember who He is because the world will try to make us forget. Satan will try to deceive us. We serve a gracious and loving Father, full of mercy and forgiveness for those who fear and follow Him.

God has taught me so much about mercy, grace, and what His sacrifice on the cross truly means for the freedom and hope I live in, and the certainty I die in.

The Creature

IN REMEMBERING WHO GOD IS we must also recognize who He is not. Romans 1:21-25 warns us about the imagination of the ungodly and unrighteous. They change God's character to corrupt Him in their minds. They change truth into lies and worship their own god-creature. When this happens, God gives their mind over to all wickedness and destruction. What a frightening place to be!

This tree looked like a creature hauling itself out of the dried creek bed, waving its eyestalks at me. It was lined with antennae creeping down its back and boasted a plethora of legs to scurry on.

It reminds me of the way things get twisted up in our mind when we don't pursue truth. By 'pursue truth' I mean reading God's word to remind ourselves what is true.

This is the ugly creature of compromise. We compromise and weaken our previously rooted convictions whenever we let sin and worldly ideas influence His truth. We slowly feed the creature in our head more of our own ideas and it becomes something else entirely. We give those false ideas legs to stand on.

When we spend time studying the word of God we will know the truth. Knowing and keeping God's word allows us to separate truth from lies (2 Tim. 2:15). Then we may take the truth and apply it to our life.

Continue to read your Bible even if you don't think it will help. God is speaking to you through it. He will use it to remind you who He is, and how much He loves you. The God that wrote it, and Jesus the Author and Finisher of our faith are alive today. You can have a meaningful relationship with Him that fully satisfies the deepest longings of your soul.

His Promises

It is essential that we take a look at what God actually promises, because He will fulfill those. For instance, Titus 1:2 and John 3:16 promise eternal life to those who believe. Psalm 34:8 promises we will be blessed when we trust in Him, and Psalm 1:1-2 says we will be blessed when we delight in God's law. Isaiah 40:29 promises God will give strength to the weak.

The Bible is full of God's promises, but we might have some false ideas of extra promises He hasn't made. For instance, I had falsely assumed that Psalm 37:4 meant God would answer all of my prayers with "yes," exactly as I wanted them. God enjoys giving us the desires of our heart but not every desire is good for us.

When we misunderstand His promises we mistake His character. We must pray for the Holy Spirit to guide us in understanding His word.

Holding Still

> *"Be still, and know that I am God." (Psalm 46:10)*
>
> *"Rest in the Lord, and wait patiently for him." (Psalm 37:7)*

I know my daughter isn't listening when she is running around interrupting me with her own thoughts. I'll be on my knee at her level, trying to get a sentence out, and she's too busy to hear it. It is only when she is standing still in front of me, looking me in the eyes that I know I have her attention.

Will we finally start listening to God in the quiet of the waiting? Will our feet slow from running away with our own agenda? Will our mouths close and cease from interrupting Him?

Making us wait can be a way of calling our attention back to Him. When we are still we hear Him. When we are watching we will see Him work.

Instead of running with patience the race set before us (Heb. 12:1), we are often limping along, wishing we had another energy bar. God is tapping us on the shoulder, calling our names and we are holding up a finger in His face, telling Him to wait until we finish one last thing.

Thank God He is so patient with us! If we remembered who God is, the almighty Creator of the universe, the Maker of our souls, Sovereign King of Heaven and earth, then perhaps we would make more time for Him. He deserves it.

There is a time and place for multi-tasking, but not when God has been reduced to a footnote at the very bottom of our life. Constantly moved from today's "To-Do" list, to tomorrow's. We forget that everything we need comes from Him.

Busy seasons happen, but let's not forsake God because we just can't fit one more thing into our day. He is the one getting us through our day! While staying busy is not a sin, we should stay conscious of our spiritual health in busy seasons.

He is With Us in the Waiting

I was laying on the couch in the dark, waiting to feel better. Or waiting to die. Whichever came first. But I wasn't waiting alone. God sits with us while we wait. He was holding my hand. He's holding yours.

During this time in my life, it felt like God was telling me, 'You've got things in your heart that don't please Me, and it's your fault. So, I'm out for now. Heal yourself and then we'll talk.' That is not the voice of God.

Yes, it is true we have things in our hearts which don't please God. He knows that our hearts are wicked by nature, and we are imperfect sinners (Jer. 17:9, Rom. 3:23). BUT why would He ever tell us to heal ourselves? He knows we cannot do that (Eph. 2:8-9). That is precisely why He came to save us. We cannot escape death and hell without Him.

He also does not tell us He is done with us. He is longsuffering (Psalm 86:15) and invested in our spiritual development, hopes and desires. He tells us He will never leave us (1 Chr. 28:20). He is not a God of abandonment but compassion, and a present help.

His Holy Spirit dwells in us as believers so that He is not just in the room with us, but in all the spaces inside us. "And when he had said this, he breathed on them, and saith unto them, Receive ye the Holy Ghost:" (John 20:22). Jesus gives His apostles the Holy Spirit, His Comforter.

With each breath of our lungs we have Him. When He decides it is time to go, we will breathe our last breath in His presence too.

The Tree Across the Street

HERE'S A TRUTH ABOUT CLOUDS: they have a spectacular capacity for color. It's best on display in the evening, when the sun sets.

On warm Summer evenings I like to sit on our front step and watch the clouds roll past the glowing branches in the crown of the tree across the street. I watch the light slide up the trunk and along each branch, until just the very tips are on fire, like hundreds of birthday candles waiting to be blown out. What do you wish for?

I wished for many things the last few Summers. The Holy Spirit helped me turn those wishes into prayers. I really needed to remember that God is good. That He cares.

When I was sorrowfully trudging along, wondering where God was and putting on a brave face for my children, God gave me this tree at the end of the day. The colors, lighting, clouds and tree were small reminders that God is good. It made me feel warm and joyful to see what He made shine.

Just like that light travelled up the tree from its roots to its tippy-top twigs as the sun set, God is moving His light through our souls. Let it fill you up.

Consider your day today. If it is just starting, purposefully look for ways to thank God even if it's difficult. If your day is coming to a close, reflect on what God did. There are mercies and blessings every day if we learn to look for them.

Learning to Be Still

While we tend to want everything now, God is in this for the long haul. Although we come to God with our own requests and timeline, God is outside of time, unbound by it. His plan can be long and it might take a while for us to see and experience the good He has promised through a particular trial. Oh, but how worthy He is to wait on!

Don't rush through His good plan for you. Trust that if He is asking you to be still and wait He has a good reason. He isn't wasting your time, because He doesn't waste His.

Catalpa

THIS CATALPA TREE grows near the road at my mom and dad's house. To me it resembles a large octopus. Its curling tentacles were splayed in a huge canopy above me.

When life gets busy it is tempting to wish I was an octopus too. Think of what we could accomplish with eight arms! But we would only have one brain. All those arms doing different things and we wouldn't be able to focus on any of them. Our brains would be incredibly stressed.

God had a reason for only giving us two hands. There's only so much we are meant to do at once. He wants us to remember how limited we are so that we run to Him. He encourages us to come when we are weary and heavy-laden so He can give us rest (Matt. 11:28).

In Genesis 2:2-3 God chooses to rest, not out of necessity, but as an example to us. The sabbath is a gift for us to rest (Mark 2:27), and for many it can be a dedicated day for spending time with the Lord. It is essential that we make time to rest with God because being in His presence restores us.

In Genesis 18:4 Abraham implores three men to rest under a tree while they get water and wash their feet. The shade provides a cool place to escape the heat of the sun. Trees are still strategically used today in hot climates as a refuge from heat (Evans 20).

God gives us rest from the heat of everyday troubles and stress too. We enter into His presence and rest in the shadow of His wings. "He shall cover thee with his feathers, and under his wings shalt thou trust:" (Psalm 91:4). When we rest with the Lord we are renewed by His strength.

He is the source of our strength (Psalm 27:1) and capable of far more than we are. "Is any thing too hard for the Lord?" (Genesis 18:14). We are in constant need of His help and direction. May we eventually make peace with the comforting reality that we are always weak and God is always strong.

If you're feeling weary, it might be time to rest in the Lord. Pray for those opportunities. What can you set down in this season to rest? What is God asking you to do (or not do) right now? Take some time alone with Him and allow Him to fill your soul.

What We Do While We Wait

My Favorite Spot in the Park

THERE WAS ONE DAY in particular that I visited this spot and sat watching the creek. I remember it fondly as a gift from God. Everything was glowing around me. Golden leaves wandered down from the trees overhanging the bank to float gently atop a lazy current. The sun was making every reflection dance. There are few times in life that I've felt fully present to just *be*. This was one of them.

It was as if God was telling me it was okay to just be there. To continue existing, breathing, quietly here. In a season when I felt like I was not enough for anyone, let alone God Almighty, He was reminding me that HE was enough for me.

He wasn't demanding anything else of me right then. I was free to be nothing more than exactly who I am with Him. There, in the quiet stillness of knowing He is God.

We are simultaneously so imperfect, and so perfectly loved by Him.

Are you ever tempted to believe that you have to be doing all the things for God, in just the right way, or you're letting Him down? Are you ever tempted to think that you must be a lazy Christian if you need to rest?

We're not disappointing Him if we can't do 'all the things' or if we do them imperfectly. It is by design that we cannot please Him on our own. We only have to do the things He call us to do with His help and for His glory.

Whatever we think we are doing for God cannot earn grace, righteousness, or extra favor. Our works fade like a leaf, and God compares our own righteousness to filthy rags (Isa. 64:6). What can we do, gain, or accomplish alone?

Anything good we do is done by His Spirit in us (Phil. 2:13). We have the luxury of being still through His Spirit because God is the one doing the work. God has also given us any godliness we claim (2 Pet. 1:3). We achieve and obtain everything by God (John 3:27).

Furthermore, we are not lazy if we genuinely need to rest. God Himself set that example for us when He rested after the six days of creation in Genesis 2. Therefore God does not condemn rest. He created us knowing full well that we would grow weary.

Corridors

HAVE YOU EVER LOOKED DOWN A LONG CORRIDOR that seemed to go on and on? The end is a tiny square in the distance that never seems to get closer. It can leave you wondering, 'Am I even moving?'

These rows of pine trees looked like long, tree-lined corridors. What hallway is God asking you to walk down in your life right now? Sometimes the season we are in feels like it will last FOREVER. But it doesn't. Each season we pass through reminds us of the very fact that it was just a season: finite.

In Genesis 39:20, we find Joseph wrongfully imprisoned. He isn't freed until Genesis 41:14. God had Joseph waiting nearby in the king's prison, ready to raise up at the right time and save Egypt from great famine.

What We Do While We Wait

But first, Joseph was in prison for two years, forgotten by almost everyone. Including the person he had just helped (Gen. 40:23)

In that long corridor of his life, "the Lord was with Joseph, and shewed him mercy," (Gen. 39:21). Everything He did in the prison prospered. God had a plan for Joseph during a season in which I am sure Joseph would have preferred to be elsewhere. He endured it and God still blessed and used him there.

Sometimes we don't see how long the corridor is. We don't know when the season will end. Do you think this might be a mercy from the Lord? How might knowing exactly how long a season will last change the way you experience it?

Accept His Peace

When we first recognize a trial in our life there is a time of confusion as we reason within ourselves over the purpose. 1 Peter 4:12-13 encourages us not to focus on those questions. Peter says we can trade confusion for joy. He encourages us to give God the glory while we suffer (vs. 14).

The Holy Spirit can help us trade feelings of confusion and injustice for joy, and that joy will bring peace while we endure. "These things I have spoken unto you, that in me ye might have peace. In the world ye shall have tribulation: but be of good cheer; I have overcome the world." John 16:33

Can you think of a time in your life when you felt confused about what God was doing? How did you handle that confusion? Did you take your questions to God? He is the one holding the answers.

Neighbor's Dead Tree

THIS TREE-SHRUB DIED after someone accidentally killed it. Landscaping gone wrong. As I was drawing this swirling chaos of a dead tree-shrub my own thoughts were just as jumbled as these branches. The enemy was whispering all kinds of lies into my ears.

Thoughts of giving up, not amounting to anything, and being utterly incapable.

During this season, there were a few lies I kept coming back to. I repeated them so often to myself that they seemed truer than God's word. No wonder the Bible tells us to take our thoughts captive (2 Cor. 10:5, Phil. 4:8).

I got so distracted trying to draw it and kept forgetting where I was. I couldn't get a good sense of where the lights and darks were. When we are confused it becomes difficult to separate God's truth (light) from the enemy's lies (darkness). Satan is a master of deception; an author of confusion.

"For God is not the author of confusion, but of peace" (1 Cor. 14:33). Learn to recognize God's voice as the one of peace. When we wrestle with chaotic thoughts and feel anxious over our trials, let's remember Isaiah 26:3 which promises perfect peace when we fully trust the Lord. Peace helps us endure the waiting and the trials.

Take some time to write down specific lies you're tempted to believe right now, and find a few scripture verses to combat them. God's truth wins.

The Tree at the Top of the Stairs

YEW TREES ARE INFAMOUS FOR THEIR POISON. I learned this later while trying to identify the tree I drew at the top of those uneven steps.

When I got to the top of the stairs that day I discovered I wasn't alone. Nearby on the grassy knoll was a gathering of young adults having a picnic. I immediately felt like an intruder at their party, though I was some distance away. I just wanted to draw the tree. Don't mind me.

The enemy knows I struggle with feelings of exclusion because the army of darkness is always watching in the spiritual realm. So I kid you not, as I drew that day it was as if I could hear snatches of their conversation. And the enemy whispered, 'They're talking about you. They think you're weird. When they're laughing, it's at you.'

Lies can seep in like poison. Even one small lie can make us sick if it takes root in us. We must speak God's truth to our hearts often, right away. With our minds stayed on Him we have peace. If God wanted me there that day then I would stay and draw.

When the darkness fights against us, we have so much light on our side. The Holy Spirit inside us is a fearsome thing to a world of non-believers. We have God's protection over us.

You know what's amazing? The light of Jesus is confusing to the darkness (John 1:5). It confounds the ones who seek to destroy us.

After putting aside the lies and finishing the drawing, I stood up to inspect the tree.

I saw this tree move as I walked around it. Warm, peeling bark created illusions; branches joined together and separated as my vantage point shifted. It is like looking at God's will in our lives. Sometimes He has us moving and sometimes He asks us to wait.

Motion and stillness; endurance can feel like both. Even those times when *we* are waiting and still, *He* is moving. He teaches us so much in the waiting. Let's continue on in His truth while we wait.

Is there something you are waiting on now? Maybe an answer to a question, a solution to a problem, or a direction in which to proceed. Wait on the Lord, and He will bring those things in His sovereign time and way.

Strengthening Our Heart

> *"But they that wait upon the Lord shall renew their strength; they shall mount up with wings as eagles; they shall run, and not be weary; and they shall walk, and not faint." (Isa. 40:31)*

I went for a drive around late November and as always, I was scanning the trees I passed. The trees looked naked without their leaves, with their true shape exposed. They remain in this naked and 'lifeless' state while they wait for Spring.

We find out what we're made of in the waiting. What if we don't have what it takes? What if we find out again and again that we're just so…weak?

Good! To realize our weakness and limitations is to invite God in – our true Strength! His very strength is made perfect in our weakness (2 Cor. 12:9). He loves to help us! He might be trying to bring you to the realization that you need Him right now.

Coincidentally, the strongest part of a tree is its "heartwood." This is the central support column within the tree. Heartwood formation occurs on a cellular level as cells begin to die (Nakada and Fukatsu, 2024). God is doing heart work in us as we endure. Just as heartwood is composed of dead cells, we too are 'dying to ourselves,' by being still, surrendering, learning, waiting and resting.

As He works on our hearts to transform them we become stronger in our faith. He is making sure our hearts are able to handle what He is preparing us for. Even when we are weak, we have God as the strength of our hearts (Psa. 73:26). When God is the strength of our heart He bears our burdens for us.

God also changes our hearts to love more like Him. Our love has to build endurance because our love is not long-suffering by nature. God's love is already long-suffering. God asks us to endure to transform our love into His love – a love that is patient, selfless, and kind, like charity (1 Cor. 13:4-7). This love endures all things.

Sometimes God waits until He has brought us to a place where we are spiritually and emotionally ready to know something. He knows when our heart is ready. This is a great mercy.

A strong heart is one that trusts in the Lord. It is a guarded fortress pursuing perfect peace by trusting God. Philippians 4:7 says our hearts are kept, or guarded, by God's peace. A weak heart, in contrast, is sickly and unaware of its need for the great Physician's strength.

Hoping in the Lord

"And now, Lord, what wait I for? my hope is in thee."
(Psalm 39:7)

God is intended to be our heart's only hope. When our hope is in the wrong thing it can become a prison for our soul. 'If only I had this, then I would be content forever.' Sound familiar? We become trapped in empty things whereas God satisfies every desire we may have (Psalm 145:16).

"The Lord is my portion, saith my soul; therefore will I hope in him" (Lam. 3:24). May our hope be in Jesus, our blessed Redeemer! When we are tempted to despair, may we remember our hope is in the Lord and not in our circumstances. Salvation means our hope finds a new home: Christ Jesus our Savior.

"As ye have therefore received Christ Jesus the Lord, so walk ye in him: Rooted and built up in him, and stablished in the faith, as ye have been taught, abounding therein with thanksgiving" (Col. 2:6-7). When we are rooted and built up in the Lord we may give thanks in all seasons; the waiting, the trials, the fruition, the answers.

First Thessalonians 5:18 calls us to be thankful in all things as it is the will of God for us.

I love when David speaks to his soul in Psalm 42:11. He investigates his heart and finds a godly motivation. "Why art thou cast down, O my soul? and why art thou disquieted within me? hope thou in God:" When we remember who God is, and how faithful He is, we have hope.

God will assist us with all our needs, granting us contentment as we wait and hope in Him. Philippians 4:11 offers a great example of Paul's reliance on the Lord for everything. "...for I have learned, in whatsoever state I am, therewith to be content."

He is worthy of our patient, expectant hope in Him. He promises to be good to those that patiently wait for Him and seek Him (Lam. 3:25-26).

Waiting means we are not acting rashly. We are waiting on His direction. We are not relying on ourselves for rescue. Thank the Lord! I'm learning that it's a gift from the Lord not to be able to do anything about a situation. Because it also means that I don't HAVE to do anything. God will take care of me, and He will do His good work.

"...Continue in the faith grounded and settled, and be not moved away from the hope of the gospel," (Col. 1:23). May we be firmly rooted in the hope He offers! The God of hope is able to fill us with "all joy and peace in believing," (Rom. 15:13). Our source of hope lives inside us. Our 'roots' will absorb all the mercy and grace He offers in our hour of need so that we "abound in hope" throughout the trials.

Instead of hoping the trial will end, hope in the Lord through it.

Hopeful Anticipation

There is a park near us full of magnolia trees. It is a stunning sight in the Spring when they all bloom. Before those trees burst into color though, they are filled with closed buds. Each bud holds the anticipation of the flower that will come.

Waiting on the Lord also forces us to hope in what we cannot see. "…then do we with patience wait for it" (Rom. 8:24-25). It is important and necessary for Him to build our patience and increase our faith. Hebrews 11:1 says, "faith is the substance of things hoped for, the evidence of things not seen."

Is your hope in the Lord, or in what He will do for you?

If we ever feel disappointed in how things are going and start to hope in anything else, let us remember Psalm 62:5, "My soul, wait thou only upon God; for my expectation is from him." A hope that is willing to wait becomes a pleasing expectation in the Lord rather than an unmet expectation of our own.

Trees have an expectation in their waiting. While dormant, they are waiting to resume life and begin growing again. We as Christians, however, are grown by Christ through the waiting. He is our living hope in every season.

Remember what He's already done for you and thank Him. Pray for reminders of the times He met your needs before. Look ahead trusting He is capable.

Preparing for What's Next

Trees know how to prepare for what's next. They pay attention to the seasons.

Deciduous trees stop growing in Summer, lose their foliage in Autumn, and prepare for dormancy. The cold weather acts as a cue for the tree's hormones to begin separating the leaf stem from the branch (Smithsonian Science Education Center, 2023).

The Winter dormancy in trees is broken down into three phases: "early rest, winter rest, and after-rest" ("What do Trees do in the Winter?," 2024). Yes, the tree is resting, waiting for Spring. But there are other metabolic processes happening within the tree while it waits. Therefore, the waiting is active.

When God asks us to wait on Him, we are relying on Him to provide all we need for whatever comes next. To meet Him. To handle the next thing. To become like Christ. He equips us for His good work.

As we prepare for what's next, God strengthens our faith too. First Peter 3:15 exhorts us to be ready to give an answer for the hope that is in us. God can use our trials to better prepare us to testify of our hope in Him. Continue to read your Bible and remember His truth as you prepare for whatever He has next in your life.

Preparing while we wait means we aren't frantically scrambling around when He calls us to act.

We also wait on His return, knowing He is coming back for us. It could be as soon as tomorrow. "My soul waiteth for the Lord more than they that watch for the morning:" Psalm 130:6). Let's look for Him with faithful certainty, even more so than in the sun rising. A heart that hopes in Jesus is seeking Him.

Don't pick up your roots and wander away when it feels like God isn't moving in a season of your life.
Stay rooted in the Source of life and love as you wait, knowing full well that waiting is sometimes part of His plan for your good and His glory.

What Our Disappointment Can Teach Us

Reevaluating Priorities

"Jesus said unto him, Thou shalt love the Lord thy God with all thy heart, and with all thy soul, and with all thy mind." (Matt. 22:37)

God can use our disappointment as a wake-up call. I did not realize how much time and energy I was devoting to the issues I struggled with. Then, when I was devastated by disappointment, God opened my eyes to where my priorities should be instead.

We need to give God's plan and truth the preference. He must be the priority in our life. What He calls us to do should be what we do. We come to God praying, 'God, can You please make this happen?' but we can learn to move toward, "teach me to do thy will" (Psalm 143:10). We should not care about our hearts' desires more than what God wants for us now.

The Holy Spirit can help us love God more than all the things we're consumed with. Come to Him asking what desires He wants to plant within your heart. Ask Him to remind you what your priorities should be.

Revealing Expectations

Disappointment is born from unmet expectations. If we break down the word "disappointment," we get the prefix "dis," meaning 'not' or 'the opposite of,' and "appointment," which is an arranged meeting or the assigning of a task to a particular individual.

Have you ever felt upset with God because you didn't see Him 'show up' for you? God doesn't miss appointments; He sets them.

When we try to force God into doing something, and our misplaced expectation is not met, we then think God did not hold up His end of the bargain. God doesn't bargain with us, and is unable to break His own commitments because it goes against His very nature.

To be disappointed in Him is to imply that He has failed us. It exposes our hearts' true desires. Even when we are forced to admit, "I failed," our heart might be saying, "God failed me." He will never fail us, and when *we* fail He still loves us. His love does not depend on our perfect performance because He knows we are imperfect.

When we are disappointed in an outcome we recognize our expectation. That expectation can be filled with our pride. In our pride we expect God to perform for us. Have you ever boasted about what He might do (Lam. 3:37) forgetting to consult His will first?

What message does it send to an unbeliever if we claim God will do something He never promised to do? They will see Him as a God who doesn't follow through. God always follows through on His own promises. How could we ever be disappointed in Him? We are not God's instructor (Job 40:2). He is ours!

We are supposed to love Him for who He is, but more often we love Him for what He does. He knows this about us, so He reminds us every day of His love. He knows that the things He has done for us will become a history of His faithfulness in our life, and spur on our faith in the future.

What Our Disappointment Can Teach Us

Disgruntled Bird

AS I SAT ON MY OLD COLLEGE CAMPUS drawing this tree, with the art building in the distance, I began to laugh.

Why was I laughing? Because this tree looked like a disgruntled bird, bent and battered by whatever gust of wind dropped it there in the grass. The bark was furrowed and layered like ruffled feathers. I kept laughing at the irony of this tree which seemed to sum up my college experience so well.

This was a shaping place for me, mostly in unexpected ways. What I thought I wanted and what I actually got from my college experience was informative and disillusioning. I watched my classmates succeed in ways that demonstrated just how incapable I was.

I watched their success from the sideline and discovered that I was going to walk a different path.

At a prestigious award ceremony where several classmates won awards and made business contacts for their future, I was in the stall of a nearby restroom accepting my own defeat. God told me, 'This is not for you…but it will be okay.'

My vision for success at what felt like such a pivotal point slowly crumbled around me. God had blessed me with artistic gifts, but there's a lot more to 'making it' and the more I learned about it the more I doubted myself. God used my doubt too.

I struggled with my faith in college and experienced emotional burdens that seemed to penetrate my core. I would not choose to go back to that time in my life. But God taught me so much more through the experience than He did about achieving the success I thought I was supposed to have.

God used everything I went through during that season of my life to help shape me. I sat there years later as someone who once kind of belonged at that school, and drew an okay-looking tree without having to prove anything or achieve pristine realism or write a paper on it. I was allowed to be imperfect.

My paper and pen reflect my shortcomings and it is okay. I practice and try again and can achieve a level of satisfaction with my work. Confronting our limits forces us to cede to the One True King, our perfect Creator. Any gift He has given me exists to glorify Him.

"Tree of Life"

I WAS INCREDIBLY STOKED to draw this former tree. When I arrived, it was more amazing than I imagined. This massive beast split years ago and its two halves were moved to flank a trail running through the park.

You can see the way the limbs twist, and even climb all over it now that it's on the ground. The wood grain captures so much movement. I had that rush of a tree feeling where I am sitting before greatness and have only to put pen to paper. 'I get to draw this thing?! Bring it on. I want to sing about this thing that God made!'

But then I started drawing it. I started over a few times because I just couldn't seem to get an accurate sense of its proportions. I started to outline its shape but every time I got back around to where I started none of it lined up.

My disappointment in my own ability to render this thing with my pens was acute. It was humbling. I couldn't make my hand do what my eyes saw. When I tried to draw this tree my expectation was in my own ability. Instead, God let me marvel at His.

I got some of it down on paper and instead of fleshing out a full drawing of this awesome tree, I closed my sketchbook. I explored as much of this tree-sculpture as I could. Then I sat there atop it, thankful. God wanted to remind me that HE is to be praised, because He made this. We have the privilege of exalting the Lord for His creation and excellency.

Our limitations can frustrate us, or they can liberate us to run to God, who is limitless. Mark 10:27 discusses one very important limitation: entering the kingdom of God. But Jesus makes it clear that while man is not able to do this alone, all things are possible with God. Our salvation is not a result of our own striving or action. "Not of works, lest any man should boast" (Eph. 2:9).

What We Held Dear

Have you ever held onto something so tightly your whole body began to ache? Your fingers cramp up. Your arms begin to protest as your muscles grow sore. Your shoulders grow tense and weary. Your back begins to strain from supporting the effort.

Yet you think you'll feel better the longer you hold on.

Strangler vines will wrap themselves around anything they think will give them life. They hold on so tightly, with so many tiny tethers, that removing them is almost impossible. Especially the longer they've been holding on.

My own heart was attached like a strangler vine to its idol, and separating it meant ripping all those little misplaced roots from their life source. I felt those roots shrivel and die.

We have an idol in our heart anytime we feel we desperately need something in addition to the Lord. Satan can even use our heart's desire to deceive us. We might pray for it often, not realizing it has become an idol to us. God can use disappointment to open our eyes to the idols we may be blind to. He alone is worthy of our time, honor, glory and worship.

We hold our idols so tight, not realizing those things steal our hearts away from God. "We know that an idol is nothing in the world, and that there is none other God but one" (1 Cor. 8:4). God helps us identify the idol and remove it. He helps us hold onto Him instead.

Isn't it wonderful that God holds *us* dear? May He be dear to us as we remember His great love, mercy and grace toward us. May we never turn to idols when we feel God doesn't satisfy. "Thou openest thine hand, and satisfiest the desire of every living thing" (Psalm 145:16).

Will we obey His good plan, and trust the One who holds the nations of the earth like dust in His hand, who weighs mountains and measures water in ways no man can (Isa. 40:12-15)?

Or will we seek to make our own gods, ones we understand, pursuing trees that don't rot to fashion them out of (Isa. 40:20)? Anything we create will pass away from this earth. God's creation, however, and whatever He does shall remain (Ecc. 3:14-15) because He alone is God and Sovereign Creator.

Think back to a time when an idol was removed from your heart. How did you recognize it as an idol? Did God help you choose to walk away from it, or did He remove it for you? Take time to thank Him for revealing to you what you held dearer than Him.

Pine Line-Up

THIS CLUSTER OF TREES STANDS TOGETHER in proximity but differs greatly in stature. The tree on the left reminded me how the Lord is above all heaven and earth. The two trees beside it had their heads lopped off to protect the power lines running above them.

God is like the "Cedars of Lebanon" prized in biblical times for their tall, straight frames of valuable timber. Only God stands tall and straight like these precious cedars. When other idols we turn to are cut down like the evergreens to the right in this drawing, it reminds us where our faith and trust truly belong: the Lord. "Who is like unto thee, O Lord, among the gods? who is like thee, glorious in holiness, fearful in praises, doing wonders?" (Exo. 15:11).

God showed His glory and power over the idols of the Philistines. When Israel's enemy removes the ark of the Lord from Israel they bring it into the house of one of their idols, Dagon. They set it in front of the false-god statue and leave for the day. In the morning,

1 Samuel 5:3 records that the statue of Dagon is laying face-down, bowed before the ark of the Lord.

The next day, after having righted the statue again, they return to find Dagon again bowing before the ark, except this time the statue is in pieces. The head and hands have been cut off.

God was sending a message that idols do not stand against the true Lord. "...Thou shalt worship the Lord thy God, and him only shalt thou serve" (Matt. 4:10). God's word says "Their sorrows shall be multiplied that hasten after another god:" (Psalm 16:4).

God's power is on display against idols again in 1 Kings 18:22-39. The false god Baal could not consume the offering presented.

However, when it is Elijah's turn, He gives the glory to God, stating that what will happen next is only by God's power. "Then the fire of the Lord fell, and consumed the burnt sacrifice, and the wood" (vs. 38).

God's fire consumed even the water drenching the wood and pooled around it. Competition over. God wins.

May we glorify God always, knowing true power rests with Him alone and not in broken idols. " I am the Lord: that is my name: and my glory will I not give to another, neither my praise to graven images" (Isa. 42:8).

Removing an idol can be incredibly painful. But any idol burns up by the holy competition. God is the giver of life, and He is everything we need and crave every moment of our lives. God removes our idols to remind us we can only be satisfied by Him. What a gracious God!

Loving What's True

> *"For the Lord is good; his mercy is everlasting; and his truth endureth to all generations." (Psalm 100:5)*

> *"Lead me in thy truth, and teach me: for thou art the God of my salvation; on thee do I wait all the day." (Psalm 25:5)*

Leaning unto our own understanding (Prov. 3:5) means we give it preference. Our own understanding does not hinder the will of God, but it muddies our minds in the midst of it. It keeps us from fully trusting in Him. It reveals a heart that is not ready to surrender to the good that God has chosen for our lives.

Our understanding comes from the imagination of our wicked hearts and can lead us to foolish, errant behavior and "presumptuous sins" (Psalm 19:13). It can be downright false, while we are called to think on what is honest (Phil. 4:8).

Our understanding is full of misconceptions and changes to fit our agenda. We also tend to be blinded to our own motives, too eager to overlook them. "All the ways of a man are clean in his own eyes; but the Lord weigheth the spirits" (Prov. 16:2). The Lord weighs our intentions and measures our motives. There is no fooling Him.

Proverbs 2:3-11 says that when we seek godly wisdom and understanding in fear of the Lord, then He will give the righteous "sound wisdom" and be a "buckler" (shield) for those that walk uprightly (vs. 7). We will be able to understand righteousness and every good path (vs. 9). Verse 6 makes it clear that wisdom, knowledge and understanding come from the Lord.

When all is said and done on earth, His truth is here guiding each generation, battling and triumphing over every lie of the world. His word is tried (Psalm 18:30), tested, and stands firm. We too stand firmly rooted when our foundation is His word.

May the Lord help us to love what's true!

The Stories We Tell Ourselves

Periodically I have to go through my inbox and sort through my junk mail. I can delete the emails I don't need, but I'll keep receiving them unless I unsubscribe.

Have you ever subscribed to your own narrative? Oh, I had bought a subscription to mine alright. We tell our brains, 'I want to hear more of this. It is the story I enjoy best.'

We all enter into situations wanting to believe something about it. What are some stories you enjoy telling yourself? Are they true? Why do you enjoy hearing them?

When you examine that narrative you love, does it line up with God's word and will? We may need to deconstruct those false narratives entirely. God can reveal to us the ways we have been deceived, and the ways we have deceived ourselves.

I don't like being wrong about something, but God is teaching me to focus on the fact that He is right. If *I* had been right in my understanding during this season then I would have missed out on a lot of blessings He gave me. He can teach us to submit to His truth if we're willing.

What Our Disappointment Can Teach Us

God reminded me that it is not a personal fault of mine to be wrong sometimes. It is an illusion that we could get to a point where we understand everything and do it all correctly. God allows us to be wrong and make mistakes because it points our imperfect selves to our perfect and all-knowing God.

Root Hut

I SAT LEANING AGAINST THE HILL GRADE to draw this, and the whole time I worried that I was going to fall backwards into the creek. You could say I was leaning forward in my chair to stay upright. In our faith, God warns us not to lean toward our own understanding (Pro. 3:5).

Our own narratives can feel like a little place to hide, just like this root hut. Our favorite stories make us feel warm. They are familiar and cozy. But when you look closely you begin to spot the holes in them. They fall short because they are not God's truth.

In this season I really wanted something to be true. It was completely selfish of me, but I still wanted that thing to be true. I even convinced myself it must be true. I sorted through all my 'evidence' of memories like my theory was on trial and I could prove it true.

I built a whole plan around it. The roots forming this hut are like the prayer walls I pulled in around me, sealing myself in to live and die by my own plan.

Sometimes God opens our eyes to our true heart in painful and humbling ways. But in His kindness He is right there with us. What a good God to show us our faults and then clean up our heart (Psalm 51:10)! May what we desire never be greater than our desire for God.

My disappointment in the fall out of this misguided and flawed plan revealed to me that I loved the story I was telling myself more than the one God was writing for me.

It is impossible for the story we imagine, that one originating from us, to be better than God's true word and will for our lives. This is true of our life on earth, and it is true of our eternal life in Heaven. "..men have not heard, nor perceived by the ear, neither hath the eye seen, O God, beside thee, what he hath prepared for him that waiteth for him" (Isaiah 64:4). 1 Corinthians 2:9 adds, "…for them that love him."

He has a wonderful plan and reward beyond our wildest imagination – beyond all of mankind's imagination. It is a promise for those that love and wait on Him.

The Gift of Disillusionment

It may not seem like it at the time, but the Lord is merciful to show us how wrong we are. He watches as we continue to act out of a certain belief, gently reminding us that we are incorrect. Gently calling us back to His own good truth. But we are stubborn.

I remember several uncomfortable moments which God used to correct my understanding. I imagined a situation going one way, and it definitely did not. And God had to allow that several times before He got my attention. He called me out of my own head to see the truth.

What Our Disappointment Can Teach Us

You probably have your own specific examples of how God used a circumstance, interaction or event to disillusion your illusion. The illusion in my head was shattered, and it hurt. But afterwards His peace found me.

Through the Holy Spirit I first repented, and then thanked God for what happened and how good He was in it. God had nothing to apologize for, being holy and righteous in all His ways. After those painful realizations and instances where God helped me see clearly, I realized that I want the truth more than my own story. I didn't want to walk around blind, continually pierced by the shards of my own broken understanding.

I had to confront what I had imagined for myself in certain areas of my life, with what He has given me (and what I have chosen). God is teaching me much about contentment and that He is unfailing in His love, goodness, and fulfillment.

He is changing the way I think for the better. God can teach us to love truth.

Two Understandings

A FEW YEARS AGO, I was driving to my grandmother's house. Out my driver's window I saw an incredible sunset flooded with colors. I turned to the passenger window and saw a quiet, gray sky. I looked from one to the other, wondering how the same sky could contain both.

It reminded me how my imagination can be right there coloring what I see and experience. I sometimes prefer it to the gray of every day. But if we really look we can see God coloring each day with blessings!

When I drew this tree, I was wrestling with my own understanding. It was a battle between what I wanted to believe, and what God was telling me. In the tree, you can see one of the main trunks has died, while the second prevailed. Which would prevail in my life: my understanding or God's truth?

In and of itself, imagination is not necessarily a bad thing. If God designed us with the capacity to imagine, then He can use it for good. Our imaginations can help us design and create. The danger comes when we prefer our own imagination to the reality God presents.

Our imaginations can also pose a danger when left unchecked because they can influence our understanding. When we want to believe something is true we will gravitate toward anything that supports it.

Having a fondness for one understanding also means that it hurts when it is shattered. We might convince ourselves something is true, and then events unfold in a completely different way than we expect. We had forgotten that this 'truth' was just an understanding that lived in our head.

What Our Disappointment Can Teach Us

We are left cradling the pieces of the story we loved. We then have to mourn an idea. An idea is a difficult thing to mourn because it is cruelly tenacious and intangible.

We fill in holes with our imagination, using it as a shortcut. We can be blinded by what we want to see. Halfway through this drawing I realized there were branches I hadn't even drawn yet. I hadn't seen them because I was distracted. The details can escape us when we are busy inventing our own.

"…Let thy lovingkindness and thy truth continually preserve me" (Psalm 40:11). We need to stay vigilant and pray for the right understanding – the truth of God. We know His wisdom is without hidden agenda or motive. Remember, God's understanding contains both mercy and truth.

> *Tree roots are not disappointed with the water and sunlight provided for the tree. They are programmed to suck in that water and photosynthesize that light. May we too gratefully accept all that God offers us as we are rooted in His great love. That is where we are filled with His fulness.*

When Our Faith Is Tested

Accepting the Trial

> *"For I reckon that the sufferings of this present time are not worthy to be compared with the glory which shall be revealed in us." (Rom. 8:18)*

All of the trees He allowed me to draw come back to this very subject.

When God tries our faith, we tend to mistake it for injustice. What did I do wrong? Why am I suffering? Why is this happening to me, of all people?

Remember, 1 Peter 4:12-13 offers the encouragement that in times of struggle we actually have cause to rejoice. When we endure "fiery trials," we are "partakers of Christ's sufferings" and are therefore promised to be partakers of His glory.

Romans 8:18 builds on this, reminding us that our suffering is not worthy to be compared to the glory we will share with Christ in Heaven. Let's pray that God reminds us in every single trial that there is no comparison to be made. Let's remember, as believers, where we are going.

All the ways we stumble and fail, our sin and faults…it all burns up like vapors and disintegrates like ash when we are surrounded by His glory in Heaven.

We are called not to view our trial as some strange thing happening to us, but to focus on the eternal ramification of enduring it in a way that is pleasing to the Lord. "Yet if any man suffer as a Christian, let him not be ashamed; but let him glorify God on this behalf" (1 Pet. 4:16).

Even when we are crippled with disappointment, weighed down by circumstances, swallowed up in sadness or pain...there is always hope in Christ. In the trial we get to experience how it feels to be held by God. There are times when the God holding us is the only One holding us together.

God uses our trials for His good purpose, and when we are faithful and obedient servants during those trials, we know we have not "labored in vain" and may "rejoice in the day of Christ" (Phil. 2:16). May we be found faithful as we endure, for the crown of life everlasting (Rev. 2:10).

Enduring the Trial

Trees that struggle are hardier.

They can endure their need because they are used to it. One study showed that spruces growing in soil with less water seemed to thrive in times of drought over spruces growing in soil with extra moisture. Those trees didn't know what to do in drought, having already used up their water. They had not learned to endure, so they dried and split open (Wohlleben 44-45).

Those hardy trees learned what it meant to be thirsty. "...my soul thirsteth for thee, my flesh longeth for thee in a dry and thirsty land, where no water is;" (Psalm 63:1). For Christians, trials teach us who to thirst for; God will satisfy with all the living water we need.

Throughout our life God teaches us to become 'hardy.' "The process of learning stability is triggered by painful micro-tears that occur when trees bend way over in the wind, first in one direction and then in the other. Wherever it hurts, that's where the tree must strengthen its support structure" (Wohlleben 46).

What are the micro-tears, the splitting-open droughts, the pulling and rending in your own life?

Endurance is learned over time through an indefinite trial or series of trials that builds godly character within us. It is hard to learn endurance if we consistently avoid problems. "Thou therefore endure hardness, as a good soldier of Jesus Christ" (2 Tim. 2:3).

Endurance is God asking us to proceed forward with Him. To rely on Him. If we knew the timeline of every trial, we would try and muster the strength ourselves. It would not take nearly as much faith in the Lord.

In 1 Peter 4:19, God promises that He will faithfully watch over and protect our soul if we are suffering as part of His will. What an incredible comfort while we endure!

The world is telling us, 'we only live once.' 'Get it now.' 'Do what makes you feel good.' We've forgotten our life is a marathon (Heb. 12:1) and that God has promised to work on us for the entirety of it (Phil. 1:6). Praise the Lord for that!

Endurance is part of sanctification, the process of becoming holy like Jesus. Can you look back at a difficult season and see the good that came from it? What did God teach you? In what ways has struggle made you stronger?

Refining Faith

> *"That the trial of your faith, being much more precious than of gold that perisheth, though it be tried with fire, might be found unto praise and honour and glory at the appearing of Jesus Christ." (1 Pet. 1:7)*

Lamentations 3:33 tells us that God does not afflict us willingly. While that verse implies His reluctance to allow affliction, "He is not reluctant about the ultimate good that is going to be brought about through that pain; that indeed is why he is doing it" (Ortlund 138). He does not enjoy our suffering, nor does He allow it without feeling it Himself. He is full of mercy and goodness.

There is a concept in Christianity of 'refiner's fire,' referring to how our trials refine our faith in a similar way to gold getting refined by intense heat (1 Pet. 1:7). Our faith is tried so that when Jesus returns, we might be found praising, honoring, and glorifying the Lord. The salvation of our souls, that end of our faith when we meet Jesus, is described as "joy unspeakable" and "full of glory" (1 Pet. 1:8).

As the gold is refined it becomes more valuable and impurities are removed. "…When he hath tried me, I shall come forth as gold" (Job 23:10).

Our faith becomes valuable and purer when it is strengthened by trials. The impurities that might exist in our faith, such as misplaced beliefs, untrue doctrine, misunderstandings, and a weak relationship with the Lord, get removed in the heat. We are forced to learn and grow in our knowledge of Him, burning away all that is contrary to our good and His glory.

Chimney Tree

THIS TREE IN A FRIEND'S YARD captivated me with its hallowed out middle and unique shape. It looks like a wood stove and chimney. If that rotting cavern in the middle was the firebox, then it was singed black and holding ashes from the remains of a fire.

If you turned them over, would the coals still glow with heat?

We have a woodstove in our home and we love to sit by the fire soaking in the warmth. After we've burned a few fires the glass on our load door becomes smeared with ash and residue.

When the firebox has completely cooled, my husband mixes a little bit of water with the ash to clean the glass. I thought surely that would make it dirtier, but he said the ash is slightly abrasive, like a fine sandpaper to rub away the grit. When he is done, it becomes a crystal-clear window where we watch the flames dance again.

Ashes are evidence that fire existed. The ashes of our fiery trials can tell a beautiful, yet humbling tale of the fires that came and went. They represent all that God taught us during those trials. Something purer and more pleasing to the Lord came out of that fire.

When we are in a fiery trial we desperately want to know why it is happening, but God waits to show us. It's usually not until the coals are cooling and the ashes are forming that we see more clearly what God did inside us with those flames.

The water of our tears mixes with those ashes and reveals a picture of what God did for us.

Something like ash, which should make things dirtier, helps to clean instead. There's something wonderfully redemptive about that. The wretchedness of our sin wakes us up to the incredible and perfect love of the Lord because He died for us while we were yet sinners (Rom. 5:8). He made us clean.

In the Bible we see instances of people mourning by sitting among ashes. After Job loses everything, "he sat down among the ashes" to mourn (Job 2:8). When the king of Nineveh hears God's warning of destruction from His prophet Jonah, he is grieved over his and his people's sin and "covered him with sackcloth, and sat in ashes" (Jon. 3:6). When David's daughter Tamar is raped and then sent away, she "put ashes on her head…and went on crying" (2 Sam. 13:19). When Mordecai hears his people will be destroyed he "put on sackcloth with ashes" and "cried with a loud and bitter cry" (Est. 4:1).

God's people mourn in ashes when they either realize their grievous sin before the Lord and repent, *or* endure heavy and sorrowful affliction at no fault of their own.

When we sit among the remains of a fire of sin or mourning, we too might feel like ashes. We might feel like we were ground into the smallest of pieces and the slightest breeze will blow us away. There is a place for ashes, but God doesn't leave us there.

Our sin and the fall-out from it can be a devastating inferno. Sin can burn down homes, burn up the atmosphere and suffocate us, and engulf everything in its path. The ashes become a reminder never to choose that sin again because of how it burned us, and perhaps those around us.

Even if we lit it ourselves, God can still use that fire as refiner's fire.

Reflect on the trials in your own life. Have the ashes cooled, or do the coals still smolder? Be careful, lest you add any kindling to a sin that tempts you and the fire light again.

Tower Tree

THIS TREE IS IN THE MIDDLE OF A FIELD in Oklahoma, but it's not growing in the ground. It is sprouting from inside an old silo. How it got there is a mystery, but you could argue that it has been 'moved away' from its proper growing place.

Just as this tree sits at a great height, God may choose to remove us from the earthly safety and comforts we rely on because He wants us to rely on Him instead.

WHEN OUR FAITH IS TESTED

We might be tempted and tried as Jesus was at the top of the temple (Matt. 4:5-6). The devil asked Him to cast Himself down if He was really the Son of God. Jesus did not give in to the temptation.

Sometimes our anger in the trial is misdirected at God, because we think the temptation comes from Him. There are specific truths to combat this. We are tempted by our own lusts and led away from what pleases God (James 1:14). We are also spiritually attacked by the devil. When we submit ourselves to God and resist the devil he will flee from us (Jam. 4:7).

"For God cannot be tempted with evil, neither tempteth he any man" (James 1:13). God stays with us through the temptation, "… but will with the temptation also make a way to escape, that ye may be able to bear it" (1 Cor. 10:13).

Jesus understands our troubles because He too was tempted as we are, but did not sin (Heb. 4:15). We have the power of God in us through His Holy Spirit and are therefore fully equipped to withstand temptation, or flee it with God's escape route.

Wherever He chooses to plant us, may we trust Him and know that He will be with us.

Will it Stand?

"We can learn a lot about what land is like by what is already growing on it" (Evans 36). If we want to know what type of soil we are dealing with, let's look at the trees growing there. Are they growing well?

If we apply this to our spiritual walk of faith, then what is the current condition of our heart? What is growing well there? Why is it growing well there? May we grow to better please and obey the Lord, changing the soil of our heart to facilitate good growth.

We want our trees to stand firm, rooted in God's great love through faith.

Even if the soil is poor, a forest may thrive with firm and well-developed root systems. "The fabulously rich and diverse tropical rain forests are mostly on very poor soils…but they achieve such exuberance owing to astonishing root networks that pretty well capture and recycle again and again every nutrient there is" (Evans 37).

"Capturing and recycling every nutrient" amongst the root system is an accurate description of meditating on God's word. Through the direction of the Holy Spirit, we find meaning in His word and it blesses and teaches us. All scripture is given by God to instruct us in righteousness, so there is always something to learn (2 Tim. 3:16).

As we read His word He builds our faith. Will it stand when it's on trial? What is our faith really made of? What is it founded in? If our faith has no rooted foundation in God's love and truth, if we think we can hope in anything other than Him and His grace, then we will topple over like trees without roots.

Building Faith

At first, we might feel as if we fail every test of faith He gives us. What does God do when our faith 'fails'? Punish us? No. He gives us grace, slowly building in us a stronger faith for next time. When He tries our reins (Jer. 17:10) and we fail, we also learn.

Do we want our faith to be mushy, soft, decaying wood, easily broken down by decomposers? Or strong, healthy wood, protected by thick bark, and resistant to rot?

"Live wood is of no use to organisms that live in dead wood" (Wohlleben 134). The devil and workers of darkness are like those organisms that live in the dead wood.

We as believers are like that living wood. We have submitted ourselves to God and He is the one sustaining and protecting us. His spirit is in us, making us alive. "Healthy trees growing in their natural range withstand almost all attacks if they are well nourished" (Wohlleben 134).

There is a progression of growth as our trials drive us back to God. Our tribulation or trials work our patience (James 1:3). That patience builds endurance through our experiences, and those experiences build hope in God as we see His continued faithfulness while we labor (Rom. 5:3-5).

God builds our faith in every trial with every corresponding move of His faithfulness. We run to Him in our distress and all we know, there at the end of ourselves, is GOD.

Fighting the Battle

> *"For our light affliction, which is but for a moment, worketh for us a far more exceeding and eternal weight of glory." (2 Cor. 4:17)*

There are some pretty amazing stories in the Bible where God helps His people defeat their enemies. He sends hailstone upon the kings of the Amorites (Josh. 10:11), He made the Syrians hear the noise of a great army and flee from an imagined attack (2 Kin. 7:5-7), and He raised up a small shepherd boy to defeat a giant with a slingshot and win a war (1 Sam. 17:33-49).

These accounts and many more in scripture, along with our own stories of battles won with the Lord are all an encouragement to trust Him. When they go to battle He asks Israel to have courage and know that He will be with them (Josh. 1:9). He is with us as we fight our battles too.

At the end of his life, Paul says, "I have fought a good fight, I have finished my course, I have kept the faith:" (2 Tim. 4:7). Because of this he has secured a crown of righteousness in Heaven. In this life we labor to share the gospel and demonstrate God's great love and grace to the world, for the prize of righteousness in eternity.

We are more than conquerors because we have Him (Rom. 8:37). God fights for us. Even when we endure injustice, we are told not to avenge ourselves because vengeance belongs to the Lord (Rom. 12:19). We may be of good cheer because God has overcome the world (John 16:33).

Keep Your Armor On

Christians are called to be peacemakers pursuing peace (Rom. 12:18, Heb. 12:14). Yet we are also instructed to put on our armor. There are battles happening around us all the time and we are asked to prepare. God does not tell us to take the armor off.

We fight to protect ourselves and others, to defend the gospel, to pursue peace.

Doing life on this side of Heaven requires each element of armor mentioned in Ephesians 6:11-17: the belt of truth, breastplate of righteousness, the preparation of the gospel, shield of faith, helmet of salvation and sword of the Spirit.

Remember that the people we encounter are not the flesh and blood we fight. We fight the wickedness inside them. Inside us. All the evil around us. But we don't fight alone. We labor alongside fellow brothers and sisters in Christ clad in armor on the battlefield with us. We labor with God who has already won the victory of salvation and life over death.

God helps us fight each battle the whole way through. Someday when God calls us home, we may take off that armor and know the battle is finished. His soldiers are coming Home.

Mosquitos

I WAS SET UP IN MOSQUITO-INFESTED WOODS as I drew, and my cupholder held bug spray instead of coffee. The sun was bright on my paper, and the eeriness of what I saw there unsettled me: flickering shadows cast by a hoard of tenacious mosquitos.

The invaders ducked around this thin layer of bug spray looking for openings. It was a meager line of defense against this angry swarm of blood-suckers. They thought I was lunch.

I could see their shadows all over my paper ducking down at my head, which was covered by my dad's old ballcap. It was a reminder that something dangerous lay in wait just outside my actual vision. Waiting for their chance to prey.

We forget we do life in a very real spiritual battle waging outside the tangible world. It is a battle that God protects us from when we put on the "armour of God" (Eph. 6:11). The shield mentioned in Ephesians 6:16 is our faith, used to "quench all the fiery darts of the wicked." My "fiery darts" here may have been mosquitos, but they only represent the attacks from a real threat.

Who are the "wicked" mentioned? Those that lay in wait for our soul. Not flesh and blood alone, but we wrestle against principalities and spiritual wickedness in high places (vs. 12). All of these evil forces can influence others to act as our enemies. They will try to influence us as well but we have our armor, shield and sword. Anyone who is against God is also against us as His children.

God is "…a buckler to all those that trust in him" (Psalm 18:30)." A buckler is a handheld shield. When we trust in the Lord, our faith becomes a shield against our enemies. "For whatsoever is born of God overcometh the world: and this is the victory that overcometh the world, even our faith" (1 John 5:4).

We are called to be sober and vigilant, on guard against the roaring lion Satan who seeks to devour us (1 Pet. 5:8). David describes his perils like this: "My soul is among lions: and I lie even among them that are set on fire…" (Psalm 57:4).

Have you ever felt that you were 'among lions'? Who, or what, are the lions in your life and how may you combat them?

Don't Put Your Sword Down

My daughter once brought me a piece of tree bark she found in the driveway. I studied this tree bark and realized it was extraordinary. These dead cells making up the outer bark were all gathered together to create paper-thin layers, arranged in ridges like stacked mountain ranges.

God used the layers to remind me of Hebrews 4:12. As we turn to scripture and the Holy Spirit convicts us, we are putting that sharp sword of God's word to use, dividing those tightly compacted layers of intent, desire, and thoughts so we can be on guard for our heart's deception and the lies of Satan.

It is a delicate and precise work to separate those fine layers.

Remember to read God's word and keep your ultimate weapon, the sword of the Spirit, sharp and ready. God's Spirit stands ready within us wielding that sword as we read, convicting us and opening our eyes and heart to truth (Heb. 4:12, Eph. 6:17). Don't put your sword down.

Trees wear this outer bark mentioned above like armor to protect their inner, living wood from inclement weather, elements of nature, and pests. If you want to infiltrate the tree and get to the juicy sapwood inside, you have to get through the bark.

"There are specialized sap-sucking pests for every tree" (Wohlleben 115) that will suck up the sap flowing out of wounds in the tree branches, trunk, or in the leaves themselves. These pests want to suck out the life essence from the tree.

"The rulers of the darkness" and "spiritual wickedness" mentioned in Ephesians 6:12 want to do the same for us because we are the children of God. They want to destroy us, render us inactive and out of the fight.

"…it helps if trees form a thick layer of outer bark to finally get rid of the sap-sucking pests (Wohlleben 116). Just as trees have bark, thank goodness we have that valuable armor of God, including the helmet of salvation and sword of the Spirit.

God Sees and Hears Us

"I sought the Lord, and he heard me, and delivered me from all my fears." (Psalm 34:4)

"The righteous cry, and the Lord heareth, and delivereth them out of all their troubles." (Psalm 34:17)

When the angel of the Lord finds Hagar in the wilderness, pregnant and alone, He gives her a direction and a promise. He instructs her to name her child Ishmael, "because the Lord hath heard thy affliction" (Gen. 16:9-11). Ishmael means "God hears."

In Genesis 21:16-17 we find Hagar in the wilderness again. She is weeping, fully expecting her child to die. The angel of God comforts her, telling her that God has heard Ishmael's cries and not to fear. He reminds her of His promise to make a nation of Ishmael as well. God opens her eyes to show her a well of water where she and her baby can drink (vs. 18-19).

Both times God met her in the wilderness when she was alone without a plan. Even though Hagar's pregnancy was Sarah's misguided plan, God still brought good out of it. He heard Hagar, had compassion, and gave her and her son a future.

We might think, 'I'm fighting my battle alone. God's way up there and I'm down here.' We feel a distance between us, letting our trouble push us away when it could bring us closer. We might acknowledge our sin before Him but do we acknowledge our troubles?

Hebrews 4:15-16 specifically tells us that Jesus is accessible and we may come to Him for mercy, grace, and help in our time of need (which, let's face it, is always). What a beautiful encouragement to approach our Lord for help.

If we open our hearts to the Lord we can rest with our trusted Savior. "Behold, the Lord's hand is not shortened, that it cannot save; neither his ear heavy, that it cannot hear:" (Isa. 59:1). His ears are open to our cries (Psalm 34:15). He is capable, and He is listening. Will you turn to Him?

When Our Faith Is Tested

In Psalm 116:1-2, David vows to call upon the Lord for his entire life because he knows that God has heard His prayers. It is a wonderful comfort to know God hears our prayers! May our prayers pour out to Him all our days, and our love for Him increase as we witness His answer.

Down in the Valley

I WALKED BY THIS TREE A FEW DIFFERENT TIMES and wondered if it would be possible to draw. I couldn't see where the ground was because it sloped away too sharply into the brush. Plus the way was littered with pricker bushes. I would have to draw it from the path above.

If you never turned your head you'd have no idea this tree existed. When we endure trials it can feel so lonely. We feel that no one sees us struggling. God sees and cares deeply. If He didn't care, why would He deliver us out of our afflictions (Psalm 34:19)?

Sometimes we are in the valley climbing out. Sometimes we are on the upper path looking down where we came from. We see our own hardships because we live them, but there are people all around us that God is carrying.

God knows exactly where this tree is, how it fell, and how long it has been there. Luke 12:6 tells us that even sparrows are not forgotten before the Lord. God sees them and their value. Jesus says we are worth more than many sparrows (vs. 7).

He doesn't lose sight of us. Doesn't misplace us. We are before His sight, part of His plan, accounted for, pursued, and in His thoughts.

That's right. He thinks about us. "How precious also are thy thoughts unto me, O God! how great is the sum of them!" (Psalm 139:17). His word says His thoughts toward us are more in number than the sand! They are "thoughts of peace, and not of evil" (Jer. 29:11).

We are also never beyond His reach. Psalm 139:7-10 explains that wherever we go, He will be there with us. He saw Zacchaeus in the sycamore tree, and Nathanael under the fig tree too.

Woolly Mammoth Tree

MY DAUGHTER LIKES TO PLAY A GAME where she throws a blanket over herself and waits for me to find her. She giggles with glee when I uncover her. "There you are!" I exclaim, as if I didn't know where she had been hiding the whole time. Then I scoop her up and hug her tight.

Sometimes we just want to hide. From the world, from others, from our own sin and trials. From facing ourselves, our mistakes, our fears. We pull up a blanket, or a big wall of ivy and hope that if our problems can't see us, they can't find us. If God can't find us, He won't see how we messed up.

God will seek His children too. Trials can be a blessing when He uses them to chase us out of hiding. "Can any hide himself in secret places that I shall not see him?" (Jer. 23:24). God always knows where we are. Instead of hiding *from* Him, we are instead called to hide *with* Him (Psalm 32:7).

It should be a comfort that God always knows where we are (Psalms 139:7-10). His compassionate, loving arms are always ready to embrace us with mercy and grace (Lam. 3:22, Matt. 11:28, Rom. 8:38-39). God has already seen the worst in us and sent His son to die to save us (Rom. 5:8, John 3:16-17).

This silver maple in my grandmother's backyard is slathered in a crazy mess of vines. I cannot remember a time when it was not wearing them. The vines may be disguising the true form of this tree, but God sees right through our own disguises to our very heart (Jer. 17:9-10).

And He loves us anyways.

We might think we have this grand, lofty faith. Then God starts trimming it back and we see the bare, naked form of our own inadequate belief. It is as if we had someone else's vines on our tree. Maybe we saw the faith of others and strung it around ourselves because it sounded good, or we looked good dressed in it.

In the trimming and pruning, God begins to grow our faith the right way. God will lovingly pursue us when we feel the need to hide, and He will pursue a better faith for us over our lifetime. He uncovers us in our sin and clothes us in righteousness.

God reminds us of His presence in many ways as we do life. He surrounds us with moments that show His hand working out the details. There are huge faith trials, and many smaller acts of God's grand orchestration and goodness. Both build our faith.

Those moments of His goodness are greater in quantity over a lifetime than the flowers swept up after they fall from this tree.

Keep Your Eyes on God

There is a practice in landscaping called 'pollarding,' where large tree limbs are chopped off close to where they divide from the trunk. It is often done as a decorative form of landscaping. All the limbs have been 'brutally' chopped, but what happens next is exactly the goal.

The tree begins an upward thrust of desperate branches. Likewise, God has every right to shape us as we grow in our walk with Him. Any part of us reaching out for the things of the world gets brought back into obedience. He knows that everything we long for will be found and satisfied in Him, so He brings us to a position where we are looking up, growing toward Him.

He is also more merciful in His chastisement than the landscaper might be in pollarding. "My son, despise not thou the chastening of the Lord… For whom the Lord loveth he chasteneth," (Heb. 12:5-6). When God brings us back into obedience through correction, it shows His great love and care in the keeping of our soul.

Surviving

> *"He giveth power to the faint; and to them that have no might he increaseth strength." (Isa. 40:29)*

When Our Faith Is Tested

"Restore unto me the joy of thy salvation; and uphold me with thy free spirit." (Psalm 51:12)

God is our living hope. When I was drowning in darkness, I was tempted to believe that there was no joy in this life and anything good must be in Heaven. Psalm 27:13 says, "I had fainted, unless I had believed to see the goodness of the Lord in the land of the living."

His goodness is here too. His goodness is all around us and inside us because of His Spirit. He is the one who hears us in the dungeon of sin and rescues us (Lam. 3:55-57), flying to our aid whenever we call upon Him. He is the one who pleads the causes of our soul and redeems us (vs. 58).

Are we merely surviving? Or are we firmly rooted in our Savior's love, believing in His promises, sustained by all that He is? Keep going. You are still here, and God is still good. It is enough to know our Savior lives and loves us. He will fill and sustain us in our struggles. There is new mercy for tomorrow (Lam. 3:22-23).

In Job 1:21, Job says, "...the Lord gave, and the Lord hath taken away; blessed be the name of the Lord." In this life, we will experience seasons of God giving and taking. May we too have the courage and faith in those circumstances to bless His name. Job had just experienced the devastating loss of his children and livelihood, and with God's help he was able to praise His name in the midst of his sorrow and anguish over it. God restored Job at the end, blessing him abundantly.

God is here ready to comfort us. He is "the lifter up of mine head" (Psalm 3:3). May we run into His arms in every trial.

He Carries Us Forward

Sometimes all we have is *now*, and now there is pain. We are drowning in 'now.' It is everywhere around us. It consumes and swallows us. Where is there, but now? What else could possibly exist, but now?

But somehow…'now' transitions to 'then,' and 'here' becomes 'there.' We are moving forward. When we still have steps to take and no idea how to take them, God is there. He is in the midst of sorrow, not absent from it.

Romans 12:12 calls us to continue "instant in prayer." May we take it all to the Lord, in prayer, often. When it is all too heavy for our heart God stands ready to bear it for us. 2 Corinthians 4:17 reminds us our afflictions are light and "for a moment" when compared to eternity and glory with God.

Sometimes survival means it is not even us moving forward, but God carrying us. There were many times when I told God, "I need You to carry me. Carry me through this because I have no strength myself." And He did every time. I don't think He ever puts us down. "…no man is able to pluck them out of my Father's hand" (John 10:29).

It is not within my power to reconcile everything you may have been through with who God is and how He works. That is for you to do with the Holy Spirit. That is what he asks us to do, to work out our own salvation (Phil. 2:12) by studying His word, clinging to what is true, and believing in Him as your Savior.

Before salvation, we endured alone. Our troubles crushed us because we had not yet met our Hope and Savior. Now, with Christ accepted into our hearts, our afflictions may be endured with a sense of purpose and even joy because God is with us, and for us.

He carries us forward. Forever.

Survivor Tree

THIS "SURVIVOR TREE" IS MEMORABLE because it withstood the blast from a domestic terrorist attack on the Alfred P. Murrah Federal Building in Oklahoma City on April 19th, 1995. A huge portion of the building was destroyed, many adults and children lost their lives, and hundreds were injured.

How do we wrestle with horrific acts of violence?

When Our Faith Is Tested

Walking around this tree was sobering. We visited the memorial at a time that I was mourning in my own way, and I remember thinking how those circumstances, while significant to me, paled to what was before me.

The memorial for this attack captures the haunting suddenness of unexpected violence. In one second everything changed. We tend to wake up and go about our day with the unspoken, unconscious expectation that life will continue uninterrupted. What do we do, what *can* we do, when it doesn't?

What happened to this tree is in the very shape of it. It is an American Elm that now symbolizes resilience to bereaved family, rescue workers, and others who know its story. It looks like everything stopped halfway up the tree, like the moment you know nothing will ever be the same.

Then it kept growing. The branches continued outward at odd angles as it began to find its way again.

Before the attack it provided coveted shade in the parking lot downtown. But after, "what was once an ignored, unassuming urban tree is now an iconic symbol of hope" (Oklahoma City National Memorial Museum, 2024). It was very close to the blast site and could easily have been destroyed.

We too might go through an ordinary life without much belief beyond what we see and touch, until the trials rage in us and through us, demanding something different out of us after.

It's trunk and bark still bear old injuries, but the tree is growing and green, looking for light. When we visited it with friends a few years ago there were leaves sprouting.

During suffering we as believers "have a strong consolation" because we have taken refuge and hold fast to the hope of eternal life with God (Heb. 6:18). This hope, that was promised "before the world began" (Tit.1:2), is an anchor for our soul, making it sure and steadfast (Heb. 6:19).

> *When our hope is in God, our soul is grounded during the chaos and turmoil around us. We are able to endure, fight, and overcome with the Lord on our side. The battles around us and in us do not quench the love He has for us. We understand that love better during each trial.*

Reluctant to Obey

Crucified with Christ

"I am crucified with Christ: nevertheless I live; yet not I, but Christ liveth in me: and the life which I now live in the flesh I live by the faith of the Son of God, who loved me, and gave himself for me." (Gal. 2:20)

When Christians talk about 'dying to themselves,' the world sees it as waste-of-a-life craziness, and thinks we do life on a silver platter of sacrifice. It's not a true picture of what it means to die to one's self.

It is our thankfulness that spurs obedience and devotion to the Lord.

When we begin to understand and believe the gospel, we come to realize God's grace and kindness toward us. Because of His love for us, my Savior Jesus has died on the cross for my sins, paying the price instead of me (Rom. 6:23, 5:8). Believing in Him and His sacrifice brings His great gift of grace into my 'account' with the Lord (Eph. 2:8).

This new understanding of His love and sacrifice convicts us to repent of the sins that are grievous to the Lord. His Holy Spirit grows in us a desire to please Him instead of our flesh. We begin to see how obedience to His word is of great value to Him because it both shows our love for Him and brings us back into His love (John 14:15, 15:10).

"And he said to them all, If any man will come after me, let him deny himself, and take up his cross daily, and follow me" (Luke 9:23). That word 'deny' means to say no to our flesh.

When we are bombarded with worldly pleasures we should consult God's word to see how He views those things. The world tells us we should do whatever we want, while God tells us to do what pleases Him (because it is also in our best interest).

Dying to ourselves means we choose God over sin.

If we find we are not willing to die to ourselves, let's examine our heart to determine why, repent, and return to a right relationship with the Lord. Acts 5:29 says we ought to obey God rather than men.

When we are believers we face a battle between our flesh and the Holy Spirit. Our flesh cries out for whatever feels good, with only now in mind. God's Spirit in us seeks to do God's will and desires the holiness and righteousness of God for us.

Obedience Fosters Life and Righteousness

The truth is that dying to ourselves hurts. It just does. It is a death of self that happens throughout our lifetime. It is to say that we love the Lord more than ourselves. It means that we put our heart's desire on the cross if what we want is not pleasing to God, nor in His will for our lives.

Let's look at Galatians 2:20 in terms of what God does for us, instead of what we have to do for Him.

- "I am crucified with Christ:" Our old self that was full of sin has died in a spiritual sense because of Jesus' sacrifice on the cross. What a relief! He has redeemed us by paying for our sins Himself.
- "…nevertheless I live; yet not I, but Christ liveth in me." We go on living after this death of sinful self, but we don't have to do it alone! We can't. Remember it is God who inspires and enables us to do His will (Phil. 2:13). We have our compassionate,

loving Savior living in us to guide us. We get to put on His righteousness instead of our sin.
- "…and the life which I now live in the flesh I live by the faith of the Son of God…" We can live this life with joy believing that God is faithful and capable. Our lives become about His purpose and work. We become more mission-minded in bringing Him glory and working to build His kingdom here by sharing the gospel.
- "…who loved me and gave himself for me." God's love for us is so vast that we can never be separated from it (Rom. 8:38-39). His love is demonstrated in the death of His son on the cross to save us. He had compassion on us when we could not help ourselves, being lost in sin and darkness.

Wow! God has given us so much and been so good to us! We have only to obey with gratitude. And He helps us do it!

His Mercy Over Our Pride

In our pride we might want to prove how obedient we are to God (we often fail at this). Obedience does not need to wait for a specific time, place, or thing that tempts us. It can begin now in our hearts. We may obey God at any time with the help of the Holy Spirit, beginning with our thoughts, speech and actions. Then, when we are tempted, we are already better prepared to obey God instead of bowing to the temptation.

Are there idols in your heart that you're struggling to let go of? Ones that keep you from obeying? Building a spiritual habit of dying to ourselves daily can help us remove idols before they get out of hand.

If we are not vigilant, we may get to a point where an idol is so big and warped in our life that we would rather physically die than die to ourselves spiritually. It's a devastating pride and hardness of heart. If we die, let it be to ourselves. God will call us Home in His own time. He will bless us with mercy and help until then!

We now live under grace through Jesus' sacrifice on the cross. We are not condemned for not being able to uphold God's standard of perfection through perfect obedience. God asks that we choose to obey under grace. "…to love the Lord your God, and to walk in all his ways, and to keep his commandments, and to cleave unto him, and to serve him with all your heart and with all your soul" (Josh. 22:5).

"He must increase, but I must decrease" (John 3:30). Pride steals the glory that belongs to God and inflates a character that won't surrender to Him. We need the Lord's help to obey and we can pray for it.

Instead of seeing all the ways we have to die to ourselves, what if we look for opportunities to cultivate gratitude and rejoice in God's will for our life? "Teach me to do thy will; for thou art my God: thy spirit is good; lead me into the land of uprightness" (Psalm 143:10).

The Creekbed

IN OUR DRIVES AROUND TOWN we kept passing this one tree leaning over the creek bed. Its two branches curl right down to the water's surface, but just before they breach it they curve abruptly back upward.

I was fascinated and I wanted to draw it. One day God showed me where to park and I took that as a yes to finally draw the tree. I walked along the road, carefully traversed the tricky section I had to cross, and made my way down to the greenery of the creekbed.

Except…where was the tree? Did I walk too far? I doubled back, thinking perhaps it looked different from below. I scanned the trees around me and decided I must not have reached it yet. Then I doubled back again, sat on a rock, and asked God why I couldn't find it.

"Order my steps in thy word: and let not any iniquity have dominion over me" (Psalm 119:133). Sitting on that rock was an emotional realization that I had been foolish. I hadn't been trusting in God to order my steps. I had become prideful about tree drawing, thinking I was entitled to the outings. I'd force my way into them if I had to.

I was relying on myself and my own strength to reach it. In our spiritual life, when we don't let God's word guide our path we can end up with sin our master again (self-appointed this time). Psalm 25:4-5 offers a reminder to let God lead us down His good paths.

I prayed, picked up my drawing bag, and kept going. God provided the blessing of natural beauty on my walk. There were delicate fern fronds uncoiling in the sunlight. The trees on the ridge above me were trailing roots all the way down the embankment to the water. At one point a heron flew down for a short hello.

I held onto roots, listened to bullfrogs and watched sunlight glitter like diamonds on the water. He even provided a different tree to draw, because of His mercy. Despite my pride.

God is so patient with us. "…for God resisteth the proud, and giveth grace to the humble" (1 Pet. 5:5). Slipping and sliding in the mud and completely missing the tree I came to draw was humbling. There I was crashing into my own plan but God was gracious enough to work it out for good.

Eventually I came to another sort of wetland area and sat on a low branch, wondering what to do. Sometimes we consult Him more as a pretense. There I was without a plan and I still had to make my way back along the creek with nothing to show for the journey.

I looked to my right and saw what looked like a little cottage in a stump. Would I too make myself a home in a dead stump of pride? When I really look at my life, I see my pride everywhere.

It is my pride that makes it so difficult to accept when I am wrong. That fuels a desperate need to explain and rectify mistakes. That desires to be seen in the best light by others. That keeps me from approaching the Lord when I mess up.

On the way to my car I looked up briefly as I crossed the last section. There was the tree: the one I had come to draw. It was close to where I'd parked and I had walked right by it.

May God help us exchange our pride for obedience.

My Plan Changed

I IMAGINED THE MORNING that I drew this tree going one way and it just didn't. At the time, I did not know the layout of the park. I had randomly wandered off the path in desperate search for a tree to draw.

There are incredible trees at this park; this is not one of them.

God knows that we are tenacious, stubborn people who tend to wander and go our own way. He reminds us in Isaiah 55:9 that His ways and thoughts are not our ways and thoughts. He is the sovereign leader of our lives; His ways are better.

In our haste for an answered prayer, in our desperation for some good we feel God has promised, we might leave His path. We decide to get it done ourselves, forgetting how incapable we are alone. We search for whatever seems good and end up disappointed. The good that God has promised is worth waiting for.

I had big ideas full of trees and they didn't go as planned. I'm learning to accept that sometimes God scatters our best laid plans so we will remember to trust His. He is merciful to remind us over and over to trust Him.

Reluctant to Obey

He is kind and patient to break down our pride in these humbling ways. A humble heart is one He can teach.

God Delights in Our Obedience

In 1 Samuel 15:1-23, King Saul takes sheep and oxen belonging to Israel's enemy (also the enemy of the Lord) back home to sacrifice for the Lord. While the Lord did at the time have very specific instructions regarding the proper way to sacrifice an animal and make atonement for one's sins, this particular instance is different.

Here He has explicitly told King Saul (via the prophet Samuel) to destroy their enemy's livestock as well. Instead, in his pride, Saul decides to bring back these animals alive to sacrifice to the Lord.

You can see the prophet Samuel's frustration here when he says, "Hath the Lord as great delight in burnt offerings and sacrifices, as in obeying the voice of the Lord? Behold, to obey is better than sacrifice, and to hearken than the fat of rams" (1 Sam. 15:22). Because it was done in disobedience the intended sacrifice is corrupted.

In this context, even though one might argue that King Saul is trying to please the Lord, it is a rebellion against God to disobey (1 Sam. 15:23). This was serious enough that God revokes his right to rule Israel.

Avoiding Destruction

There was a tree I wanted to draw once that I couldn't get to safely. If I stepped off the path to approach it I might break some limbs. I considered going down anyways.

It reminds me how dangerous it is to walk that line of sin, almost on the edge. That place where slipping would be so easy and things could get so much worse.

Because you're already so close to the danger.

Psalm 37:30-31 speaks of how the righteous have the law of God in their heart so that their steps will not slide. When we keep the truth of God before us, His laws of life, we stand firm on the solid ground of righteousness. Even amidst our struggles and heartache our steps will not slide when we trust in the Lord and His promises.

When we walk in the Spirit we are called God's children and Jesus' friends. The carnal mind, however, makes us God's enemy and those walking in the flesh cannot please God (Rom. 8:7-8). We must bring every thought into obedience with Christ, having even a readiness to rectify our disobedience (2 Cor. 10:3-6). Daniel's desire to obey God was greater than his fear of being fed to lions (Dan. 6)!

Have you ever experienced that sick feeling of your flesh fighting against the Spirit inside you? It makes it very difficult to obey. There were moments when they were fighting in me and it completely incapacitated me. I couldn't get a word or action out (Gal. 5:16-17).

Be careful not to sow to the flesh. What we plant is what we will harvest. The destruction of sin is very real. It separates us from God and leads to death. It has consequences, sometimes devastating ones.

Have you experienced destruction from your disobedience to God? Maybe it was destruction through addiction, which can be categorized as idolatry. It is to have an unquenchable thirst for the thing that is drowning you.

Maybe we are broken by hate (ours, or another's). The Bible says hating a brother is to murder him in your heart (1 John 3:15). 'Murder' is a strong word, but that's how concerned God is with our heart.

Maybe the struggle is adultery. Again, the Bible says even looking at someone with lust is laying with them in your heart (Matt. 5:28). We are warned not to provide an occasion for the flesh to lust (Rom. 13:14).

God is bigger than all of these things, and gives grace to cover them. "But where sin abounded, grace did much more abound" (Rom. 5:20). Hallelujah! Our decisions matter. Yes, we live under grace, but that grace is not an occasion to sin (Rom. 6:1-2). Our decisions have an eternal weight. Romans 6:2 mentions we are dead to sin. Do we act in a way that reflects a heart dead to sin and unable to respond to it?

Oatka Tree

I KNEW SOME OF THE LIMBS on this tree were living because they were growing leaves. Some of the limbs were dead. The wood was missing its bark there and no leaves were present.

A tree can seal off a limb that is growing in shade; it will not waste resources growing leaves there. Leaves are for photosynthesis, and how can they photosynthesize in the dark? How can we as believers satisfy ourselves in the dark either, once we belong to the Lord? Only His light nourishes our soul.

As believers we are instructed to use our members, our limbs and being, as instruments of righteousness and not sin (Rom. 6:11-16). We are instructed not to obey sin, nor serve it anymore (vs. 6). Instead we are free.

Just as this tree was shutting off resources to any limbs that were dying, may we likewise starve the sin in our life, choosing instead to nourish our relationship with God.

May God help us find the limb in our life that needs to be sealed off: whatever sin or temptation we struggle with, and may we likewise die to ourselves for the benefit of the whole tree. Dying to ourselves may be emotionally and mentally painful, but it preserves our spiritual health.

The Effects of Obedience

The death of a tree affects the environment around it. It decomposes, sometimes over centuries, and its nutrients are shared with the living organisms around it (Franklin et al, Tree Death as an Ecological Process).

In chapter one we discussed how after a tree dies the understory responds, and trees that were suppressed can launch upward in the opening to seize the light. Just as tree death is not wasted, our death to self and sin is not wasted either. When we die to ourselves we also create more room for Christ and the good work He can do in us.

We thrive when we remove what is warring against the Spirit. Our obedience in dying to ourselves can bless those around us as well, just as the decomposing tree nourishes life.

Think of who the Lord could bless through your obedience. Your family, friends, any unbelievers witnessing your walk of faith… If your sin affected others, how might turning from it benefit them? God can do so much with a humble, obedient heart.

A War of Two Wills

TWO TRUNKS EXTEND UPWARD but this ash tree will never grow another leaf. It is likely a victim of the Emerald Ash Borer (EAB), which is an invasive beetle causing the death of millions of ash trees (NYSDEC, 2024).

Our sin can act like the EAB. The EAB attacks ash trees by inhibiting the flow of nutrients and water in the vascular system beneath the bark (Prendergast and Prendergast 103). Sin can disrupt our relationship with the Lord, driving us away from our loving Father until a time when we are willing to repent.

Meanwhile, we sacrifice His loving embrace, protection, and all the fruit of the Spirit.

One sign of a beetle infestation in an ash tree is crown thinning. This means branches from the upper canopy (the crown) have fallen. They are dropped to conserve resources for the fight.

When our own sin infests us, it can impede the righteousness that God is trying to grow in us. Think of that crown of righteousness being at stake.

If you lift up the bark on an infected Ash tree, you can see S-shaped trails in the wood from where the beetle has been. If left unchecked our own thoughts will move similarly to damage our mind, body, and soul. They twist around in our minds and become actions.

This tree had another element working against it: its structure. When a tree forks too early and grows two main limbs instead of one it can stress and weaken the whole tree. They both grow a separate crown that is impacted differently by natural forces such as wind (Wohlleben 39).

Because of this, they end up moving out of sync with each other. This rending can cause a break in the trunk, and the wound may be difficult to heal.

Our own will is similar when it rebels against the Lord. Just as those two trunks cannot peaceably coexist, the righteousness of God doesn't coexist with our own obstinate self. We cannot serve two masters (Matt. 6:24). We pursue our own will, or the Lord's. He is the only one worthy of that crown.

Since drawing this the tree has split in half. Only one trunk now stands. Will you choose to follow the Lord, laying down your sin and self to do so?

Robertson Rd. Ruins

THIS TREE SITS NEAR THE ROAD on the way to a dear friend's house. Every time I drove past it I thought to myself, 'Wow, I really need to draw that tree.' When I finally did I got a strange sunburn as a souvenir and God taught me about obedience.

When a tree dies, it might die a 'snag' (standing dead wood) or fall as a log that is gradually decomposed. In some ways, when we die to ourselves spiritually, we become like a snag. As we read in Galatians 2:20, we are still living life but it is no longer we who live. We live a life of faith in Jesus, our own sinful self being crucified with Him on the cross.

This tree still stands, but many of its massive limbs are scattered nearby. It is slowly being consumed by the life around it, thereby becoming less of itself and more of the life it can nourish.

Romans 12:1 tells us that we offer ourselves as a "living sacrifice" when we obey. We embody all that we want, say, or think, that is contrary to what God wants for us. We roar against the chains of not getting to do what we want but we also know those chains are a lie. Those chains were actually the sin binding us when we didn't know Christ and had no choice but to sin.

We are now chainless and free, choosing to submit to the Lord and thankful for His grace over us. The death to self is actually life and peace. I can rest in obedience when I remember that submitting to our gracious and merciful Lord IS rest. Obedience brings peace. We can lay there as that living sacrifice, dead to sin yet alive in Christ, and flourish.

Submission Simplifies Life

In dying to ourselves, we might think we have to deny ourselves all our needs and wants. We'll just toughen up and become a figurative martyr by proving how spiritual we are. 'Look at me, God! Look how I sacrifice for you!'

Or maybe we think, 'I'm so righteous, I don't even have desires apart from God's will.' No, we still have those desires because we still do life in bodies of flesh and sin. But we give those desires to God and obey.

What do we do when we want things we can't have? When our flesh wants to take over? We obey, because God says to. We do what His word says in each situation, because He says to. It is the sin that complicates our life. Obedience brings peace, even if it is difficult at first.

We cannot perform our way to righteousness, nor save our own souls. Is that defeating? No! It's incredibly freeing. God has done the work for us. We just need to accept Him.

Joyful Obedience

"If ye love me, keep my commandments." (John 14:15)

Trees don't disobey. They are growing where they are planted and performing how they are made. It might look like obedience but it lacks choice. Obedience, on the other hand, is not just a response. God wants us to *choose* to obey.

Why are we reluctant to obey? The blessings far outweigh the 'cost.'

God reminded me that any true joy and peace has come at a time when I was obeying Him. He reminded me that good change involves good loss. What might 'good loss' look like? Laying aside anything that comes between us and the Lord so that we might not have any gods before Him (Exo. 20:3).

A good loss means laying aside the sin that so easily besets us (Heb. 12:1). But God's good blessings await to fill any void we think we might feel after a loss in the flesh.

We demonstrate our love for God through following His word, just as Jesus modeled His obedience (John 15:10). Scripture draws a clear connection between love and obedience.

Who do we love more: God or ourselves? If we love ourselves more we will obey ourselves (that fickle, wicked heart steering our life). If we love the Lord more, we obey Him and continue in His love. The Bible goes on to mention all the good that comes from obedience and doing it God's way (long-life, prosperity, blessings, protection, joy...).

The Holy Spirit can shift our thinking from the world's to God's. A.W. Tozer writes that being crucified with Christ means three things:

1. The believer is only looking in one direction, toward Christ and away from all that is behind us.
2. We are not going back, we are going to die to the sins of our flesh (not a physical death).
3. We have no plans of our own. All plans are now made by God (Tozer 86-87).

Tozer writes further, "In every Christian's heart, there is a cross and a throne, and the Christian is on the throne till he puts himself on the cross; if he refuses the cross, he remains on the throne" (Tozer, 2024).

Jesus is the only one meant to be on the throne. Are we willing to give up the seat?

Reflect on a time where you had to die to yourself. In what way(s) did you need to surrender your will and accept the Lord's? What did you learn in that season? From this side of the trial, do you see God's love, compassion, and mercy in it?

Our Shepherd's Protection

John 10:3-5 is a beautiful picture of obedience and trust, as well as the overwhelming care of the Lord. Jesus is our shepherd, and we the sheep follow our shepherd because we know His voice. We trust Him; therefore we go where He leads us.

We learn to recognize our Shepherd's voice by reading His truth and committing it to heart and memory so that we will not be led astray.

Reluctant to Obey

We do not follow a stranger, because his voice is unfamiliar to us. "The thief cometh not, but for to steal, and to kill, and to destroy:" (vs. 10). The thief referred to here is Satan.

Can you think of the voices you've heard calling out for your time and attention? Calling out to take your soul captive? May we learn to love God's voice more.

In verse 7 Jesus says He is the door by which the sheep go in and out to find pasture. Jesus offers us abundant life (vs. 10). Before salvation we were like sheep going astray, but we have now been restored to the Shepherd of our soul (1 Pet. 2:25). Obedience keeps us in His protection.

By One Man's Obedience

Jesus does not hide from His death. He heads into the garden of Gethsemane with His disciples. "And Judas also, which betrayed him, knew the place: for Jesus ofttimes resorted thither with his disciples" (John 18:2). Jesus goes to a place He is known to go. And He knows they will find Him there.

In the garden He prays to God about His coming death on the cross. It is an example to us to pray for help in obeying the Lord. We too must seek God for strength in our need. We do not desire to obey and please God on our own – the Spirit of God motivates us.

It is God's will to allow Jesus to die on the cross, and Jesus obeys (Luke 22:42). He experiences great emotion about enduring the cross (vs. 43-44). Yet Jesus also has joy in saving us! "…who for the joy that was set before him endured the cross" (Heb. 12:2). He knew that life and hope would come for so many sinners when saved through His sacrifice.

"For as by one man's disobedience many were made sinners, so by the obedience of one shall many be made righteous" (Rom. 5:19). Adam is credited with disobedience, bringing sin and death to the world. But Jesus obeyed, and brought life and salvation.

"Father, into thy hands I commend my spirit" (Luke 23:46). When we discuss how difficult it can be to obey, let's remember the ultimate example of obedience: Jesus' sacrifice to save our souls. God understands it's hard, and He will help.

What if our obedience could set someone free to live the life God has planned for them? What if obedience could set us free?

"…He humbled himself, and became obedient unto death, even the death of the cross" (Phil. 2:8). Because of His obedience we have the choice to accept freedom from sin, help for all our days, and eternal life in Heaven instead of Hell. Thank You, Lord Jesus, for obeying!

God Blesses Obedience

God promises us abundant blessings when we do life with Him. Remember, those that delight in the law of the Lord "shall be like a tree planted by the rivers of water, that bringeth forth his fruit in his season; his leaf also shall not wither; and whatsoever he doeth shall prosper" (Psalm 1:3).

That tree sounds like it's thriving. We too can thrive when we obey the Lord and trust Him.

When we disobey He takes the time to teach us and correct us, which brings us back into the blessings of obedience. "Now no chastening for the present seemeth to be joyous, but grievous: nevertheless afterward it yieldeth the peaceable fruit of righteousness unto them which are exercised thereby" (Heb. 12:11). That fruit in us is the righteousness and joy He promises when we learn to obey.

Is there something in your life that you're coveting right now? God's transformative love can help us let go of those things. We might think, 'I can't possibly put this down.' But He is gently opening our hand and telling us He is enough for us. Remember the line from that hymn: the things of this world grow dim "in the light of His glory and grace."

We lift up the Lord and remember who He is: our portion (Lam. 3:24). When we remember this, those things of the world that we were clutching to our chest return to the emptiness they always were.

Grow where He plants you, in the way He tells you to grow. When we are rooted in His love, in the way of life, filled with the fulness of God, we get to stay there! Our roots will not be looking to slurp in anything that doesn't foster life. We already have everything we need.

Returning to Our Fortress

Hiding with God

"The Lord is my rock, and my fortress, and my deliverer; my God, my strength, in whom I will trust; my buckler, and the horn of my salvation, and my high tower." (Psalm 18:2)

God is not a shack we run into to keep the rain off our heads. He is the stronghold holding us fast, keeping out the deluge and shielding us from the onslaught. When the enemy feels too close, and whenever you are troubled or afraid, run to your Strong Tower (Prov. 18:10). You will be safe there.

We protect what we love; we preserve what is precious to us. Who is God loving and protecting? Us! As believers we get to hide in the shadow of God's wings because of His lovingkindness (Psalm 36:7).

As believers we will never be without God's miraculous help. No trouble will be faced alone. Our God is not some lofty deity that descends when summoned in the face of danger. He is already here with us. His Holy Spirit lives in us when we are saved, which means He is here already. He is a "very present help in trouble" (Psalm 46:1).

When we are "troubled on every side," we are not in despair (2 Cor. 4:8). This is only possible when we trust the Lord to keep us safe. Psalm 27:5 mentions He will hide us when trouble comes.

Don't Abandon Your Fortress

In the Bible, our Protector God is often described as physical safety we can enter into. "Be thou my strong habitation, whereunto I may continually resort...my fortress" (Psalm 71:3).

God does not need fortifying or reinforcing. For our enemies that tower is impenetrable.

Will we retreat into the safety and power of the Lord? Too often we trust in Him – not 'when' but 'until' - things get tough. That's when we decide to trust ourselves instead. To do so is to forsake our best defense from all the evil in this world.

I had wandered from God and grown complacent during this season. My Bible was gathering dust on my shelf. It seemed like too much work for an already overworked mama to pursue God at the end of my day. Already-breaking things were not being fixed.

The enemy saw an opportunity to strike because I was mulling around outside my Fortress instead of safely inside. Satan saw an opportunity to attack me indirectly and directly. He raised up temptation, whispered lies, deceived, pushed apart and tore down whatever he could, wherever he could, in my heart and life.

"It is of the Lord's mercies that we are not consumed," (Lam. 3:22). God protected me, restored my soul, healed me, brought together, redeemed, rooted my faith in His love again, forgave and taught me so much about grace. Why? Because I am His child and He is a good Father.

Even if others in our life have wronged us, we may deal with that biblically when we are in our Strong Tower.

When we see the enemy approaching we turn and flee into our Strong Tower. But often the enemy comes creeping much more subtly than this. It's never too late to run to the Lord. "But the salvation of the righteous is of the Lord: he is their strength in the time of trouble." God will help and deliver those that trust Him (Psalm 37:39-40).

Returning to Our Fortress

Was there a time in your life when you were running from God? Do your circumstances drive you from Him, or into His embrace? God is the stronghold that stands when all else falls into ruin. He is the one keeping your soul *from* ruin.

Abandoned Fortress

I STARTED DRAWING THIS FORMER TREE, thinking it resembled some old crown a giant had dropped. This would be a painful crown to wear with its stalactite-bark-spears. Not unlike the crown of thorns placed atop our Savior's head to mock Him.

When Jesus died to save us from our sins He made the Strong Tower accessible to everyone who believes and accepts Him into their heart.

As I continued drawing it became an abandoned fortress in my imagination, like a castle covered in spiderwebs and crumbling into ruin. It reminds me of the danger of forgetting our Safe Place!

If we wander from His protection we allow ourselves be ensnared by anything that seeks to prey on us. Our heart falls into disrepair. We are out there alone, battered by circumstances and temptation.

God doesn't want us to leave our Fortress. It is why He demonstrates complete faithfulness in all He does. He knows that by building our reliance on Him He is forging a real relationship with us. We will run to the safety we have learned to trust.

We will feel so many things in life, and we are called to take them all to God. We have a God living inside us who can do anything and helps us when we ask.

There is one fortress that we must abandon: the contaminated stronghold of sin. God storms that corrupted castle and carries us back to His kingdom.

Clinging to Your Rock

WHEN EVERYTHING IS GOING SMOOTHLY in life we tend to leave our rock. When our heart is overwhelmed, however, we run and cling to it: "When my heart is overwhelmed: lead me to the rock that is higher than I. For thou hast been a shelter for me, and a strong tower from the enemy" (Psalm 61:2-3). The cares of this world are too much for us to bear alone. We are created needing our Creator.

This scraggly pine was clinging to the cliff face at Letchworth State Park one Fall. We were stunned by the trees in all their fiery plumes of Autumn splendor. This tree drew me because of the way it was clinging to the rock and looking for the light.

The rocky soil tethers it to safety. As we hold onto our Rock, He is holding onto us. He keeps us safe and sustains us as we surrender and endure. He is with us the entirety of anything we bear. "The sorrow that feels so isolating, so unique, was endured by him in the past and is now shouldered by him in the present" (Ortlund 48).

We do not endure alone. Any suffering we experience is a tiny glimpse of what Jesus endured for us on the cross. He is familiar with our sorrow and intimately acquainted with us. He blesses us during every trial and His goodness has no end.

Honey Locust

THE BASE OF THIS TREE looks like it's wrapped in barbed wire. I believe this is a Honey Locust, a species of tree which has patches of thorny sprouts on the trunk. Those dastardly thorns are over two inches long!

I started drawing it one warm afternoon in March, bringing my daughter with me. She colored her pictures while I stared at the tree before me and wondered how to draw it.

All I saw was chaos and distraction. The tangled branches hanging off it seemed like confused roots searching for soil. Those thirsty 'roots' were drying out, dangling in the air and exposed to the elements.

As believers we know our roots can draw in the life-giving water of Jesus when we are rooted and grounded in His love. Psalm 42:1 says, "As the hart panteth after the water brooks, so panteth my soul after thee, O God." Like the deer pants for water, may we thirst for a closer walk with the Lord!

We may want to seek Him, but let's not forget that we also know where to find Him. God's word provides the wisdom we need to grow and thrive as Christians. It is how we hear God speak to us, and how we begin to believe.

The zigzagging pandemonium of twigs and branches also reminded me how desperate we can be to misdirect others from our real self in a difficult season. Misdirection hides the mess. It provides no chance to see the heart of what is before you and address it.

God is always present with us, and His eyes are always upon us. He sees every sin, but He also sees every trouble and is there to help. "For I said in my haste, I am cut off from before thine eyes: nevertheless thou heardest the voice of my supplications when I cried unto thee" (Psalm 31:22).

Why would we fear the goodness and help of the Lord when we need it? We can't hide from God. Let's instead train our eyes to foresee the *evil* and hide ourselves from that (Prov. 22:3). Satan delights in our circles of doubt and confusion, doing anything he can to worsen our spiraling. May we trust in the Lord and not fall into confusion (Psalm 71:1).

Songs of Deliverance

Psalm 32:7 says that God is our hiding place. He will preserve us from trouble and give us songs to sing of His deliverance. That means He protects us in a way that makes us want to tell others those stories of His protection.

Generations of God's people have handed down songs of deliverance to remember God's faithfulness. Songs about all that God has done for them; it was their history lesson. Moses and the people sing praise for the Lord's deliverance from Pharaoh (Exo. 15). Psalm 105 is just one recount of God delivering the Israelites from Egypt's oppression, and preparing Joseph to help save them from famine.

What songs of deliverance has God given you? Have you witnessed His divine protection during a moment of danger or need? Remember those moments as part of your testimony of God's love toward you. Sing them and remember the way back to your fortress.

Guarding Your Heart

> *"Keep thy heart with all diligence; for out of it are the issues of life." (Pro. 4:23)*

I once watched the changing of the guard at Buckingham Palace. It was this grand ceremony with marching and music. And then the old guard left and the new guard took its place.

With less outward fanfare, we too could change the guard. We are not as diligent as we should be about guarding our hearts. When we get saved we have God's Holy Spirit to help guard our heart. The Holy Spirit reminds us of the truth, love, and protection that forms God's stronghold around us.

During this season I made so many plans guided by my heart instead of guarding it. My counselor stopped me in one of our sessions and said, "It sounds like you're listening to your heart. Speak truth to your heart instead." She was right.

The world tells us to listen to our heart. But allowing our heart to guide us is like a tree ripping off all its protective bark and yelling, "I'm ready to feel something!" Imagine the insects, fungi, and pests that would love to take hold of it.

Just as God gave trees their bark to protect the sapwood inside, He offers us His strength, protection and sovereign direction. With His help, we are to guard our heart diligently, not slothfully. It is much more difficult to get the things that don't belong there out once they are already inside.

A well-guarded heart is one that listens to wisdom and Godly counsel, fixing them in place within us (Prov. 4:20-21). But when you give your heart to the world you're inviting in what is against God (James 4:4). If we go looking for trouble we will find it. In all things we must ask, is this likely to grow righteousness in me? Does it please God?

If we don't guard our hearts we are likely to be deceived by them. We will become discontented with the good blessings God has for us (real substance), and waste our lives chasing the world's vapors.

God protected me from some poor choices and their repercussions in ways I am still recognizing. He has been my Guardian from the moment I trusted Him, and saved me from destruction many times.

When we are saved our eyes are opened to sin and evil. We might look around with new eyes to see darkness dwelling with us, burrowing into our heart. Pride, disobedience, lust, deceit, wickedness, addiction, whatever it might be. Don't grow complacent. Complacency breeds compromise.

Guarding our heart means weighing everything against the truth of scripture with discernment.

Returning to Our Fortress

The Issues of Life

"…When the Bible speaks of the heart, whether Old Testament or New, it is not speaking of our emotional life only but of the central animating center of all we do" (Ortlund 18). It is where the "issues of life" arise, deeply connected to all that happens around us and in us.

If our heart is what animates all we say and do, and it is filled with muck, the result is a regurgitation of all the filth inside us.

When we don't guard our heart it becomes filled with all sorts of unpleasant things. Envying and strife, which breeds confusion and evil (James 3:16), foolish talking, idolatry, and fornication (Eph. 5:3-5). God tells us that we will reap what we sow, and challenges us to sow to the Spirit (Gal. 6:7-8). Then we will reap its fruit.

If filled with scripture and truth, held safe in our fortress, then our hearts will flourish and pour forth joy, peace, patience, and goodness.

This Old Stump

THIS HUGE, MANGLED STUMP full of holes had an uncanny resemblance to my heart. I remember thinking, 'This stump is my future. My heart is going to end up like this stump if I can't change it.'

But hadn't God already changed my heart? I had accepted Him as my Savior many years ago. Why was this season such a struggle for me? He is always working on us and we always need to run to Him.

As I was drawing this stump my load-bearing heart was bowed under too much weight. My flesh and Spirit were warring inside me (Gal. 5:17) and my war-torn heart was paying the price; I became weak, riddled, and ineffective.

I am thankful to say my heart did not end up like that stump (to God's glory and goodness). I called to Him in my distress and He heard me (Psalm 120:1). He preserved my soul. These afflictions strengthen our faith and become a song we can sing for Him (Psalm 98:1); a testimony of what He did.

I returned to the park a year later to find the stump had been ground down. In its place were sawdust and woodchips. In a way, I enjoyed the destruction of that former analogy to my heart. I felt like God was telling me my heart was a living, beating thing again, and He had new plans for it. Every beat is a beautiful continuation; I am still here, He is still good.

Heart Concept

THIS IS A CONCEPTUAL DRAWING OF THE HEART made up of different trees. I had looked up a picture of an actual heart and realized the blood vessels and arteries looked a bit like roots. The heart pumps blood throughout the body, and phloem pumps water from the roots up through the tree.

May we stay vigilant over what gets planted in our hearts. Any emotion we don't take to God, any sin we don't repent from, can begin to change us.

Returning to Our Fortress

When we read about Jonah's unrighteous anger in Jonah 4 it should give us pause to consider our own hearts. Anger can rise up so easily within us and it is most often full of personal offense and pride.

Jonah was angry at the Lord for sparing the people of Nineveh after they repented. He did not feel compassion toward them, nor did he desire their rescue from the Lord's judgement. We might think we are much better than Jonah and would have acted differently. But how many times have we let pride, arrogance, and anger fuel our actions?

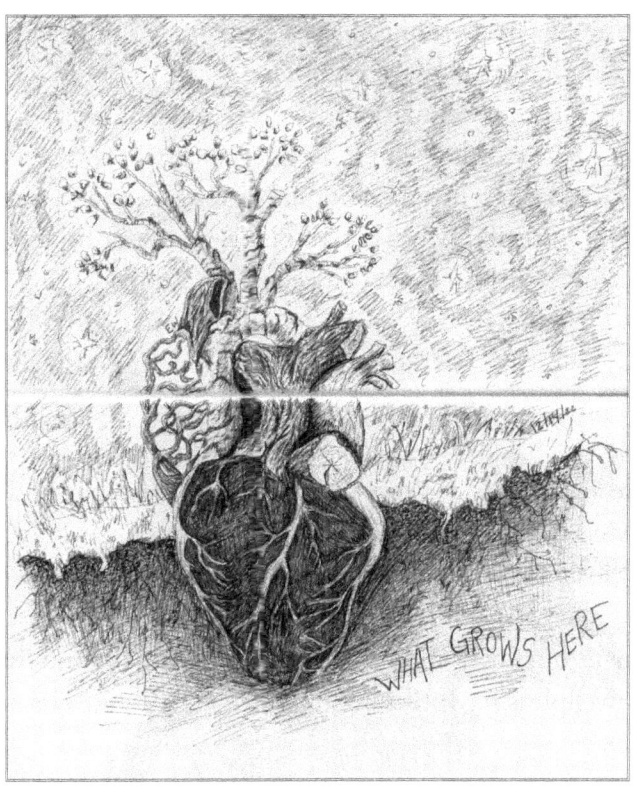

Remember to assess what is growing in your heart often. We might be surprised to find how wicked our hearts truly are on their own. It makes the work God does in our heart so important! When God begins to heal our hearts it is like walking with Him in a garden where He shows us all the good He is growing there.

What We Ingest

Have you ever been reading a book, listening to a song, or watching a show that began to grieve the Spirit of God in you? Our souls can feel heavier after ingesting something dark. It is subtly changing our thoughts, influencing our behavior, and directing our conversations.

Be careful not to quiet your convictions; it is the Holy Spirit warning you. There's nothing wrong with closing a half-finished book and returning it to the library early. Turning off the song because the lyrics praise the wrong things. Leaving the show unfinished (and yes, never finding out what happens next).

Setting healthy boundaries for what we ingest glorifies the Lord. It means we love Him enough to be grieved by what grieves Him. The Holy Spirit can help us love Him enough to obey and choose what pleases Him instead of what entertains, distracts, or numbs us.

Guarding our hearts means we are always inspecting the water we draw up through our roots. Is your water contaminated? Are you drawing up life-giving water, or poison? Ingesting something that does not please the Lord sows to our flesh and gives the enemy a foothold.

There are sins God is very clear about in the Bible, and then sins that convict specific people in how He designed us. Pray for direction, do life as He leads, and 'consume' media with discernment. We are not good masters of our own emotions and thoughts. Let's not overestimate our own ability to please Him. He works in us "that which is wellpleasing in his sight" and helps us do His will (Heb. 13:20-21).

Take Your Thoughts Captive

When we are sinning, our thoughts can change to make excuses for our sin. We stop listening to truth. We cling to the idea that maybe what we are doing could be okay. We think it's not that bad and we don't take it to God.

Returning to Our Fortress

When we are spiraling in anxiety, depression, and overwhelmed with the cares of life we might find ourselves in a dark place with dark thoughts. Our thinking gets warped. We start to consider and do things we would never have before.

If this is you now, please ask for help. Please continue to read your Bible, and also seek additional resources for help if needed. Our thoughts can be exceptionally hard to break out of on our own. God is there for you, has never left you, and will provide a way to heal.

We can remain trapped in a prison of our own lies and flawed thinking, or we can build a prison for the thoughts that lead to lies, flawed thinking, sin, and any imagination competing against God's truth. We are instructed to take our thoughts captive, bringing them into obedience along with our actions (2 Cor. 10:5).

If our thoughts are running us, may we continue to walk in faith following God and obeying Him. He will make our thoughts to follow (Pro. 16:3).

Mind Paths

HAVE YOU EVER GOTTEN LOST IN THE WOODS? Do you remember the fear and confusion you felt? If we don't know the way we will wander aimlessly.

One day, while I was walking a common trail at a park, I spotted another path leading away into the grass. While unimpressive and a meager two inches wide, it was nonetheless a path. Somehow the paths that are frequently travelled are always evident.

The paths in our mind can be the same. God showed me how specific neural pathways in my brain had become the only pathways I ever took. Some were circular. Others contained memories I couldn't stop revisiting (regardless of whether the memories were pleasant). Some of them were filled with lies like a familiar scavenger hunt.

They all had the same problem: none of them lead me where I needed to go. I wore very deep grooves into my mind-park traveling those wayward paths.

We forget where we're going and lose our way when we step off God's path. This singular, narrow path to righteousness is always moving toward the Lord, walking in His commandments.

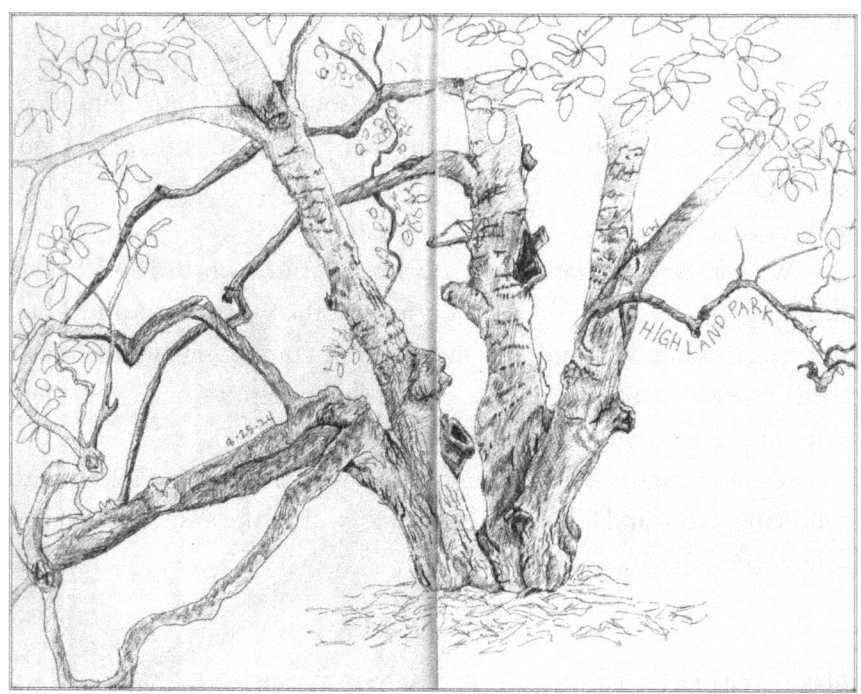

Our downward spirals can be so unwillingly addictive. If I wanted to change my heart, I had to change the way I think. That meant not taking those paths anymore. I had to stop myself the moment I started down one, backtrack, and find a new one.

What I needed were trail markers to remind me where the right path was. Our trail markers might look like memorized scripture verses for our specific trials. They could be memories of God's goodness. Tack them up along the way.

In writing this book I was forced to revisit many verses God gave me during this season of my life and each of them was a trail marker from God to stay on the right path. May He leave you trail markers in your spiritual walk to remember the way back into His love.

Stopping the thought before I travelled it was exhausting. By the grace and help of God it was possible. It becomes easier. Did you know that God designed your brain with the ability to change neural connections?

When we learn new information, the proteins forming our synapses change to make them stronger or weaker (Making and Breaking Connections in the Brain, 2024). We can pray for the Holy Spirit to help us abandon any path that leads us away from God's life-giving truth and strengthen the connections of truth that fortifies our faith.

If we are able, God allows us to become active participants in our healing, because He has a lot to teach us in the process. I was so thankful to see those old pathways start to shrink the less I travelled them.

Are you following the path He set for you? Those that don't believe wander around lost. We as believers know the Way: Jesus. Why would we choose an endless, lonely labyrinth when we have a clear path to life laid before us, guided by the all-knowing God?

Taking Refuge

> *"Trust in him at all times; ye people, pour out your heart before him: God is a refuge for us. Selah." (Psalm 62:8).*

When you played tag as a kid, did you ever have a 'safe'? This nickname meant the agreed-upon location where you could not be tagged. It was a safe zone. And when you were running from whoever was "it" you knew you were running hard for that safe place.

May we run to God with more vigor, knowing He protects our life and soul.

A Safe Place for All of Us

God asks you to "pour out your heart before him" (Psalm 62:8). Tell Him every single thing. All your fears, all your sins. Your feelings. He is a safe place filled with grace. We can trust Him with all of it.

In your time with God you can yell, cry, give thanks, ask all your questions, and be as weak as you are. No more disguises. God has already seen all of you. He is with us as we face ourselves too.

Cling to the truth that God wants to heal and restore us. We do not have to fear coming to the Lord in whatever state we are in. "Though I walk in the midst of trouble, thou wilt revive me:" (Psalm 138:7). When we are weak, He is the strength we need (2 Cor. 12:9).

I had to take it all to God and I still do every day, with whatever comes up in my heart. He welcomes it. He is the only true refuge of unconditional love in this universe.

At first I prayed the generic prayers. Over time He broke down my walls. I was telling Him my deepest fears. I was surprised because they weren't known to me until I said them to God. We may not know our true heart until He shows us.

When we tell Him everything, ask for help, and give thinks, He gives us the supernatural peace of God to guard our hearts and minds (Phil. 4:6-7). There is nothing like His peace.

Remember, don't hide from God. Hide with Him.

> *As we trust Him we find rest and peace. God wraps us in protection while we grow, so that we remain grounded in the fortress of His love, safety, grace and mercy.*

Redemption Over Resolution

The Cross

"For all have sinned, and come short of the glory of God; Being justified freely by his grace through the redemption that is in Christ Jesus." (Rom. 3:23-24)

The greatest story of redemption is the cross.

We are born with sin that separates us from God (Psa. 51:5). We cannot get to Heaven on our own because the sins we commit keep us from measuring up to God's standard (Rom. 3:10, 3:23). Our sin earns us death (Rom. 6:23a); that is how much God hates sin!

Yet, because of His great redeeming love, God sent His son Jesus to die on the cross in our place. Jesus paid the penalty of sin so we don't have to (Rom. 6:23b, John 3:16). He saw our wretched need for a Savior and He answered.

Crux of the Cross

When the Lord spoke to Israel about their redemption, He called even His creation –the heavens, mountains and trees – to praise Him for it (Isa. 44:23)!

Redemption has always been part of God's story for us. He had a perfect plan from the very beginning to redeem the entirety of sin through the salvation found in the sacrifice of His son (John 3:16, Eph. 1:7).

Redemption is not the ending; it is the entire purpose of the story. It's not about our trials working out perfectly in the end, but God's redemption and grace during them.

Rotting Apple Tree

YOU WOULDN'T KNOW THIS TREE WAS ROTTEN from the outside. When it was cut down that inside (and rotting stink) was exposed. Just as its outward appearance deceived the homeowners into keeping it around too long, sin deceives us too. It looks good from the outside but it is full of destruction.

In Psalm 38:4-8, David says his sin wounds "stink and are corrupt," that his loins are filled with a "loathsome disease." He is "feeble" and "sore broken."

But wait, doesn't it feel good to do what we want? Maybe for one fleshy second. Then it destroys us, corrupts us, and breeds filthiness in our soul. We become a story that could have ended differently.

"Because the carnal mind is enmity against God: for it is not subject to the law of God, neither indeed can be" (Rom. 8:7). Giving ourselves over to sin and following our flesh makes us God's enemy. We must confess our sin to the Lord as the Holy Spirit convicts us and then turn from it. Then the rot of sin cannot split us down the middle like this tree. We accept His grace and forgiveness to heal.

Jesus has both broken and healed my heart with His kindness and grace (Rom. 2:4). We can't earn grace. Every time I try to, He reminds me I can't. If we think we can earn grace, then we set ourselves up to think we've lost it when we fail (which we do because we're imperfect).

Forsaking sin and choosing the Lord's life and righteousness brings us back into a right relationship with Him. He restores our soul and heals us (Psalm 23:3, Titus 3:3-5). Our story becomes a testimony of His goodness and mercy that we can carry all our life.

A Godly Sorrow

MY FIRST IMPRESSION OF THIS TREE was that it resembled a snail slowly rippling forward with a large hole in its deformed shell. As if it just accepted the wound; it would be there forever. What is so alluring about our pain, weakness, or affliction, that we wouldn't take it to God who promises to carry it for us?

It looks like it suffered a fatal blow that took the heart right out of it. One measly buttress is supporting that upper side to connect the tree around that hole. When we don't have Jesus in our heart we are like this tree; doing life unaware that we have a hole inside us.

Without the Lord our sorrow has no place to go. There is a hole in us that cannot be filled: a cavity of confusion and pain. There is very little to hold us up and we are barely functioning. How sad for pain to be the end of the story!

When we have the hope of Jesus and the blessing of knowing Him as our Savior, the holes in our life are filled again…by Him. He is all the substance for our emptiness. He is abundant life. With Him there is no wanting (Psalm 34:10).

Is there a time and place for a healthy sorrow? 2 Corinthians 7 discusses how sorrow can have a God-honoring purpose. A "godly sorrow" is the term used in the King James translation, referring to sorrow that leads us to repentance and salvation (vs. 10). It is a heaviness of heart from the Lord; grief that causes us to run to God. The consequences of sin include sorrow.

After salvation the debt of our sins is already paid by Jesus. We still need to confess those sins to God and turn from them. Paul is rejoicing in verse 9, not because the Corinthians are sad, but because their sorrow has led them to repentance, so that they may better perfect holiness in the fear of God (2 Cor. 7:1).

Sorrow can lead us to healing. It did for me. Now, when I am confronted by unexpected sadness, I can run to the Lord who has forgiven me and remains a safe place for all of me. I do not need to sin in order to fix the way I feel; I know God will do that.

Was there a time you sinned and experienced great sadness and regret over it? Satan will use sin and guilt as a wedge between us and the Lord. God does not delight in our sorrow, but rather uses the natural ramification of sin to drive us to Him.

The salvation that comes from the godly sorrow is unregretted (2 Cor. 7:10). The blessings of a godly sorrow for those that believe are carefulness, the cleaning of our hearts, fear of the Lord, and earnestness of the Spirit (vs. 11).

Why would we mosey forward with our holes, accepting the drudgery? Why choose the trial over God? The Lord can give us joy amidst our suffering, hope for now and tomorrow, strength in weakness, and healing in brokenness. He came to heal us.

Forever

When I was a kid I thought Heaven was a place you could get to if you went high enough in the sky. I wondered how airplanes could avoid hitting it. Did rocket ships travel through it on the way to the stars?

When I was older, how would I get there? Did I need a really long ladder? Would one of those planes take me there? Then I learned it wasn't a place you could climb to. You couldn't just stumble upon it either. I could only go there if I believed and accepted Jesus as my Savior.

Only Jesus' blood shed for our sins can cover us with grace. Only through true faith and a relationship with Jesus can we enter Heaven. If we die before we accept Jesus, then our sin will separate us from Him forever.

In a world that has forgotten what 'forever' means, God reminds us there is no end. Eternity is not marked in days or moments, but is absent of them.

When we believe on Him, yes, our physical bodies will still die someday, but our souls will go to Heaven because we have peace with God. He sees the righteousness of Jesus instead of our sin. We will wake up in glory, forever in the everlasting life and joy of our Savior's embrace.

Waiting for Redemption

"In whom we have redemption through his blood, the forgiveness of sins, according to the riches of his grace." (Eph. 1:7)

When Jesus died on the cross He was rejected, mocked, scorned, wounded and marred. And He still died for those very people doing it, because of His love.

Do you know what Jesus prayed when those people were crucifying Him? "Then said Jesus, Father, forgive them; for they know not what they do" (Luke 23:34). Jesus died for His mother, the disciples with her, His friends, and all the scorners standing next to them, cheering for His death. This is a God of compassion.

If Jesus died to save "whosoever believeth" then that includes you (John 3:16). Do you believe that God can and has forgiven you from every single sin, as soon as you believed and confessed it to Him?

Maybe what you've been through in your life doesn't look pretty. Maybe you feel no one would love you if they saw the ugliness inside you. Guess what, friend? God already sees it and He still loves you!

Maybe the idea that God could love someone like you is absolutely terrifying and incredulous. What if it's also the greatest loving kindness you'll ever experience?

God has chosen us, not because of our strength and ability, but because His strength is on display when we are weak (2 Cor. 12:9). Even our own salvation is nothing we can boast of (Eph.2:8-9). When we begin to understand our sin, we realize we certainly don't deserve His grace. But there it is, ready and available to us when we believe.

If you have been through things, or done things that you don't think God can possibly rectify or redeem, may I compassionately point out that His word tells us the truth? His redemption is lived out in little old imperfect us.

Redemption Over Resolution

Already Redeemed

The Holy Spirit can help us accept with confidence that we have been redeemed. "…receive not the grace of God in vain" (2 Cor. 6:1). As believers we live in the Lord's great grace.

It diminishes our perception of the power of Jesus' blood when we live in condemnation and fear, and hide in anything but the Lord. It shows that we do not believe we will ever be anything more than what we did. We have redemption through his blood and our sins are forgiven (Col. 1:14)

As believers, are we doing God's work, praising His name, and moving forward confidently with Him as our hope? Or are we still waiting for a soul redemption that has already happened? Satan would love nothing more than for us to feel stuck and focused on everything we did or that happened to us.

Remember the liberty and grace of Jesus' sacrifice. Don't wait for redemption; hope in the Redeemer.

Our Cherry Tree

AS I DREW THIS CHERRY TREE I was mesmerized by its simultaneous ugly-beauty. If we are personifying the tree here, it has a commendable confidence in being present. The rippling mass of scars, tears, and mismatched proportions would give it every reason to hide. This thing has a past – an unpleasant one. A past full of mistakes, and injuries inflicted upon it.

Yet here it is. It knows exactly what it is and what it has been through and it is still standing.

Do you ever feel like this tree? Sometimes we go through things that completely wreck us. We are tempted to just stop showing up. Probably best if no one sees us struggling right now, right? Been there.

There is something incredibly powerful about being exactly who we are in Christ and accepting everything we have been through in these temporal bodies. Being completely vulnerable, yet so strong in the Lord. That kind of confidence comes from walking with Christ and knowing where you are going at the end of this life.

He is our hiding place, yes, but sometimes that hiding place is in plain sight of others. When we show up to do the work He has called us to do exactly as we are, entirely needing Him for everything, it speaks loudly to a world that is largely self-serving and self-reliant. It shouts in quiet ways that after all we have been through, we still believe God is good.

It adds truth to our faith. Because if God doesn't see us as ugly and broken, it shouldn't matter if anyone else does. May we show up firmly rooted in the knowledge that we are fully loved and accepted by God.

Not the World's 'Redemption'

The world tells us to measure our life in defining moments. Think about that. What if the moment is bad? Painful? If it helps define your life then it remains a fixed regret. Through God's redemption and grace these moments can be reconsidered, or let go.

Or say that defining moment is wonderful. That can be tricky too. It sets up other moments to fail if they don't compare. It could rob us of the beauty of everyday life. Leave us chasing the high of the next perfect moment.

Take it from someone who used to trap herself in moments, reliving them indefinitely. It's not an ideal way to approach life.

Have you ever wanted to redeem a moment in your life? It's tempting to redeem ourselves when we feel embarrassed or struggle to accept a failure. God sometimes chooses to redeem those moments for us. But consider what hoping for our own redemption would gain us.

Redeeming ourselves in a worldly sense brings us glory. It appeals to our flesh. True redemption is not to be confused with getting your hearts' desire if you are 'faithful enough.' It is not about our reputation being saved or personal vindication.

True redemption is found in the blood of Jesus.

Yes, what we do with our time matters, but we can easily crumble under the pressure to get every moment right. We fail sometimes. We get it wrong. We sin and make mistakes. And God is so good to redeem that for us!

When God redeems our moments it looks like His goodness and mercy where we least expect it. He brings something of value out of something that seems to have none. Each moment *He* redeems is a picture of His redemption for us.

If you characterize your life in single moments you will be denying the power of God's transformative work. Those moments come and go; God stays to do His good work in us.

Can you think of a time in your life when you or your circumstances felt redeemed? Was that redemption from the Lord, or did it look more like the world's definition of redemption?

Grace Reigns

> *"Moreover the law entered, that the offence might abound. But where sin abounded, grace did much more abound: That as sin hath reigned unto death, even so might grace reign through righteousness unto eternal life by Jesus Christ our Lord." (Rom. 5:20-21)*

The first time I read this section of scripture I was overwhelmed by the possibility – the *certainty* – that God's grace could rule over me. Freedom and redemption ruling me? Setting me free? The cruel king of sin is overthrown by the benevolent King of grace. He claims us as His own, takes the throne, and we are forever free.

The Lord already knows all of His children. He knows we are sinners and He delights in saving us. We cannot hide from His love, mercy or grace. Our sins are already blotted out. We can boldly approach the throne of grace as we are because He has redeemed us (Heb. 4:16, Isa. 44:22)!

When grace reigns over us we are new creatures (2 Cor. 5:17)! "…saith the Lord: for I will forgive their iniquity, and I will remember their sin no more" (Jer. 31:34). Originally spoken to Israel (God's chosen people), this is the promise we are now adopted into because He died for whosoever believes (John 3:16). That's you and me!

When God looks at His children, who are still struggling in these temporal bodies here on earth, desiring to please Him but often failing as we miss the mark, He does not condemn us. We get His grace instead. That grace is transformative, and fully capable of redeeming us for His purpose and glory. *And our good.*

Tacconi's Cherry Tree

THIS TREE WAS RECOMMENDED by a friend at our church. When I drew it God was teaching me about redemption. I stared at a wound sitting right where its heart should be and wondered how this tree could look so much like me.

Maybe you've been this cherry tree too: peeling apart, mottled and knobby. Nothing in its right place. Misunderstood. Maybe you've got a heart wound from something precious lost or part of yourself severed.

Guess what, friend? I've been there too. God can redeem that! His love for us is full of redemption. This supernatural love of God is almost inconceivable. Ephesians 3:17-19 says that when we are rooted and grounded in love, we will know His love, which *"passeth knowledge."*

The cherry bark here may be full of scars, almost busting out of its bark-seams, but the tree itself has a redemptive beauty too. In Spring it has the most beautiful blossoms. In Summer it bears sweet fruit.

Don't judge by a simple day, or one season. Don't judge by appearances. God is still working.

Four Arms and No Back

MY DAD RECOMMENDED A VERY SPECIFIC TREE for me to draw at one of his favorite parks. Then, as I had never been there before, I had no idea where in that (enormous) park it actually was. I drew this one instead.

I drew this tree before approaching it. When I finished I went up to meet it and noticed that some of the spots I'd drawn were actually deep crevices going all the way through the tree! The backside was a gaping wound.

As we learn to love others, we tend to expect healthy, normal interactions. Sometimes we get something else, because of a story that only God knows the entirety of. The people we meet in life might be going through things we can't understand. Let's be kind when they don't get to explain. When we don't get to explain. If we never have an opportunity to explain something to others, then we aren't meant to. God will work either way.

We expect everything to be fine, like this tree with its four branches. Then we get up close and we are disappointed, or maybe others are disappointed in us, because we are not what they expected.

We can strive toward this heart with one another: "With all lowliness and meekness, with longsuffering, forbearing one another in love" (Eph. 4:2). Let's run to God and allow Him to love through us. We can trade, 'I just don't care right now,' for 'I care because God cares.'

1 John 3:17 discusses the heart of compassion we are called to have for those in need. The love of God dwells in us when we have compassion for others. Was there a time when you struggled to find compassion for someone in a conflict? Why do you think it was a struggle for you?

Living Victorious in Freedom

We ask for His help and accept His forgiveness (1 John 1:9), repenting and living with a transformed heart. "…and this is the victory that overcometh the world, even our faith. Who is he that overcometh the world, but he that believeth that Jesus is the Son of God?" (1 John 5:4-5)

We are victorious over sin and free from its bondage through Jesus. Be careful not to use your freedom from the eternal consequences of sin as an incentive to do it. We still experience natural consequences of sin in this life, and it doesn't please God to use His great gift of grace this way. "What shall we say then? Shall we continue in sin, that grace may abound? God forbid. How shall we, that are dead to sin, live any longer therein?" (Rom. 6:1-2).

When we are redeemed we are free from who we were before, and can learn to release the guilt that came with it.

Red Maple

WHEN I WAS A CHILD my grandfather would take us for walks in the park to collect leaves. So many colors, shapes, and sizes! These mere leaves that fell became treasure collected with great anticipation.

I still look forward to the foliage display in our yard every Fall. This red maple in particular takes the stage. Resplendent red bursts from every leaf.

Leaves that turn red in the Fall have undergone a chemical change. Sugars get trapped in the leaf and produce new pigments that were not present during the growing season (Smithsonian Science Education Center, 2024).

Sin is similar. While sin may seem sweet and pleasurable to our flesh for a season, like the sugar our body craves, it does not nourish or satisfy. Instead, our hunger only grows. The sugar in the leaf of the red maple gets imprisoned, turning the whole leaf red.

Did you ever get to a point where the sin and shame in your life was yelling so loudly that it became this hot, bright color inside you? We can feel trapped, unable to escape it, just like the sugar in those red leaves. Praise the Lord that we have not been chemically changed to remain in that state. "…Though your sins be as scarlet;" Jesus washes us white as snow (Isa. 1:18).

It doesn't matter if someone else still sees us as the Red Maple; if all they remember is your sin, or that thing you did or said in one season that you wish we had done or said differently. Maybe the words they said to you still make you feel like the Red Maple and nothing more. In your dark moments you look at yourself and all you see is their shade of red.

We can and should make amends for sin as necessary, but ultimately we don't answer to those people. We answer to the living God, but thankfully as believers He sees us as His beloved children, covered by His grace and mercy, and fellow heirs to His Son, Jesus. We are undeservedly loved!

Our godly character and good works of faith can speak mightily to others such that they would glorify God (1 Pet. 2:12) regardless of how they see or speak about us now. God may still use us in their lives. The transformation of our hearts alone is a great testimony.

It is called a red maple because of those memorable leaves in one specific season. At the end of Fall, all those red leaves will drop off the tree like our old identity. New growth will spring forward after Winter.

Likewise, God does not forever label us based on sinful or misguided actions in our own seasons. Jesus already carried that sin and shame to the cross (Heb. 12:2) and God remembers it no more (10:17). We are capable of change. Let God direct it.

Forgiveness

Only God can offer perfect forgiveness. He forgives us with a clean slate. "If we confess our sins, he is faithful and just to forgive us our sins, and to cleanse us from all unrighteousness" (1 John 1:9).

We tend to hold grudges, keeping others' offenses in front of our face. Instead of walking around as record-keepers and score-settlers, let's let the Holy Spirit work a forgiving heart in us. Remember how grateful you are to have His grace and forgiveness over your own soul,

"...forgiving one another, even as God for Christ's sake hath forgiven you" (Eph. 4:32).

God asks us to forgive others. You might be telling yourself right now, 'but this person does not deserve forgiveness!' Neither did you. Jesus bore all the sin of mankind AND God's wrath over it so that we could be forgiven.

If forgiveness feels impossible for your situation, bring it before the Lord for His help.

The redemption He has given us through his blood *is* the forgiveness of our sins (Eph. 1:7). He has forgiven us for all the debt we owed (death for all our sins) because Jesus already paid that debt.

"Then came Peter to him, and said, Lord, how oft shall my brother sin against me, and I forgive him? till seven times? Jesus saith unto him, I say not unto thee, Until seven times: but, Until seventy times seven" (Matt. 18:21-22). We must forgive others because God has forgiven us.

We may pray and let God lead us in creating healthy space and boundaries for our healing and others' if necessary. We are always called to forgive but forgiveness does not mean we stay in a place of perpetual hurt.

When we have been forgiven for something we did or said, by the Lord, and have made it right with whoever else our actions impacted, then we do not need to remember that offense anymore, nor live in continual shame. That condemnation of guilt comes from the accuser, Satan. "And they overcame him by the blood of the Lamb..." (Rev. 12:10-12).

Even when the people closest to us betray us and inflict their own sin upon us, we may learn to forgive them through the supernatural love of God within us. Impossible in our flesh, yes, but possible with God. This forgiveness humbles us as we realize a fraction of how it must feel when we sin against God, who gave us everything, and He forgives us.

For Our Good

> *"And we know that all things work together for good to them that love God, to them who are the called according to his purpose" (Rom. 8:28).*

If we trust God's promise to work good from our circumstances, then we will experience His peace in the midst of them. His Spirit helps us to trust Him and carry onward.

We may have our own idea of what redemption will look like. Will we accept the good He chooses to bring, even if it's different than we thought?

Are we willing to accept sanctification (working holiness in us) as the "good" that is promised in Romans 8:28? Is sanctification 'good enough' for us? Or do we have another plan for a better good that God can bring? We want to keep scanning the horizon for the good things coming our way after a trial, but holiness and righteousness is His blessing to us. It pleases Him.

Redeeming the Struggle

Sometimes we are tempted to take charge of redemption. We want to redeem our own circumstances because even though we know that God promises good will come from them, we don't trust Him enough to let Him work. We make reinforcements and back-up plans because we can't stand not being able to see what He is doing.

We cannot redeem ourselves, or others (Psalm 49:7-9). We have this desperate need for our pain to mean something. That search for meaning is a cry for redemption that only God can answer.

Durand Tree

THIS TREE TWISTS AND WRITHES before my eyes, so slowly that it doesn't appear to move at all. Its progress was impossible to measure in the forty minutes I sat before it putting pen to paper. So much of it embodies endurance and struggle.

We too twist and writhe as we wrestle with our own sins. When we struggle God is always there to help us avoid temptation and obey. We can reduce the power of sin over us when we are rooted in God's great love. "Keep yourselves in the love of God, looking for the mercy of our Lord Jesus Christ unto eternal life" (Jude 1:21).

When we mess up in life, our great Redeemer is right there. He is "plenteous in mercy" (Psalm 86:15).

This tree seemed to tell me many stories as I walked around to inspect and climb it. How did it get this way? What appeared to be a story of brokenness and anguish could easily be a larger, longer story of redemption. Each wound was somehow part of that story.

I learned that a tree can try to repair itself when injured. Sometimes tree wounds will even weep a sort of black substance from their wounds, as if bleeding. If fungus has penetrated the exposed wood, then no matter how the tree tries to repair itself, it will not be able to heal that wound (Wohlleben 44). The rot stays.

Which of this tree's wounds are still trying to heal? What rot and decay are eating away at it? When I drew this, I was struggling with a wound that wouldn't heal. With our wounds, however, we have God's redeeming love and incredible healing power to bind them up. He will hear our cry (Psalm 38:15).

Because of our sin we deserve death…but God has redeemed us. He offers us freedom and glory instead. He has exchanged condemnation for life and grace. Instead of a grave when we die, we get the Lord!

> *When we are rooted and grounded in God's love we know that we are redeemed, and our Redeemer will continue to grow and transform us our entire life. May we continue growing that crown of righteousness while we are here, knowing God will help and gets the glory.*

A Light That Won't Go Out

Looking for Light

"For thou wilt light my candle: the Lord my God will enlighten my darkness." (Psalm 18:28)

"If I say, Surely the darkness shall cover me; even the night shall be light about me." (Psalm 139:11)

Sometimes our light is a blazing sun for the whole world to see, and sometimes it is a small, flickering flame that will not go out. God's light does not go out.

I remember how great the darkness was for me, and how persistent God's light. I believe the enemy's agenda was to utterly destroy me so that I would never shine light again in this world. He almost succeeded.

Darkness can take many forms. My darkness took the form of anxiety and depression, which led to despair. No single situation caused it; it was a compilation of darkness that left me stuck.

But God's light found me everywhere. Literal sunshine breaking through, trickling down to find me. And spiritual light shared by encouraging sisters in Christ, family, Bible verses and many prayers. His light flooded my soul.

The light of Christ in our hearts is what lights us, and when we are His, we are His forever. For any in darkness now, please remember

God loves you and Jesus is a light for your darkness. The light of hope is still lit, and you are still here. God is still good.

When His Light Shines Through Us

In the darkness of night, trees continue breathing ('transpiring'). They wait for light. When the sun rises they continue to absorb the life that light gives them.

Before we experienced the reconciliation and redemption of Christ, we were sitting in a dark room, waiting. Matthew 4:16 says, "The people which sat in darkness saw great light; and to them which sat in the region and shadow of death light is sprung up." These are people stunned by light and hope.

"Then spake Jesus again unto them, saying, I am the light of the world: he that followeth me shall not walk in darkness, but shall have the light of life" (John 8:12). Our path in life as believers is a shining light and we get to walk it (Pro. 4:18)! We are no longer stumbling around in darkness, unable to see (vs. 19). We see the darkness of the world for what it is: the absence of the light and life of Jesus.

Trees in a stand compete for light, fighting to take up as much space in as little time as possible to maximize resources for photosynthesis. While trees fight for light, we have it in abundance through God: our eternal light source nourishing our souls.

Cathedral

ONE OF MY FAVORITE THINGS about waking up for morning trees was watching the light change as the sky was gradually flooded with color in celebration of the coming sun. The hues in the bark of this tree remind me of stained glass.

I travelled to Europe on a school trip years ago and we visited so many cathedrals. They display intricate windows of precisely arranged glass of varying color. The pictures made of glass tell a story and evoke a mood.

They are just waiting for one thing: the sun.

"For the Lord God is a sun and shield: the Lord will give grace and glory:" (Psalm 84:11). Those glass pictures are revived by the dazzling hues shimmering in the light of the sun. God is like a sun for us, giving light, warmth, and life. We are like colored glass waiting for the Lord to shine light through us.

The presence of light completely changes the glass. Jesus' light shining in our heart changes us as well. When He shines His light we can better assess the state of our heart. What else lives in there competing for our attention? Let's get rid of the idols in our heart, lest we build churches for the wrong things.

If we think of our heart like a church, are we in the back pew observing from a safe distance? What questions are you asking God back there as you watch the light move? We could end up staying in that pew a long time before we get to the altar beyond it.

We could stay a bypasser to our faith, or we could do life in our Savior's loving embrace, bowed on our knees at the foot of the cross. As believers we have the privilege of walking in His light all our life.

A Light for Our Darkness

Biological motors, driven by turgor variation (alternating water pressure), located down in the base of a leaf can close it for the night and reopen it for the day (Lüttge and Hertel, 684). This is part of the circadian rhythm of certain trees. We can take a lesson from those leaves and close ourselves off to darkness.

Darkness hides sin. It smothers our joy. It is not where God is.

Jesus is our light, representing God who is light. In God there is "no darkness at all" (1 John 1:5). I would rather find refuge in the light than the darkness. Our temporary trials in this life throw no shade over the glorious brilliance of God's promises and His great salvation leading us to eternal life.

The Bible is full of people asking the Lord to make His face to shine upon them. Additionally, it is a way of blessing someone else to ask God to make His face shine upon them. He is a light we can bask in.

Moses' face shines after spending time in God's holy presence on Mount Sinai (Exo. 34:29). When we spend time with Him, our light is bright because it is closest to its source.

Sycamore Silhouettes

I WAS THREE-QUARTERS OF THE WAY through this drawing when the sun crested over the hill and blinded me. In an instant all the trees turned to black silhouettes. Where did all my details go? Only dark shapes remained.

Darkness makes it hard to see. Our eyes need to take in light in order to process images and then understand them. How could I draw the details hidden in shadow?

In the very real spiritual realm, our enemy is moving, working darkness in details we can't always see. But Jesus' light shines in that darkness and confounds it (John 1:4-5).

God has a plan for allowing the shadows sometimes too. They might scatter the light for a time but they can give that light greater definition. The trials in our lives can refine our hearts and faith. They can reveal a lot about how we are living.

We never really know what shadows are over the people around us. Other believers are walking through trials with the Lord too. We can pray and come alongside them to be lights that help chase away that darkness for a time.

Pray for those who haven't accepted the Lord and don't yet have His brilliant light to send their darkness fleeing. Keep shining and God will use that light in the life of others, just as Jesus' light gave us life too.

Color as a Quality of Light

Even the most ordinary of objects can be rendered beautiful by the light shining on them.

Color is not possible without light. It is the quality of light reflected by an object. The sun can change the color of things, depending on how it shines and gets reflected. We observe the light, measure it, and give it a value with a name.

Color must be seen or it has no meaning. It is no coincidence that God made the sky blue and the grass green. What an absolute delight! He gives us sunsets and so many bright colors in nature all for His glory.

Darkness can confuse our perception of color. We are tempted to call an object by the same color name even if the light has changed. Say you put a red apple on a table and turn off the light. In the dark you are asked to name the color of the apple. You want to say 'red,' because you know it is supposed to be true. But the apple is no longer red.

Perhaps you could make an argument that it has no color there in the dark, in the absence of light. When we stay in darkness too long, our souls can become colorless as well. We forget who we are supposed to be.

God's truth acts as a light. It illuminates lies to help us see clearly and make the right choices. We are able to identify and understand the proper 'colors' of any outside influences without confusion.

Thankful for Color

WHILE I WAS DRAWING THIS TREE, I just felt thankful to be doing it. Any other time of day it would probably be an unremarkable tree. In the sunlight it was extraordinary.

God prepares the light and colors, and sends us to encounter them in His creation at a time and place when we will be astounded.

The light we see is made up of colors. Romans 5:5 says that God's love is shed abroad in our hearts by the Holy Spirit. 2 Corinthians 4:6 says His light has shined in our hearts too. The Holy Spirit inside us is like a prism for the light of God shining in us, allowing us to see and understand the rainbow of God's great love.

Shining His Light

"Let your light so shine before men, that they may see your good works, and glorify your Father which is in heaven" (Matt. 5:16).

Light and darkness are opposites. As Christians we are warned away from darkness, and indeed are not darkness because we have the light of Christ in us. "…whosoever believeth on me should not abide in darkness" (John 12:46).

We are called to be like Christ in this life, so we too shine the light of Christ to others. Matthew 5:14 says we are the light of the world. We act and speak in a way that reflects the love and holiness of Jesus instead of sounding and acting like the world.

It is easier to shine His light when we are not following darkness. May we cast off the works of darkness, evil and sin (Rom. 13:12). As children of light we shine in a "crooked and perverse nation" (Phil.

2:15). We are called to shine His light as evidence of Him and for His glory (2 Cor. 4:6).

We are not flashlights that can turn off anytime we want to. A candle is placed where it can give light to the household, not hidden away where it is of no use (Matt. 5:15). We shine for the Lord because He asks us to. That light does not depend on earthly circumstances. We are called to shine through them.

Like trees, we are nourished by light. Our light source is our Savior Jesus living in our hearts, giving us life. "The Lord is my light and my salvation…" (Psalm 27:1). Darkness is starvation. Why would we choose to dwell there?

Trees say, 'I am soaking in as much light as possible because this is what I need to survive.' Christians just take it a step further. We take that light and shine it for others as well.

Whatever season you are in, it's okay if the light you're able to shine with Him looks different than it used to. He is still with you, still has a good plan, and still has that light lit in your heart. He loves you dearly.

May we "arise, shine" because our light has come: salvation through Jesus. May our light shine that hope of salvation to unbelievers wandering in darkness (Isa. 60:1-3).

Who Lights Your Candle?

I once read a quote that said if you feel your light diminishing you just need to reach out to the flame next to you to be relit. There's at least some truth to that. Those around us can certainly lift our spirits by making us laugh, showing love, and encouraging us. After spending time with them our own flame can be a little brighter.

But we can't rely on others to keep our flames lit. Psalm 18:28 says, "For thou wilt light my candle: the Lord my God will enlighten my darkness." It is God who lights our candle and keeps it lit. Only our unfailing and inextinguishable God can be our steadfast light.

I had relied on others to keep my flame lit. When they failed me I was plunged into darkness over and over. Every single candle in the world will go out; God's unfailing love will not. If you rely on another person for light, strength, or joy, then your flame will eventually go out because people are imperfect: they will fail you.

It is not fair to expect someone else to be everything you need. They are not designed to be. You cannot *be* their flame, nor can you *carry* their flame. And they cannot carry yours. Only God can satisfy our every need and longing.

Melting Candle

THE SHORTER TREE IN THE FOREGROUND here reminds me of a candle that has been lit for too long. The burls and bumps look like wax that dripped all the way down. Then the wick was extinguished and the candle grew cold.

Maybe this tree-candle was lit for the wrong reason. Now it remains stuck in a state of decay. We too will suffer destruction if we are walking in darkness, tripping over snares and breaking ankles in the dark.

Every day we wake up with breath in our lungs and light in our soul because we know the One who put it there. He keeps that flame lit. He brings us out of darkness.

Don't look to the reflected flames of the world around us, which draw us with the promise of light but hold no warmth or strength, being altogether a lie. "…be content with such things as ye have: for he hath said, I will never leave thee, nor forsake thee" (Heb. 13:5).

For God's Glory

Any spiritual light emitted from us as Christians originates from God's Holy Spirit inside us. We do not shine for our own glory. The purpose of His light shining out of us is to inspire others to glorify God in Heaven (Matt. 5:16).

Our Heavenly Father is described as light Himself (1 John 1:5), and we are His children. We have become light-givers on a mission to cast off darkness in His name, for His glory.

During this season I prayed God would allow me to shine His light even in my brokenness. He revealed to me that my heart was not in the right place with that prayer. Really, I wanted to control that light and shine in a specific way for specific people.

God reminded me that we are supposed to let Him direct His light through us. Me wanting to be a light in my own way was really me trying to fabricate redemption for myself. I'm so thankful He is patient as we learn!

Do you desire to be a light for others? Remember to examine your motive for shining. Remember it is not your own light pouring out of you.

Before the Sun

The creation account in Genesis has a specific order to it. On day one, God creates light and dark. On day three, God creates the trees. One day four, God makes the sun and moon. Wait…God created light *before* He made the sun?

A Light That Won't Go Out

In Genesis 1:3, God speaks light into being. In verse 4, He divides the light from darkness. They are separate. The entire first day and night are without a moon or sun. This is astonishing!

In this order, the trees are created before the sun. But we know trees need sunlight in order to complete the vital process of photosynthesis. It allows them to transform carbon and water into sugar and oxygen.

God is described numerous places in the Bible as light. God creates light in these verses, so the light comes from Him. This supernatural light sustains the trees before they have a sun. God also waters the ground before a drop of rain is spilled from the heavens (Gen. 2:6).

To us, it might seem like God did it out of order, but God is demonstrating His sovereignty over creation by being the One to sustain it. He has full power and control over it. "And he is before all things, and by him all things consist" (Col. 1:17).

This is also before sin entered the world, and the curse of sin affects all of God's creation. So those trees created on day three did not experience drought or detriment from lack of sun exposure. They had everything they needed and God said it was all "good."

The sun is described as a "greater light to rule the day" (vs. 16), and it is created by God to nourish life. Here on this earth we need that sun.

In Heaven, there is no bright burning star to act as our sun. We don't need one. The Bible says that God shines for us! "And there shall be no night there; and they need no candle, neither light of the sun; for the Lord God giveth them light: and they shall reign for ever and ever" (Rev. 22:5).

> *God's light shines in our soul as we remain rooted in His love. The bright light of His love does not go out. In Heaven there will be no darkness and we will live forever in His light.*

Who We Are Now

Embrace Your Identity in Christ

"But as many as received him, to them gave he power to become the sons of God, even to them that believe on his name." (John 1:12)

As a society we have broken down the topic of identity into a few key questions: Who am I? What defines me? With what or whom do I associate myself? What gives my life meaning?

All of these questions put the focus on ourselves. Discovering who we are, or 'finding ourselves' becomes this noble quest we embark on in life. It is daunting to imagine that we are solely responsible for defining our existence as a whole. And who are we to determine our own value?

A life-long pursuit of who we are is to love ourselves so much that we will spend our entire lives chasing ourselves instead of accepting who God is.

God redeems our identity when we are saved by grace through faith (Eph. 2:8). Salvation takes the focus off of us and places it on the Lord. He is the core of who we are, and He is faithful and unchanging.

While I was busy wondering who I was, God was directing me to discover who He is first. Then He revealed my true identity within the revelation of His.

Stop Redefining Your Identity

I am a 'mother,' an 'artist,' and an 'introvert.' Those labels help others understand me, and they help me understand myself. The danger is that none of those things are permanent.

Will I still 'feel like' a mother when my children are not under my direct care? I love making art, but what if there comes a day when I can't? I enjoy quiet time to rest and recharge, but does that mean I can never socialize when the situation requires it?

We are left to redefine ourselves over and over when our identity is in the wrong things.

What if you find your identity in a person or group? People fail us. We fail them. If the people we hang with stop hanging together, our identity can fall apart. Only God is incapable of failing us (Deu. 31:6).

What if we find our identity in a past trauma or mistake? Then we are forever tied to the hurt that haunts us anew. Indefinitely. We become incapable of letting it go because it is now part of who we are. We drag it into the future with us.

Redefining our identity over and over in the world sounds exhausting. Establishing your firm identity in Christ still allows for change, but it is directed by God and there is no questioning who we are. We simply grow with Him. There will be nothing to redefine because our identity is solid.

We have the incredible peace of knowing exactly who we are in Christ! There is no elusive definition of 'self' needed to pacify us. When we are saved by grace, we are children of God and He will take care of us. God has to remind me of these things often because it is easy to forget who I am. How blessed we are when He reminds us!

Can you think of a time when your identity was tangled up in something outside of the Lord? Ask yourself how it would feel if that thing were removed from your life. Would it feel like you lost part of yourself? If so, some of your identity is rooted there and it must be reassigned back to the Lord.

No One Else Gets to Define You

I once let a particular truth seep into my soul and completely color the way I perceive myself. It was as simple as a boy saying something cruel to me. This wasn't a simple insult. His words deeply wounded me.

What he said was true for him, at that time. It did not have to be true for me, but I made the mistake of dwelling on those words indirectly for over a decade. While I now understand that what he said was not a reflection of who I am, it took root in me anyways.

One small root can grow an entire tree.

Trees have tiny feeder roots that grow from their larger woody roots. Feeder roots are the primary means for absorbing water and nutrients (Iowa State University, 2024). *They make up the majority of the root system.* From that one unpleasant truth, Satan grew small feeder roots to form a whole snaking structure of lies I believed about myself.

How destructive those lies become when we mistake them for truth! Satan is described thus; "…there is no truth in him," and "he is a liar, and the father of it" (John 8:44). Because they stemmed from a root of truth, I accepted the lies as truth too. They grew with any encounter that seemed to verify and reinforce them. I made them mine.

Those feeder roots are supposed to absorb vital sustenance for the tree. Why would we choose to let something *bad* nourish us?

I had to confront those words and take them to God because I had never fully acknowledged it and it was somehow connected to this recent season. God allowed me to do so in a safe space with Him, and move past it.

It is also worth noting that we never know the words or actions someone might be desperate to take back. We can choose to forgive with God's help. I know I would not be the person I am if that boy had never said those words to me. *Not* because they determined who I am, but because of how the Holy Spirit subsequently used them to grow empathy, kindness and gentleness in me.

Do not let someone else define you or determine your worth. Choose the life-giving truth that God loves you so much. Take anyone else's words about you to your compassionate, loving Father and trade them for His great love. Put on His grace, mercy, and kindness.

God knows you by name. He calls you His own.

Tangled Roots

THIS TREE LOOKS LIKE IT WAS RIPPED from the dirt and slammed on its back in the mud. It stares skyward, asking God, "What just happened?" That is exactly what I felt God doing in my heart at the beginning of this season.

The challenging time that inspired tree-drawing was permeated with a crisis of identity. God stayed with me as He pointed out the weaknesses of my faulty identity. It was heart-rending. Eventually, it was heart-repairing, to God's glory.

I had allowed the wrong things to shape me. To my core. I felt the need to look beyond God for approval and substance. I thought

I could escape the everyday doldrums with all the other joy I chased. Instead, God compassionately rooted me back into His loving care. I found my identity in Him, and my joy returned.

When we are uprooted God has a good reason for it. We may end up on our back for a while, legs dangling above us. Sometimes we have to be uprooted in life to find out we were rooted in the wrong things.

When you yank out a plant that's deeply rooted there is usually a lot of protest from the plant. I once watched my then 83-year-old grandma spend twenty minutes trying to yank a small redbud stem from the ground: a gift from her garden to mine (I did try to assist her but that blessed lady is a bit stubborn). Unfortunately, that sucker was stuck tight.

We are like that when we resist the work God wants to do in us.

We know we can't stay there lying in the mud. We have to right ourselves. But in order to do that we first have to stand. God is the lifter up of our head (Psalm 3:3). When He has lifted us to our feet, He helps us walk in the ways we should go, and remember the truths we forget. He reminds us who we are.

Colossians 2:6-7 challenges us to be rooted in Christ and built up in Him. We are children of God when we are believers, thereby called to be set apart from the world. There are incredible blessings and protection when we are His children (Psalm 18:30, Jer. 17:7).

A Gentle Landslide

IN THIS BOOK we are using the illustration of being firmly rooted in God's love like a healthy, thriving tree whose roots are strong in the dirt, getting nourished. Consider for a moment if the analogy changes for this context.

Imagine you are standing at the bottom of this hill. You watch the soil move slowly toward you. You can see the roots emerge all the way down the hill as this takes place, warning you.

It starts with your feet. First, you lose sight of your toes. Then your ankles. Not to worry. You think you have plenty of time to lift up your feet, brush the soil off, and move to safety. After all, it's moving so slowly that it's barely an inconvenience.

The slender trees growing at the top of this hill are victims of what I'll call a 'gentle landslide.' The soil erosion gradually exposes more of them, revealing their meanderings on the slope. Erosion will change the hill grade over time as soil gets deposited in other places and steepness varies. It is like a slow-motion landslide, taking all that holds the trees firm with it.

Sin can come in the same subtle, creeping ways until it buries us. Yet the entire process feels like we are still in control. We can get out any time we want. The danger is manageable. Satan sows lies and deceit like a professional.

Will you be buried by a gentle, lulling landslide, until the dirt is over your head? Or will you move to safety, toward the Lord, the moment you lose sight of your toes? The moment you see the soil coming for you.

Is there sin in your life that you are not addressing? What warning signs do you see? Stay vigilant and discerning in your walk with the Lord (1 Pet. 5:8). We are instructed to "...follow after righteousness, godliness," and "fight the good fight of faith," holding onto eternal life (1 Tim. 6:11-12).

Rooted and Grounded in Love

I am tempted to only see the worst parts of myself, what I was before, and the ways I don't measure up. We can be so cruel to ourselves. This is not how God sees us!

We are each "fearfully and wonderfully made" by God (Psalm 139:14). If your Creator loves you – His creation – then you are loved absolutely. You are not a mistake. Every part of you as a believer was fashioned for a good purpose and plan.

Upon salvation we are valuable because we become the righteousness of Jesus (2 Cor. 5:21). We are valuable to the Lord simply because He loves us. He knows us thoroughly and has precious thoughts toward us (Psalm 139:17).

Who I am in God's eyes, after Jesus has restored me with the peace and righteousness of salvation, is who I get to be always. I want to embrace the way He sees me. The way He loves me. He's working on me and I'm still learning.

Here's the struggle: finding identity in Christ is not a one-time thing, but an ongoing mission. We must continually root ourselves in Christ and remember who we are as His children. The Holy Spirit will help.

"That Christ may dwell in your hearts by faith; that ye, being rooted and grounded in love, May be able to comprehend with all saints what is the breadth, and length, and depth, and height; And to know the love of Christ…" (Eph. 3:17-19). This is a multidimensional love that we can enter into, and be surrounded by.

We matter so dearly to the Lord. When the world rejects us (as it did Him), when our care for others is met with indifference, and when we feel invisible – being both unseen and unheard - we rejoice and rest in the blessed truth that God feels very differently about us.

Our Heavenly Father is the very definition of love (1 John 4:8). We matter to Him. God loved us so much that He made a plan to rescue us from our sin by sending His son Jesus to die on the cross so that our sin would no longer condemn us (John 3:16-17). Does this sound like a God that doesn't care?

"And we have known and believed the love that God hath to us. God is love; and he that dwelleth in love dwelleth in God, and God in him" (1 John 4:16). When we understand true love as defined and modeled by the Lord – the love that casts out fear (1 John 4:18), we will realize that the love the world offers does not compare.

God's love gives its life (John 15:13), does not envy or boast but suffers all things (1 Cor. 13), and saves and redeems the lost (John 3:16, Rev. 5:9). When we begin to understand that love we will be filled with the fullness of God, and experience His love even if the enormity of it is beyond our human comprehension (Eph. 3:19).

This is a love that will never leave us wanting.

Putting on Godly Character

> *"And be renewed in the spirit of your mind; And that ye put on the new man, which after God is created in righteousness and true holiness." (Eph. 4:23-24)*

God begins an incredible work when we are saved, starting with the redemption of our very identity! In Ephesians 4 He commands us to put off our former ways. The "old man" in verse 22 refers to who we were before, being "corrupt" and walking in darkness and sin.

Who We Are Now

God loved you even before you loved Him. So much so that He died to save you from your sins. He saw your sins, but He also saw who you could be with Him in your heart.

The 'old man' of sin is dead upon salvation and remains the only one buried in the grave. We who believe are alive in Christ, living in His mercy and grace, and doing His good will until He calls us Home. It is a great joy that when God looks at us He does not see that old self anymore.

We are instructed to put on the Godly character of righteousness and holiness (vs. 24), as well as kindness and forgiveness (vs. 32). We are called to walk in the Spirit, and we will then produce the fruit of the Spirit, which is godly character. Galatians 5:22 lists love, joy, peace, longsuffering, gentleness, goodness, and faith.

God knows we won't see, or do, the work that needs to be done inside us by ourselves. It is only with the help of His Holy Spirit in us that we may put on His character and wear it like a new shell.

Tree seedlings cast off their old shell too. It begins with a tiny embryo inside a seed coat buried in the dirt. It begins to take in water and grows until it cracks its hard shell. The embryo is like a soul ready to accept the Lord.

A main radicle root grows down and looks for water (Kalman 10), just as we take in the life-giving water of Christ to sustain us (John 4:14). Once the seed is free from its old shell it can emerge from the soil and grow in the sunshine. Once our old shell is cast off, we too find new life in Christ.

A New Creature in Christ

Who we were before salvation looks completely different from who we are after. If we are in Christ we are a "new creature" and the former things of our life are cast off (2 Cor. 5:17). "All things are become new." What a joyous identity we have in the Lord!

1 Corinthians 6:10-11 mentions who we were before accepting Christ – reveling in the sins that would keep us out of Heaven and dangerously unaware of them. But now we are washed, sanctified,

and justified in Jesus' name, because of His sacrifice on the cross to pay for those sins. What a relief that we don't stay the people we were before.

We have been sealed by the Holy Spirit. He is the one defining us and transforming us to be like Christ. Romans 8:9 tells us that before salvation we did not have the Spirit of God in us and did not belong to the Lord. But after salvation we are considered His children (vs. 16)!

We have received "the Spirit of adoption, whereby we cry, Abba, Father" (Rom. 8:15). God adopts us into His heavenly family and becomes our Father when we believe.

Jesus' holy and precious blood was shed to save us! When we are saved, we also have value as a co-heir with Christ (Rom. 8:17). We will be with Him in glory when we die!

We have been anointed as a "chosen generation" and a "royal priesthood" (1 Pet. 2:9). He set us apart so we can "shew forth the praises of him who hath called you out of darkness into his marvellous light:" We are now no longer darkness, but light.

When we recognize our sin and the gravity of it, we begin to see it how God does. This promise that we have become new is freeing! We are now loved without a history of who we were before; now only forgiven and redeemed as God's precious children, pleasing in His sight.

Set Apart for His Good Purpose

We think that comparing ourselves to others will help us measure our value. We are warned not to compare and measure amongst ourselves (2 Cor. 10:12). Instead of asking, 'Am I normal? Am I like everyone else?,' we can ask, 'Am I like Christ?' and know that He helps us to be.

As Christians in the world we may always feel like the odd ones out. Because we are! And it's a good thing! As believers we have been chosen, and adopted by the Lord (Rom. 8:15, John 15:19). The world walks in the flesh; we walk around with the Spirit of God inside us.

Unbelievers do not have the Spirit of God and do not belong to Him (they need our prayers and compassionate love).

God has also prepared good works for His children to do (Eph. 2:10), and we have been called out of darkness to do them with His help.

When we know we are going to Heaven it's natural to want everyone to come with us when they die. Have you ever prayed fervently for the salvation of someone dear to you? It is completely in the character of Christ to care about where someone will spend eternity. It means we love and care for their soul the way Christ does for us.

We might hesitate to share the gospel because we fear that an unbeliever will laugh at the truth we love so dearly, or dismiss it as false. Well the short answer is...they will. 1 Corinthians 1:18 says that the world thinks the gospel is foolishness. If you're telling someone about the Lord and they have already rejected Christ or aren't ready to receive Him yet, then they will not hear it (John 8:47).

Others may think we are silly but we know and trust that the gospel is the power of God to salvation for those who believe (1 Cor. 1:18). If they reject us, we have a measure of peace knowing we have still told them about our life-giving Redeemer who lives today. The result is not up to us. If they are ready to hear though, God can use you to plant and water seeds of faith.

It is not our responsibility to save anyone; it is our job to tell them the truth. God draws them to that truth, and Jesus is the only way to get the Heaven (John 14:6-7).

We cannot control how others choose to see us. We can pray for peace in simply showing the love of Jesus and modeling His character. It is not our job to be 'liked' by as many people as we can. We can live more freely knowing God is pleased with us because we have accepted His Son Jesus and are following His commands.

Redeeming Identity

Acts 8:3 introduces the character of Saul as one who "made havock of the church, entering into every house, and haling men and women committed them to prison." We hear of this infamous zealot again in Acts 9:1. "And Saul, yet breathing out threatenings and slaughter against the disciples of the Lord…"

He is on his way to Damascus to persecute more disciples and bring them bound to Jerusalem when Jesus stops him in the road, changing his life forever.

Later, in Acts 9:15, God describes him as "a chosen vessel unto me…" He had a plan to use Saul to declare Jesus Christ to the Gentiles. Saul? The one who was hunting down Christians to bind, imprison, and kill them? How could he be used for God's glory?

Because of the change in him. God redeems his identity and even gives him a new name. Acts 13:9 mentions that Saul is called Paul, and we see him referred to by this new name going forward.

Immediately after Paul accepts Jesus (and his sight) he goes about his God-given mission because He was told to. He does not let his past define Him (although it seems to in the eyes of everyone else) but focuses instead on the work God has called him to do.

God uses Paul in remarkable ways. His past is now only a testimony of how God transformed him. Paul counts all his former stature – any gain in the world - as a loss when compared to the excellency of knowing Jesus (Phil. 3:8).

Do you ever allow your past to hinder your ability to serve the Lord and fulfill His calling for you in the present? We are no longer prisoners of our past. We are God's children; saved, redeemed and loved.

Asymmetry

THERE WAS ONE NIGHT that we pulled into our friend's driveway for life group and I was stunned by this lopsided tree. A quick glance says it's clearly favoring its right side for mass.

Some of the most interesting trees are ones that lack symmetry. Their unusual shape may give them character, but I'm also learning it can be tricky for the tree when it lacks symmetry.

Who We Are Now

Trees with curved trunks have unevenly distributed weight and have to over compensate by reinforcing wood on that side (Wohlleben 38). They need to support and balance the tree.

In our sin we may feel like lopsided, broken trees; so far from the righteousness of God. But even in this drawing here, the tree has a balance to it. Two thirds of the way up it looks fairly symmetrical. Even asymmetry can become symmetry.

Salvation is similar. We are not in symmetry with God before salvation. Our sin and carnal flesh make us His enemy. When we become saved God sees Jesus' righteousness instead of our sin. We are in 'symmetry' with Jesus, reconciled to God.

What begins at salvation as a symmetry of righteousness gradually takes on a visual symmetry as the Holy Spirit works within us to transform our actions and life in a way that reflects the heart of Christ.

A Very Tall, Mostly Straight Tree

WHILE SKETCHING THIS, I glanced around at the other trees and realized that many of them were not actually alive. They were just snags: dead where they stand.

The foliage forming their deception was actually a network of vines choking them, so much so that the vines outgrew their trees. They tangled at the tops like a questionable canopy made of borrowed crowns.

It reminded me how people (sometimes us) can put on a good show of faith, saying the right Christian phrases or doing good works. They look alive on the outside, like one of God's children. They may even have a form of godliness, but they deny the power of Christ and don't truly believe (2 Tim. 3:5). Their heavenly identity is false.

If you never have a real relationship with your Savior Jesus then you will not enter heaven. "I, even I, am the Lord; and beside me there is no saviour" (Isa. 43:11). Matthew 7:21-23 says that when someone who never truly believed in their heart tries to enter Heaven, Jesus will say He never knew that person and will ask them to leave.

What does it mean to be a Christian and follow Christ? Hebrews 9:14 says that the blood of Jesus will "…purge your conscience from dead works to serve the living God." Not to merely look alive, but to BE alive. We will truly be alive when we believe in God, accept Jesus into our hearts, and repent from sin.

Last Tree Before Winter

THE LIMB AT THE BOTTOM OF THIS TREE, which moved away from the light, was perhaps sealed off and died. It looks like a poorly grafted branch onto the tree.

Grafting involves making a small wound in both the accepting tree, and the branch being grafted in. They are precisely joined together and they fuse as the wounds heal together.

Jesus gave His life to graft us in to the promise of salvation. By His wounds we too are healed. God opened up His promise just like creating an opening for new branches to enter in. The Gentiles did! So do we when we believe.

We became partakers of God's promised salvation for His people (Israel) when Jesus died for "whosoever believeth on Him" (John 3:16). If we believe in Him then we are grafted in to the promise of eternal life like wild olive branches into an olive tree (Rom. 11:17).

Unlike that dead branch we mentioned earlier, we are well-grafted branches able to partake in the sustenance and blessing of the root. The root (God) is holy and thereby makes the branches (us) holy (vs. 16). All the glory for this comes from our great God (vs. 18).

We are reminded that whoever chooses to believe may be grafted into the good olive tree. There is no competition amongst branches, nor any more deserving than the rest. All must believe in Jesus, confess, and repent to have eternal life. Even those who chose not to believe may be grafted back in when they do (Rom. 11:23-24).

Growing Bark

Trees may be identified by their bark. It is one of their defining characteristics. We are defined by the life we live now: our words and actions.

We might see someone else's 'bark,' but we don't see their soul; only God does. When we witness actions and choices in a person's life it begins to demonstrate whether or not that person has the Holy Spirit in them.

There will be a difference in us as the saving grace of Jesus reigns in our life now (Rom. 5:21). We are transformed. The outward life we live begins to change as our new identity in Christ flows out of us. We start growing different bark.

God's word teaches us that believers will spend eternity with the Lord in Heaven. Unbelievers, if they never accept Jesus, will spend eternity suffering in Hell. There is a great and unsurmountable divide between the two when we die (Luke 16:26).

This divide is like the cambium layer in trees which divides the inner living bark from the outer dead bark. Tree cells join the living or the dead on either side of that cambium layer. We too have a choice to either accept Jesus into our heart, or reject Him and the salvation He offers.

As believers we are part of the living wood, alive through faith in the grace of God.

Barking Up the Tree

JUST AS TREES CAN BE IDENTIFIED by their bark, God says that we will be known as Jesus's disciples by our love for one another (John

13:35). It identifies us as vessels of God's love in action on this earth. His love through us is visible evidence that points others to the source of that love.

Unlike bark, our identity in Christ is not merely skin-deep. It reaches into the very core of us. It redefines all parts of us through salvation when God claims us as His children. We are no longer lost and alone, but reconciled, known, and loved more deeply than we can ever fathom.

> *Our personalities may change with our likes and dislikes over a lifetime; our identity doesn't have to. We will know who we are when we know who God is, and He tells us who He is in many ways throughout our entire life, beginning with His word. Stay rooted in the blessed identity of being His beloved child.*

Straightening Our Heart Posture

Walking Uprightly

> *"That ye might walk worthy of the Lord unto all pleasing, being fruitful in every good work, and increasing in the knowledge of God." (Col. 1:10)*

> *"Be glad in the Lord, and rejoice, ye righteous: and shout for joy, all ye that are upright in heart." (Psalm 32:11)*

I am a chronic huncher. Since I don't want to end up with back problems I've been trying to walk more upright. Pulling my abdomen back to straighten it feels like falling backwards. I'm not used to it because I've been walking one way for so long.

I know myself and I recognize that hunch as the posture of someone who still wants to hide. Who still feels small. Still wants to apologize for everything she does.

Walking upright for me means believing I've been redeemed. Accepting that I'm not perfect but that I'm also under the grace of God. To walk worthy of the calling (Col. 1:10), following God's commands. To walk in the confidence that I am fearfully and wonderfully made and God has a plan for me.

Whatever our heart 'posture' was before, God can help us walk tall in righteousness and use us to do His good work. I want to walk in righteousness, following the Lord where He calls me to go, loving who He asks me to love, and glorifying Him in everything He asks me to do.

Our hearts are subject to God and He has the power to change them. "Search me, O God, and know my heart: try me, and know my thoughts: And see if there be any wicked way in me, and lead me in the way everlasting" (Psalm 139:23-24). May we humble ourselves before the Lord and ask for His help in correcting our heart posture just as David prayed in Psalm 51:10 for a clean heart and renewed spirit.

Can you think of a time when you were focused on another person's heart and the ways it needed to change? Have you ever been the one telling everyone in your path to 'straighten up already'? We can spend less time managing other people's heart posture and more time praying and examining our own heart with God.

Spiritual Posture

When we walk hunched over it affects our entire body. We end up carrying our weight differently and can end up with back or knee problems. It can cause lasting damage if we don't address poor posture.

Our physical heart is affected by our posture as well. When felling trees, your posture matters. One study showed that the posture of people felling trees had a significant impact on the load distributed across their body, including their heart (Tsioras et al).

During this season God revealed how my heart needed to change for my own spiritual survival. When I was so focused on myself and what I wanted my very heart posture changed. I had become stooped and huddled in around myself. My head was tucked down, my eyes earth-bound.

Poor spiritual posture can affect our entire life. It can negatively impact our interactions and relationships. Especially our relationship with God. It leads us to make poor choices or sin. It can lead to spiritual laziness.

Straightening Our Heart Posture

Was there a time in your faith that you felt slumped over, just slogging through the day? A time when your faith just couldn't keep you upright anymore? It is not our own mustered faith, but God that is and has always kept us standing. "My flesh and my heart faileth: but God is the strength of my heart, and my portion for ever" (Psalm 73:26). He describes Himself as the strength of our life (Psalm 27:1).

When we as Christians spot a heart issue that needs attention we are sometimes too lazy to deal with it. We would rather pretend everything is fine to mislead ourselves and others. We hide behind all our works for the Lord, our pronounced faith, and everything else stays secret, right?

No. God sees everything. Jesus will "bring to light the hidden things of darkness, and will make manifest the counsels of the hearts" (1 Cor. 4:5). When we have the correct heart posture we are standing tall, firmly rooted in the Lord's love and are nourishing a relationship with Him.

Even some devils believe (James 2:19) – but they are not saved nor going to Heaven. Serving the Lord, loving Him, seeking to please Him, obeying Him, and repenting of sin are all heart changes that demonstrate true faith and a relationship with the Lord. Believing in Jesus is not simply knowing *about* Him. It is to know and acknowledge your need for a Savior. It is accepting Him into your heart and surrendering to Him.

We maintain a proper heart posture when we follow God's commandments, meditate on the proper things, stay humble in heart, and remain obedient and hopeful. With the Holy Spirit's help, all of these things are achievable.

That Tree from My Walks

TREES GENERATE ENERGY through photosynthesis, which requires water and sunlight. The water is drawn up from the roots and distributed throughout the tree through its own equivalent of pipes (Merhaut, Scientific American, 2024). We too draw up love and life when we are rooted in God.

Leaves absorb sunlight and convert it into photosynthetic sugar to nourish the tree. God says He is our sun (Psalm 84:11). When we lift our soul up to God we are like those leaves absorbing the shining light of our Lord and savior as we worship Him. Our arms raise in worship and extend out like the branches of a tree. "I stretch forth my hands unto thee: my soul thirsteth after thee" (Psalm 143:6).

Don't Follow Your Heart

My heart has gotten me into trouble many times because it is a master of deception. Jeremiah 17:9 calls it "desperately wicked." What I think and feel is too dangerously fickle to be considered truth - especially truth to act upon.

Even when we are blind to our own heart's true intention, God "knowest the hearts of all the children of men" (1 Kin. 8:39).

There may be a time when, in order to preserve a healthy heart posture, we need to grieve or mourn because what we are holding onto is weakening our heart or hindering our obedience. The Bible says, "Blessed are they that mourn: for they shall be comforted" (Matt. 5:4). God comforts us through His Spirit.

God desires to bless us but He also wants a relationship with us. He wants to build our faith in Him. If God gave me all my hearts' desires right away then I would only come to Him demanding what I want and leave the minute I receive it.

Surrender your heart's desires to Him, pray over them and His will, and allow Him to bless you with them as He sees fit.

Don't follow your heart. Follow God's.

Following God's Commands

God commends and blesses the one who walks "uprightly," in the state of his heart (Psalm 84:11, Psalm 125:4, Prov. 11:20) God is pleased when we seek righteousness with the Spirit's help (Zep. 2:3, Phil. 2:13). "I know also, my God, that thou triest the heart, and hast pleasure in uprightness…" (1 Chr. 29:17).

God seeks humble and willing hearts. "…I dwell in the high and holy place, with him also that is of a contrite and humble spirit, to revive the spirit of the humble…" (Isa. 57:15). Staying humble allows us to rest in the strength of God. Humbleness in heart means we are not exalting ourselves and our own ideas. "…for God resisteth the proud, and giveth grace to the humble" (1 Pet. 5:5). We are submitting to the Lord's commands.

In Deuteronomy 29:25-28, Moses is telling the Israelites what will happen to them if they forsake their God and His commands. They will be cursed and led into captivity by their enemies, and perish. But when they "return and obey the voice of the Lord, and do all His commandments," and "turn unto the Lord thy God with all thine heart, and with all thy soul," then the Lord will make them and their work prosper to yield fruit everywhere in their life (Deu. 30:8-10).

We too suffer real life consequences when we do not follow God's commands. We end up serving other gods and idols. We sin and reap corruption. Let us turn back to God with all our heart and soul!

Moses reminds the people that no one needs to go and fetch God's commands anymore. "…the word is very nigh unto thee, in thy mouth, and in thy heart, that thou mayest do it" (Deu. 30:14). They knew what they should be doing. So do we.

We hold God's word in our hands every time we read our Bible. We can know His commands, and the Holy Spirit will help us follow them. Remember, Jesus says that loving Him means following His commands (John 14:15).

Heart of Stone

BEFORE WE ARE SAVED our hearts are like hardened stones. Ezekiel 11:19-20 beautifully describes the work God does in our heart upon salvation when He enters in to begin transforming us.

Verse 20 says God will do this heart work so that His people will obey, and accept Him as their God. When God works on our heart we come running back to Him! "…I will put a new spirit within you; and I will take the stony heart out of their flesh, and will give them an heart of flesh" (vs. 19).

Regardless of how this rock ended up here, the tree began to grow around it. The rock changed the structure of the tree to encompass it. When we were dead in sin, before we knew Christ, our wicked hearts warped our lives. But now God has given us a new heart and a new Spirit.

May we have a soft heart ready to receive the Spirit's direction and teaching.

Sowing the Gospel in Our Heart and Others'

In Matthew 13:3-8,13-23, we learn of the different ways our hearts are affected by the word of God. In the parable of the sower, Jesus describes a heart where seeds of the gospel never took root, being devoured by fowls before they could grow; a heart who was initially impacted by the gospel, but whose roots of faith were shallow and died in scorching trials; a heart who was overpowered by thorns; and the heart who was ready to hear, whose ground readily accepted those gospel seeds, and the growth there that yielded much fruit.

Which heart is yours?

In Hosea 10:12 we are instructed to break up "fallow ground," or inactive soil, and seek the Lord. This allows us to sow righteousness and reap mercy. Righteousness comes from the Lord. If we are sowing the seeds of the gospel in someone's heart, remember that only God knows the timing of their salvation. God knows the details and makes the plan. Keep praying for the unsaved.

God's word is full of people whose hearts were changed. There is time to accept Jesus' free gift of salvation until our final breath. While we are breathing there is hope. If we have accepted Jesus into our hearts then those seeds are growing.

There is a direct relationship between what you plant and what grows. Galatians 6:7-8 warns us of the corruption that can grow when we sow to the flesh. When we sow to the Spirit we reap everlasting life and the fruit of godly character! The choice seems clear.

He Helps Us

I sat weeping one night after church, just talking to God and feeling spent. It is frustrating and exhausting that my heart will always try to deceive me. I will always be tempted by my own understanding. I will inevitably keep sinning because I'm a sinner. And when I think I'm still carrying my cross I look around to find I've laid it down somewhere and have to go find it again.

God is so patient, compassionate, and merciful toward us (Psalm 145:8)

When our heart condemns us, He is greater than our heart (1 John 3:20). He knows when we have a desire to please Him and when we don't because He knows our hearts so well.

During this season I was weak in many things. I was mistaken in many things. I am still weak now, but I know God is my strength and His grace is sufficient for me (2 Cor. 12:9). I am only mistaken now as often as I stop relying on the Holy Spirit to guide me. And whenever I stop reading His word and think I can do it on my own.

Our faith as believers exists, but it is imperfect. Mark 9:23-24 records a conversation Jesus has with a father who comes to him in desperate need of help for his child. The father cries out that while he believes, he needs Jesus' help because his belief is imperfect. It is a wonderful admission that he knows he alone is not enough and his faith needs work. Would Jesus please help his child in spite of it? Jesus does.

While reading one day God brought me to Psalm 145. Verse 17 describes how God is "righteous in all his ways, and holy in all his works." This might cause us to believe that God is cold toward us as sinners, but it's not true. He cares about our struggles even while He is righteous and holy.

The Bible says He is "rich in mercy" (Eph. 2:4) with excellent "lovingkindness" (Psalm 36:7). Remember, He loved us when we didn't love Him. When we sin, His grace is there to cover it (Rom. 5:20) and He has already paid for it on the cross (don't forget the need to confess it to Him and repent).

God asks us to pick up our cross daily and follow Him (Luke 9:23). That means He already knows we will put it down at times. Depending on the day, that cross might feel as heavy as a hammer driving the nail (us) into the ground. Usually this is when we forget the hope we have in Jesus and are only seeing the work.

But we have another truth - Jesus says "my yoke is easy, and my burden is light" (Matt. 11:30). We get to lay our own burdens down at His feet and find rest for our souls (vs. 29). He does the work and we surrender to it. He will not ask us to do something that He will not help us do.

God teaches us to do His will and leads us in the land of uprightness (Psalm 143:10).

Kindness

One spark of kindness can wholly move us, especially if it feels undeserved. It cuts through the worst things you think about yourself. It can turn a day around, check an attitude, and inspire more kindness. It fosters life.

The world tells us to get even, take revenge, and give others 'what they deserve.' Not true for believers. God has called us to model His heart in all matters.

We are called to be kind, have a tender heart, and forgive others as we have been forgiven (Eph. 4:32). Furthermore, 1 Peter 3:8-9 tells us, "…having compassion one of another, love as brethren, be pitiful, be courteous: Not rendering evil for evil, or railing for railing: but contrariwise blessing;"

I can think of specific acts of kindness in my life shown to me by others at a time when I really needed it. It has acted as reproof, as love, as a word spoken in due season, as proof I do exist, and a light to chase away lies.

It is a marvelous mystery to see how God moves in the hearts of ourselves and others. He should be the one motivating our love and kindness in this life! When God shows us kindness it can crumble strongholds.

Pursuing Treasure

> *"But lay up for yourselves treasures in heaven, where neither moth nor rust doth corrupt, and where thieves do not break through nor steal: For where your treasure is, there will your heart be also." (Matt. 6:20-21)*

The Old Testament records instances when Israel's enemies pillaged the house of the Lord and took away the Lord's treasure. Silver and gold were carried away along with anything else thought to be of value.

This usually happened when Israel had turned from the Lord and God allowed their enemies in to conquer them. He allowed this, knowing His own house would be robbed. When Israel returned to the Lord, seeking Him and walking in His commands once more, God restored them to their land and allowed them to take back the silver and gold. They returned His treasure to His house.

It represents the condition of their heart. When His people turned from Him and set their heart elsewhere, they were carried away along with the physical treasure from His house. When their hearts returned to the Lord, the treasure returned to His house. Their hearts were once again storing up treasures with God.

God desires all of us. He pursues us. We are His treasure. Is He ours?

Straightening Our Heart Posture

Where is Your Treasure?

Proper heart posture means our whole heart belongs to the Lord. "And thou shalt love the Lord thy God with all thine heart, and with all thy soul, and with all thy might" (Deut. 6:5). "For where your treasure is, there will your heart be also" (Matt. 6:21). May we treasure the Lord, knowing our hearts belong with Him.

We are called to pursue heavenly treasure over treasures in the world. Eternal treasure and rewards in Heaven are incorruptible and forever. We begin by accepting Jesus into our hearts. That means we are going to Heaven. Thieves cannot break through and steal us away from the Lord and His love (Matt 6:20). We continue by pursuing the Lord and walking in righteousness with His help.

The Moths

I SAT WITH A TREASURED FRIEND a few years ago in the midst of sorrow and rending in my heart. She shared my silence, listened when I did speak, and didn't ask for the details I did not want to give.

Instead, this woman of God spoke life into me as the Holy Spirit directed her.

We swung gently on her tree swing and gazed out at the creek. I wondered what God was doing. I knew that He wasn't finished with me but I had no idea how He could possibly use this season of my life for good.

I remember that in between words my friend and I watched the brown moths in the tree above us. They filled the air.

Matthew 6:19 says, "Lay not up for yourselves treasures upon earth, where moth and rust doth corrupt…" Those destructive moths came right down and tried to land on us, demanding our attention. We had to swat them away.

That first Summer, if my treasure had truly been in the Lord, I would have been embracing my incorruptible reward and treasure in Heaven, where "neither moth nor rust doth corrupt." Instead, I had hidden my treasure in a heart-shaped box and the moths had found it.

I had an idol in my heart and God was removing it before it corroded me completely. "It is of the Lord's mercies that we are not consumed, because his compassions fail not" (Lam. 3:22). Thank the Lord for His intervention!

We are called to focus on the things that please God, labor to further His kingdom, and store up eternal reward as we do. "For where your treasure is, there will your heart be also" (Matt. 6:21).

Trade Temporal for Eternal

The things around us are temporary and will decay. Our own bodies are no exception. However, 1 Peter 1:3-5 explains how our eternal inheritance will not decay. "To an inheritance incorruptible, and undefiled, and that fadeth not away, reserved in heaven for you" (1 Pet. 1:4).

As a believer, your heavenly inheritance is reserved for you right now in Heaven! Wow!

STRAIGHTENING OUR HEART POSTURE

The glory and treasures stored up for us in Heaven are a permanent record of how we lived, and most importantly what God did for us (Matt. 6:19-20, Job 16:19). Therefore we put our trust not in the things of the world which decay, but in the Lord God Almighty.

"...for the things which are seen are temporal; but the things which are not seen are eternal" (2 Cor. 4:18). When we are prioritizing the Lord's work, we can have great peace knowing we labor for the Lord and are storing up treasure in Heaven. We work toward the eternal things that cannot be seen but through faith are believed.

> *Our behavior changes as our heart changes. Our souls grow strong in righteousness with hearts rooted in the love of God, sown to the Spirit. May we cultivate an eternal mindset with a heart surrendered to God.*

Redefining Beauty

What is Beautiful?

> *"Favour is deceitful, and beauty is vain: but a woman that feareth the Lord, she shall be praised." (Pro. 31:30)*

I once overheard a few junior high school girls on the swingset comparing their weights. These girls were all as thin as my pinky, and that's only a mild exaggeration. I looked at my daughter playing nearby and wondered what she would endure from a world where her peers would see her body as her identity.

Another time at church I heard a woman discussing the body of someone else's toddler, and not in a "look at those cute cheeks" kind of way. The conversation about our size begins shockingly early.

Why does beauty equal value in our society? Why are our scales weighed with social media 'likes' and our ability to keep up with fashion trends? Our heavenly value is not dependent on appearance or popularity.

God gave us the ability to assess beauty and admire it. We have eyes and brains that appreciate pleasing shapes, symmetry, order, color and skill. We have ears to hear and enjoy musical arrangements and melodies.

In the world this ability to appreciate beauty is tainted by sin such as lust, coveting and envy. It leads us to make comparisons between each other, sow to the flesh, or be unkind. It means that other people's temporary favor for us can deceive us.

But God redeems this when he helps us to see with our soul, directed by the Holy Spirit. We can look at another human and see their value apart from beauty. God loves each of us and Jesus died to save whoever believes, regardless of what they look like on the outside.

Our inner beauty is amplified by the great value we have in being His sons and daughters, and being loved by Him.

Just as a soul seeking God is beautiful, God has also created a natural world abounding in beauty and mystery. We cannot know or discover the entirety of it (Ecc. 3:11). He clothes the grass and flowers with such beauty that they surpass the clothes of King Solomon (Luk. 12:27).

He created the heavens in such splendor that all nations would know the work of His hands. "There is no speech nor language, where their voice is not heard" (Psalm 19:3).

May our ability to appreciate beauty cause us to praise God (because we admire His creative hand, and the souls He made) instead of worship our own flesh.

Inside the Willow

A FRIEND AND I MET FOR A PLAY DATE one day, and while we were talking God interrupted us with a spectacular show of beauty just to glorify Him. Glittering golden leaves from the tree above began to shower the playground. Neither of us commented on it; we just watched in awe.

I had drawn a few trees by now, and she suggested an impressive willow tree as my next candidate. It was a tree I'd seen before; shapely and boasting a thick mane of hair tendrils. When the wind blew it came alive in swirling cyclones.

Part of me would always reject it as an uninteresting subject to draw. From the outside it was just scribbles of hair. After five minutes there would be no more information to communicate with my pens.

Her suggestion got me thinking; what did it look like on the inside? A few days later I was seated inside that curtain of hair drawing the guts of the tree. From this vantage point I could truly see its character. It was full of bends, twists and tangles. Some might call it 'ugly.'

If you can learn to love beyond appearance, if you can see value where others have overlooked, you might be nearer God's heart than you realize. Outer beauty is often self-serving. The beauty of the heart comes from putting on Christ's character.

Snaggle Stump

THIS WILLOW STUMP IS BIGGER THAN ME. The tree removal company couldn't cut any lower due to all the knots in it. Now it resembles a misshapen skull sporting a snaggle tooth. It has little 'legs' that it could scuttle away on like a spider. The whole structure is punctured with holes that look like eyes.

Meanwhile, it was framed by the beautiful foliage of healthy trees beyond it. I probably should have been drawing those, but God kept teaching me through these dilapidated trees.

When God reaches out toward the suffering and needy, the neglected and overlooked, the wicked and sinful, we see His great healing power, mercy, and grace on display (Mark 2:17). He sought out their company and stopped to meet them. He came for this purpose: to call sinners to repentance. To heal us in the most profound and essential way – by removing our sin and paying our debt with His life so we don't have to pay with ours.

When we are in circumstances far from glamorous, feeling stuck in the worst version of ourselves, we can take great comfort and relief knowing God still has compassion for us. "…his compassions fail not" (Lam. 3:22). "…his mercy is everlasting;" (Psalm 100:5).

He responds with kindness, love, and mercy when we deserve death and judgement.

Even when we are made to feel incredibly small and insignificant by the cruelty or indifference of others, we know our God adores us. Not because we are beautiful, talented, or worthy, but because HE is good.

My mother-in-law planted flowers inside the hollows of this skull-stump and now they are like a crown of unexpected beauty. There is life here and God is still working.

Forever Young

Staying 'forever young' might seem appealing when we notice the signs of aging in our own bodies. Our bodies rearrange themselves into different proportions. Our hair turns gray, then white.

Our very skin changes, like that of trees as they age. Young trees have smooth outer bark. "As trees age, wrinkles gradually appear (beginning from below), and they steadily deepen as the years progress" (Wohlleben 62).

We tend to think of aging as a negative process; the process of becoming less beautiful. We imagine we are heading downhill and it all begins with that first gray hair. But God says, "The glory of young men is their strength: and the beauty of old men is the gray head" (Prov. 20:29).

What if it is a privilege to age physically, as well as spiritually? To be content in growing old, knowing God is still as good as He was yesterday and His love for us does not decrease as the number of gray hairs increases. Lord, liberate us from our temporal mindset!

My body bears scars and carries features I might wish to alter if I had the choice. But this flesh is also a vessel for the Holy Spirit to work (2 Cor. 4:6-7), and a member of Christ's body here on earth (Rom. 12:4-5).

God promises to give us a new body in Heaven. The body He gives us for eternal life with Him in Heaven will be "glorious" (Phil. 3:20-21). Not scarred. Not crippled or diseased. Not full of sin. Our very body will be redeemed.

How do you view aging? When you come across an old picture of yourself, what do you notice first?

What Is Beautiful to God?

I used to have a post-it taped to my bathroom mirror that quoted Proverbs 31:30. Every time I looked in the mirror I wanted to remember that God values the heart of a woman more than her looks. Specifically, how a heart bowed in holy awe and fear of Him is praiseworthy.

The world has its own idea of beauty, but what is beautiful to God?

When He looks at His children He sees His Son's righteousness, and holiness has a beauty to it. Even when the world merely measures us by our appearance, God sees our very heart and still loves us dearly.

In 1 Samuel 16, the Lord is commending David to His prophet, Samuel. He says, "…man looketh on the outward appearance, but the Lord looketh on the heart" (vs. 7). God reminds Samuel not to be fooled by what he sees on the outside, because He has chosen David for His specific purpose and plan.

Does our appearance affect our ability to do the "good works" that God has ordained us to do (Eph. 2:10)?

1 Peter 3:3-4 further discusses the beauty that pleases the Lord. He says to adorn our *hearts* rather than our bodies, and that a "meek and quiet spirit" is worth a great price to God. A meek and quiet spirit is beautiful to the Lord. Is that something we can see from the outside?

2 Corinthians 4:16 reminds us that our outward man will perish. The beauty of youth is fleeting. Would God in His infinite wisdom place so great a value on an outward beauty that is not designed to last? But "the inward man is renewed day by day" through His Spirit.

God's perfect love casts out fear (1 John 4:18) including the fear of others' opinions. Someone else could think the worst thing about you, and while it might hurt a lot, it ultimately does not affect your value. It does not diminish God's love for you. We can always pray for help in accepting God's perfect love for us.

We can learn to see what God has made and praise Him for it - whatever it may look like. Whether it's symmetrical or not. Whether it's blemished or not. Whether it's tall, short, purple or yellow. We can see value in others because God does and God lives in us.

A Make-Over

God's idea of beauty includes the exchange of sin, death, and mourning, for grace, life, and joy.

In Isaiah 61 the Lord promises to perform works of healing and beauty over His people. We too are now His people, having been adopted through salvation by His death on the cross. Verse 10 equates His salvation to a robe of righteousness we get to put on, as if He is adorning us for a wedding.

In verse 3, He promises to give beauty for ashes to those who mourn (cleaning them from the ashes of mourning), to exchange mourning for joy, and heaviness for praise. He equates these redeemed people to trees of righteousness planted for the Lord to bring Him glory.

Our sin is not becoming. It does not make us beautiful. It mars us. But God sent Jesus to die for us because He wanted to save us from that sin. He loved us even when we were 'unlovable.' Even when we were 'ugly' on the inside. We are cleaned and dressed by Him as He redeems us.

The Jesus We Want to See

Isaiah 53:2-3 describes Jesus as less than beautiful. He was not good looking or attractive, and had no beauty to recommend Him to others. He is said to be despised, rejected, and a "man of sorrows."

This is our great and mighty Redeemer, who was, in all ways, not what people expected. He was not a lofty rich king (in appearance).

He did not overthrow the government. He didn't hang with only the cool kids or the big players of the time. He was not attractive.

How we view Jesus will wholly impact our entire belief. Too often we look for the Jesus we want to see; the Jesus that looks like us; the Jesus who makes sense to us.

Throughout history people have wanted art that reflected them. They would commission artwork depicting the Jesus that looked like them: the Jesus most applicable to their life.

Wealthy people wanted to see a superhero Jesus. They didn't want to see the crown of thorns, the piercing, or the stripes. They wanted an idyllic, able-bodied Jesus; a pale, blonde-haired, blue-eyed, super buff figment of imagination.

But that is to deny His *suffering* on the cross, which is so pivotal to our faith.

Suffering people nearing death wanted to see the Jesus who suffered. They could relate to that Jesus. How could superhero Jesus possibly understand what they were going through? The religious artwork in those places depicted a grim and disturbing crucifixion - all of the suffering and none of the glory.

It's closer to the truth (though we know He was going to glory with God when He gave up the ghost). Jesus "went down into the horror of death and plunged out the other side in order to provide a limitless supply of mercy and grace to his people" (Ortlund 37).

How can we come to know God if we don't know Jesus Christ in truth, and accept the gospel of His death, burial, and resurrection? "…I am the way, the truth, and the life: no man cometh unto the Father, but by me" (John 14:6).

If we mistake who He is then we are in danger of never truly coming to know God. "… God hath given to us eternal life, and this life is in his Son. He that hath the Son hath life; and he that hath not the Son of God hath not life" (1 John 5:11-12).

Jesus does not conform to our image; we conform to His. We believe God's word, receive His Spirit, and are transformed and sanctified throughout our lives to be more like Christ.

If we only look for a 'Jesus' that resembles our flesh, then we are denying Him in truth. We become like the Pharisees and Priests who saw Him with their own eyes, talked with Him, knew the scriptures, yet denied Him. He was rejected by those who arguably should have known Him best.

God's standard of perfection in the flesh is Jesus. Jesus' perfect sinless life, and His teaching that our sin would keep us out of heaven is all designed to show us that we are the ones who don't measure up and can't do it alone. Realizing this puts us in a great spot to accept His help and salvation.

He isn't like us in all the ways that matter. When we are saved by believing with faith, we are counted as righteous in God's eyes, like Christ, and welcome to share His inheritance in Heaven.

Bearing Marks

"But he was wounded for our transgressions, he was bruised for our iniquities: the chastisement of our peace was upon him; and with his stripes we are healed" (Isa. 53:5).

We all carry marks of what we've been through in life. Some are visible and some are not. We might wonder, 'how could my scars be part of God's good plan?' We can't always know the answer, but we know we serve a good God worthy of our trust.

He heals us throughout our life but those scars can be a gift. May they be reminders of His faithfulness toward us during each trial. May they remind us of the 'stripes' Jesus Himself endured for all of us. He is no stranger to our suffering.

While you may carry physical marks, you also have a beauty that no one in this life can truly see or know. God is working within your heart and that is beautiful to Him.

We have the incredible hope of exchanging our marks. The 'mark' of sin can be exchanged for the mark of Christ's holiness, righteousness, and the promise of Heaven. We can pray for help in forgetting what is behind as we press toward His mark (Phil 3:13-14).

Almost Felled

THIS TREE LOOKS LIKE IT WAS MARKED for felling at some point and never gotten around to. Looks like it's dead and ready to go; a multi-trunked snag with scattered scars.

There might be seasons where we are like this tree, unable to bear what comes next because we're barely standing after the last battle. But God is there carrying and caring for us, shouldering our burdens.

Jesus too was 'marked for felling.' Matthew 26:3-4 talks of how the religious leaders plotted Jesus' death. They didn't just want Him gone; they wanted to make an example of Him. They persecuted Him. They 'cut Him down.'

REDEFINING BEAUTY

Jesus was wounded, bruised, chastised, and gave his life for our healing. He bore all of our sin, and the wrath of God over it in order to save us. They succeeded in killing Him because He allowed them to.

But He did not stay dead! Remember He is our *risen* Savior. That tomb was empty. He rose from the grave to give all those who believe victory over death and eternal life with Him.

May our scars simply become stories of God at work; tales of His healing and goodness to bless and encourage others.

Her Grandma's Tree

I DROVE UP TO THIS LOVELY HOUSE by the lake and drooled over stripes of melting orange sherbert smeared across a pale blue lake. A liquid pink ball of sunshine hung in the sky. The mourning doves were cooing, bringing back soothing memories with their gentle lullaby notes.

This beautiful scabby birch tree did not look like any other birch tree I'd seen. My experience was mainly with Paper Birches, which look 'prettier.' This one had an over-abundance of scars.

The rippling black scars are fissures in the bark where the two sides have pushed up against each other. The lenticels, or thin, horizontal lines on the bark help birch trees to exchange oxygen and carbon dioxide through the trunk (U.S. National Park Service, 2024).

Each trunk had different plates on it: black marks that appear like scabs on skin. Our own wounds scarred over fragile flesh can tell a story too. Physically, they tell the story of injury and healing. Emotionally, they speak of heart-wounds and tell the story of God's healing, redemptive work within us.

Our own scars, emotional or physical, show an exchange of suffering for God's enduring faithfulness, healing, and love during it. We may always bear them but they remind us that God stayed with us and sustained us while we endured. He does not leave His children.

Palm Tree

PALM TREES HOLD A SPECIAL INTEREST for me because they are like nothing else back home. They seem to completely embody the iconic vacation scene. As soon as you see them you know you are 'somewhere else.'

We first saw them while visiting our friends down South. Our buddy picked us up at the airport around midnight and I could just make out palm-like silhouettes in the dark sky. I knew I'd see them in the morning. For now they were just a shadow of the real thing.

"For now we see through a glass, darkly; but then face to face: now I know in part; but then shall I know even as also I am known" (1 Cor. 13:12). What we see and know now is only a portion of what God reveals to our limited human minds. When we are with Him in glory we will understand with such clarity the things He will show us.

The trunks of certain species of palm trees look like a stack of rings fitted together. I was amazed to read that those rings are actually leaf scars, where new leaves grew and then died, all the way up the tree as it grows (Broschat, 2024). Its scars are inseparable from its characteristic palm tree stem. They often wear the sheaths of dried leaves (Lanzara et al. 65).

John 12:12-15 records how the people rejoiced over Jesus' coming to Jerusalem. He rode on a donkey, as prophesied in Zechariah 9:9, and they cried "Hosanna!" and laid palm branches in the street. Thus starts what we know as Holy Week, beginning with Palm Sunday and ending with the Resurrection of Jesus.

Above, we discussed how palm fronds can leave scars when they die off the stem of the palm tree. Here were God's chosen people laying them in the path as He rode, a path which would ultimately take Him to the cross, where He would endure lashings that left 'stripes.'

Just as the palm fronds were cut from their trees, maybe leaving scars behind on the stem, Jesus would be marked as well; "wounded for our transgressions" (Isa. 53:5). "...by whose stripes ye were healed" (1 Pet. 2:24). It is His death on the cross that paid for our sins and healed us spiritually for all eternity.

Were those scars beautiful? No. But what they represented is. Our righteousness in Christ has a spiritual beauty to the Lord, who gave His life on that wooden cross, fashioned from a tree, where His blood was shed for us.

Bone Bark

THIS TREE RESEMBLES WHAT IT MIGHT LOOK LIKE to see flesh returning to bones. Smooth layers of sapwood and heartwood look like bone merging with textured bark.

Redefining Beauty

In Ezekiel 37, the prophet has an extraordinary vision in a valley of dry bones. God raises them to life before his eyes! The bones are first joined into complete skeletons, and then flesh and skin come upon them. When the bodies are restored once more, Ezekiel is called to prophesy and ask the wind to enter those bodies, giving them breath and life.

I can only imagine how astonishing such a vision would be. First, imagine how unsettling it would be to see a wasteland of human bones. Then Ezekiel watches the dead come back to life in such explicit detail.

It is this striking imagery of the bones rejoining and "the sinews and the flesh came up upon them" that God uses to illustrate His promise to restore Israel. He will gather them, revive their spirit, and bring them out of captivity into their own land. We serve a God of restoration and reconciliation.

Our bones are not a permanent home for us. When believers die we are completely separate from what happens to our bodies in the ground. That body is now an empty vessel. "We are confident, I say, and willing rather to be absent from the body, and to be present with the Lord" (2 Cor. 5:8). In death, the body of flesh is left behind and our soul goes to Heaven with God!

The body we dwell in on this side of Heaven will be reduced to bones alone after the spirit leaves it. Eternal life is found through belief and a genuine relationship with Jesus, confession to the Lord and repentance from sins.

Since all our earthly bodies will pass away with time, let's let the Holy Spirit help us look beyond physical beauty and see the value of a soul.

Leftovers

We are incredibly valuable to the Lord our God who gave His life for us, regardless of what we look like on the outside. All He saw was our need on the inside.

Even one leftover soul is of great value to God. In Luke 17:12-19 Jesus heals ten lepers. These leftovers stood apart, isolated because of their affliction and its danger to others. They were cast aside, disfigured and diseased, but Jesus moves toward them in love.

Jesus heals those ten 'leftovers' and only one turns back to give glory to God for the miracle. "And Jesus answering said, Were there not ten cleansed? but where are the nine?" (Luke 17:17). Jesus commends the one thankful enough to return.

"…joy shall be in heaven over one sinner that repenteth, more than over ninety and nine just persons, which need no repentence" (Luke 15:7). It is not about the quantity of salvation, but each individual heart. And within that heart the Holy Spirit begins adorning and transforming the soul.

We are tempted to look at those around us with gauges and scales. Against our will even we automatically assess their beauty and value. God looks at the heart. What can you do differently to try and see beyond mere appearances, and practice looking at the heart?

> *When we are rooted in God's great love we know that the way He sees us matters far more than the opinions of others or ourselves. We grow and know our tree is beautiful, not for its leaves or bark but for Who is growing it.*

God Sustains Us

Sustained and Satisfied

> *"Thou openest thine hand, and satisfiest the desire of every living thing." (Psalm 145:16)*
>
> *"But my God shall supply all your need according to his riches in glory by Christ Jesus." (Phil. 4:19)*

God sustains His children physically and spiritually throughout our life. Spiritually, He provides eternal life and salvation for any who believe through the death of His son (John 3:16). He provides the love, grace, strength, mercy and kindness we crave. Physically, He promises to meet our needs when we trust Him, and simply seek His kingdom. He'll take care of the rest (Matt. 6:31-33, Phil. 4:19).

We are further encouraged by David who says, "I have been young, and now am old; yet have I not seen the righteous forsaken, nor his seed begging bread" (Psalm 37:25). How good He is!

From the Table

I was reading through the gospels during this season in order to remember who Jesus is. In the course of reading, the Holy Spirit stopped me at an encounter between Jesus and a Canaanite woman in Matthew 15.

In this context, Jesus has not yet died on the cross, so salvation has not come to the Gentiles through His shed blood. As a woman of Canaan, she is not one of God's chosen people, Israel. It is clear, however, that she believes in Jesus. She calls Him "Lord, thou Son of David" (vs. 22) and worships Him (vs. 25). She is desperately seeking His help, fully knowing and believing that He is capable.

What gets me is the exchange in verses 26 and 27. Jesus has explained that He came for the lost sheep of Israel – which does not include this woman. In verse 26, Jesus says, "It is not meet to take the children's bread, and cast it to dogs."

It might seem harsh to us that Jesus uses this illustration for His point. His children at the time were only the Jewish people. He was teaching them, healing them, and having a relationship with them – the benefits that come from being His children. The life He was offering was for them first (Rom. 1:16).

Any other nation at the time was like a dog coming to the table to steal bread. The bread that is meant to nourish the children is not meant to go to the dogs. Jesus knew He was going to die on the cross though, and redemption from sin would come to all mankind – whoever would believe.

She responds in verse 27, "Truth, Lord: yet the dogs eat of the crumbs which fall from their master's table." This woman is fully aware of who she is and what she is asking. She knows that the "house of Israel" is the Lord's people and not her. She also knows He is the Master, the only one who is able to help her daughter. She is willing to overcome the obvious hinderance of her position in order to obtain the help and mercy she needs.

In this she is admitting, 'I know that bread doesn't belong to me, but will you allow me to take the crumbs that fall?' Jesus rewards her faith and heals her daughter (vs. 28). Sometimes when we ask for a little, fully believing, He gives us far more.

Have you ever felt like this woman? If you have accepted Jesus, was there a time before salvation when you felt like a dog at the Lord's table, looking for crumbs that didn't belong to you?

"Then hath God also to the Gentiles granted repentance unto life" (Acts 11:18). "…The Gentiles, which followed not after righteousness, have attained to righteousness, even the righteousness which is of faith" (Rom. 9:30). This woman's faith in Jesus was rewarded; He granted her request, just as our faith is rewarded with eternal life.

As a believer now, do you ever still feel like all you deserve are crumbs? Through our belief in Jesus and His sacrifice on the cross, we are now welcome at His table because we are His children! We may all partake of the Living Bread that He is. Remember your identity in Christ as His child: welcome at His table, with a portion all your own.

Our Provider

I looked out at our deck one day after a rainfall and noticed the quantity of water collected in a small basin. I tried to wrap my brain around how rainfall is actually measured. Wouldn't it depend on the container it falls into?

It turns out weather professionals use a standard gauge for measuring rainfall. The US Standard Rain Gauge involves the use of an overflow cylinder which collects the excess rain and measures that as well (Wikipedia, 2024). Even the overflow gets accounted for.

God's abundance of love, mercy and grace on the other hand, cannot be measured. He pours into and over us to fill up our earthly vessels. "…my cup runneth over" (Psalm 23:5). He sustains us our entire life, with the promise of eternity, until we enter life everlasting and are daily in His presence.

Redemption for God's people is described as, "…their soul shall be as a watered garden; and they shall not sorrow any more at all" (Jer. 31:12). Isaiah 58:11 reminds us that the Lord will "satisfy thy soul in drought…" We are no longer thirsty, but satisfied by the Lord's abundance.

In John 4, Jesus is speaking to a Samaritan woman drawing water from a well, and teaches her about a different kind of water. "But whosoever drinketh of the water that I shall give him shall never thirst; but the water that I shall give him shall be in him a well of water springing up into everlasting life" (John 4:14).

When we have Jesus living in our heart, we have a continual supply of water springing up within us. Our soul will never run dry.

The Gift of Rain

THIS SWAMPLAND WAS SATURATED in after-rain contrast. All the blues and browns of decaying leaves in mud were scattered amidst lime green shoots of grass. The greenery formed mounded islands framing pools of gray sky and reflected trees that rippled in the wind.

Deciduous trees are directly nourished by rainfall and drink gallons of water during a downpour. The rain funnels down twigs and branches all the way down to the roots (Wohlleben 102). Tree wood is made of long, hollow tubes instead of cells, which transport water all the way up from the roots to the leaves (Wohlleben 58). They catch rain so they can drink it in.

In my drawing, the rainwater collected by depressions of earth was slowly being absorbed by nearby trees. Acts 14:17 says the Lord: "… did good, and gave us rain from heaven, and fruitful seasons, filling our hearts with food and gladness." God sends the rain to give life.

Leading into this difficult season, I wasn't reading my Bible. As I drifted from the Lord my soul suffered great dehydration. When we don't read our Bibles we are without the life-giving water Christ promises.

When I started reading God's word again, I expected to feel better immediately. But God was teaching me to build a habit of returning to Him daily. "But my God shall supply all your need according to his riches in glory by Christ Jesus" (Phil. 4:19).

When my thoughts grow too loud I open God's word and He speaks life, truth, and peace into me. His word rains life to soak into my roots and satisfy my soul.

Maybe you're surrounded by floodwaters in your life, wondering what God is doing. You know He heard your prayers but you don't yet see Him answering. Just as God sent the waters that stood above mountains back into the earth (Psalm 104:6-9), He will cause the sorrows in your life to recede and once again restore you to life.

He "prepareth rain for the earth" (Psalm 147:8). There are places on this planet where rain literally changes the ecosystem; wet seasons alternate with dry. Plants and animals endure the dry season to get to the wet, and along the way God is providing for them, even though it is difficult.

When we are saved, God's grace reigns in our heart and changes that environment completely. Imagine what He can plant and grow there!

Vineyard Tree

I ARRIVED JUST BEFORE SUNRISE and a friend met me in her yard to introduce the tree candidates. This one stood out for the variety of life it supported, so I set up to draw it.

This tree sustained other plants. To the vine growing up its trunk it played host. It also hoisted the tangle of grape vines covering it toward the sun.

Jesus is the vine sustaining our life. In John 15, Jesus explains that we have a relationship with God as the Giver of Life, through

Him. He asks His disciples to abide in Him and reminds them that it is the only way to bear fruit.

In John 15:1 Jesus says, "I am the true vine, and my Father is the husbandman." God is the farmer, Jesus is the vine, and we are the branches. The vine is where life flows.

Branches that are not connected to the vine are on the ground, lifeless. They have no root system. Nothing sustains them. In and of ourselves we can do nothing; the power is all God's.

If we are abiding in Christ, relying on Him for strength and life, then we are clinging to the life-giving Vine that sustains us in our Christian walk. He will grow good fruit in us.

Bearing good fruit is evidence of Christ at work within us. "Either make the tree good, and his fruit good; or else make the tree corrupt, and his fruit corrupt: for the tree is known by his fruit" (Matt. 12:33). We will be known by our works of faith as believers, as well as the godly character within us.

God Sustains Us

In nature, mushrooms are considered the above-ground fruiting body of fungi. When present on bark or wood, they can be a sign of rot and decay within the tree. It's a fitting picture of corrupt fruit signaling a heart against the Lord. It signals the presence of unrepented sin within a person.

Remember, abiding in Christ brings the good fruit of patience, gentleness, goodness, joy, peace, love and faith (Gal. 5:22). They are evidence of His Holy Spirit dwelling within us.

What spiritual fruit have you seen God growing in you as you walk more closely with Him? We would be fruitless and lifeless without our Vine, the Lord Jesus, and God the farmer tending it. If your spiritual walk doesn't seem to be bearing much fruit of His godly character in you, study out why that might be and pray that God would help you grow in your faith.

He Sustains All Creation

Job 38-41 discuss how God is the one sustaining His creation and establishing His design for it. Psalm 104 discusses the great things that God made, and how He is still sustaining them. Verses 10 and 11 discuss the water that God sends into the hills, which allows beasts to quench their thirst.

Verse 16 mentions how "the trees of the Lord are full of sap." This sap is a sugary liquid composed of water and photosynthetic sugars. Verse 21 says even the lions seek their meat from God. His plan for sustaining His creation is evident. We may see it each morning in the delicate droplets on the very grass under our feet.

He is even nourishing life far from bodies of water, because of the transpiration of trees. As they release water vapor into the atmosphere they create clouds (Wohlleben 106) which yield rain to help things grow.

He has also designed some intricate relationships in nature to sustain His creation. For instance, in the forest's soil the roots of trees interact with a web of fungi to exchange nutrients and even communicate important information from tree to tree (Simard 60).

He has sustained His children throughout our history. Nehemiah 9:20-21 describes the great provision and sustenance of the Lord even during Israel's years of wandering in the desert. God gave them His "good spirit to instruct them," and made sure they lacked nothing. During 40 years of wandering, God gave Israel bread from heaven, water, and held their very clothing together.

Our God will satisfy and nourish us when we long for Him and seek Him! "For he satisfieth the longing soul, and filleth the hungry soul with goodness" (Psalm 107:9).

> *May we too catch all the rain God sends down to water our soul as we stay rooted in His great love. We are nourished by a compassionate Gardener who continually sustains us.*

When We Delight in God

Loving and Living His Word

> *"I delight to do thy will, O my God: yea, thy law is within my heart." (Psalm 40:8)*

> *"Praise ye the Lord. Blessed is the man that feareth the Lord, that delighteth greatly in his commandments." (Psalm 112:1)*

God blesses those who delight in Him. We are blessed when we do not follow the counsel of the world, but rather delight in the law of the Lord, meditating on His word (Psalm 1:1-2). God compares those believers to a tree planted by the water which is sustained and thriving (vs. 3). Loving His word and following His commands is a primary way to delight in Him.

His Word is Sweet

In the Spring my daughter and I love to sit on the front steps of our house and watch the bees swarm our anemone plant. Their legs collect pollen from the silky pink flowers and it looks like they're wearing fuzzy yellow bell-bottoms.

I recently learned that honey is a mixture of nectar, pollen, and bee saliva (this is a simplification). I didn't realize the spoonful of honey I add to my tea in the afternoon is actually part bug saliva. It's both amazing, and faintly unsettling.

A spoonful of straight honey can be overpoweringly sweet. The Bible compares God's word to honey. "How sweet are thy words unto my taste! yea, sweeter than honey to my mouth!" (Psalms 119:103).

Imagine if you normally consumed a bland diet. What a decadent treat honey would be to your tongue! Everything apart from God's word is that bland diet. Maybe some nutrition can come from it, but it doesn't amaze and move us like the sweet honey of the Lord's word.

"My son, eat thou honey, because it is good; and the honeycomb, which is sweet to thy taste: So shall the knowledge of wisdom be unto thy soul:" (Prov. 24:13-14). Wisdom is compared to sweet honey for the soul. It sustains it and flavors it. Oh, that we would love God's wisdom enough to long for sweet drops of His word on our tongue!

Honey has the capacity to absorb different flavors depending on the pollen gathered by the bees. That's how we get lavender honey, orange blossom honey, and blueberry honey. Scripture is similar. There are sections of scripture that become words "spoken in due season" (Prov. 15:23), ministering to us in the exact ways we crave.

Maybe another believer has dropped honey on your tongue with the scripture they shared for a specific need. It is wisdom flavored for the occasion, based on what the Holy Spirit knows we need at that moment. Just like the variations of honey, His word speaks specific wisdom to our soul.

The fruit of the Spirit, which comes from a relationship with God, offers so much flavor in life! When we taste and see that the Lord is good (Psalm 34:8) we will want more of Him. As believers, we have tasted His righteousness and goodness and we prefer that taste over the world's. God refines our 'taste buds' as we mature in our faith.

Mulberry Tree

THIS MULBERRY TREE DROPPED A LIMB after becoming overly encumbered with honey. The hive hanging on that limb, fashioned by little architect honey bees, became too heavy for the limb to sustain. You can see the wound left behind in the drawing.

The pleasing aroma and tastes of the world might beckon like honey at times. But we soon realize that the world's 'honey' is tainted with sin. One example is Proverbs 5:3 which warns that "the lips of a strange woman drop as an honeycomb." Verse 4 goes on to say, "But her end is bitter as wormwood…" Her sweet words were actually a lure to evil.

"The full soul loatheth an honeycomb; but to the hungry soul every bitter thing is sweet" (Prov. 27:7). Are we longing for the world's pleasures that will never satisfy, mistaking the bitter taste as sweet? If you are only concerned with filling yourself and don't discern what you consume then you'll try and satisfy yourself in any way possible. If we instead hunger after righteousness, we will be filled (Matt. 5:6).

Craving His Word

Our spiritual tastes are influenced by our satisfaction and contentment. The Holy Spirit can teach us to crave God's wisdom over the world's. We know His word leads to life and righteousness. May we be content with truth. It sets us free (John 8:32).

If a tree was thirsty and dying, and there was water in the soil, wouldn't the roots absorb as much as the tree needed to thrive? Our soul receives nourishment straight from God's truth. "Wherefore lay apart all filthiness and superfluity of naughtiness, and receive with meekness the engrafted word, which is able to save your souls" (James 1:21).

"The law of the Lord is perfect, converting the soul:" (Psalm 19:7), and "The statutes of the Lord are right, rejoicing the heart: the commandment of the Lord is pure, enlightening the eyes" (vs. 8). Verse 12 says His word can help clean us from secret faults and errors we may not even be aware of.

When we read God's living word we feel it prick our hearts and convict us. Sometimes even our own ways are a mystery to us; we don't always notice when we are straying away from the Lord. But God will reveal any hidden error or motive to us (Phil. 3:15).

The Psalms are full of praise for God's word. We crave His word because we want to understand life and God, and because we want to please Him and the Bible tells us how.

A Little Teapot

THIS TREE RESEMBLES A TEAPOT with a giant open mouth spilling loose-leaf tea. The suspended animation is striking; it might come to life at any moment and start speaking, waving its long arm as it talks.

Just like tea leaves yield their aroma and flavor when steeped in hot water, sometimes it takes a trial to make us sweat a little and run to God. He draws us out and we yield. When we are steeped in God's word, we draw out the meaning in it. God's Holy Spirit helps us understand and apply what we've read to our lives.

May we "Study to shew thyself approved unto God, a workman that needeth not to be ashamed, rightly dividing the word of truth" (2

Tim. 2:15). May our words and heart meditation be pleasing to the Lord (Psalm 19:14). What we are meditating on will spill out of our mouth.

Matthew 15:18-19 warns that the things which defile us come from within, out of the heart. What kind of 'tea leaves' do we have steeping inside us? Are we nourishing our relationship with the Spirit by reading God's holy word, or allowing our own corruption to flow out of us?

As Christians, our words should not fall casually like partially steeped tea leaves from our mouth as it flaps. We instead speak purposefully, directed by the Holy Spirit. For us women, "She openeth her mouth with wisdom; and in her tongue is the law of kindness" (Prov. 31:26).

Remember, when we know God's word, we can offer "a word spoken in due season" to others (Prov. 15:23). It might look like timely advice, encouragement, exhortation or reproof. Our speech will be full of grace, and we'll know how to answer others (Col. 4:6).

Let's steep ourselves in the rich truth His word has to offer. As we read and His word convicts us, we will change to be more like Him. We will become saturated in all the flavors of who we are as His children.

A Sweet Savor

God's word tells us that a sacrifice to God is like a "sweetsmelling savour" (Eph. 5:2). This verse specifically mentions Jesus Christ's sacrifice on the cross being that sweet fragrance offered to God.

In Leviticus we learn of God's instructions for the atoning Old Testament sacrifices that His people were to make for their sins. These detailed, specific instructions involved the priest burning the animals brought for each person's sins. They are described in Leviticus 1:13 as "a sweet savour unto the Lord."

The best smelling aroma for God is the sacrifice that reconciled us all to Him when we choose to believe. We no longer need to sacrifice animals because Jesus died once and for all, to cleanse us sinners from all unrighteousness! God 'smells' that righteous sacrifice of Jesus on us as believers (2 Cor. 2:15-16).

2 Corinthians 2:14-17 equates us believers to a savour for the Lord. We offer the sweet aroma of the knowledge of Him wherever we go. For some it is rejected unto death, and for some it is accepted unto life. Either way we are a "sweet savour of Christ, in them that are saved, and in them that perish:" (vs. 15).

We are instructed to offer up spiritual sacrifices which are pleasing to the Lord. God accepts these spiritual sacrifices because they are seen as holy through Jesus' blood (1 Pet. 2:5). These spiritual sacrifices include a broken heart, righteousness (Psalm 51:17-19) and offering sacrifices of joy (such as continuing to praise Him in our sorrow) (Psalm 27:6).

In the vision shown to John in Revelation 5:8, God's word mentions "golden vials full of odours" held by those worshiping, and that those odors are the prayers of saints.

Our own lives surrendered and lived in submission to His glorious will are a living sacrifice (Rom. 12:1). We take all that we are and put it on the alter before Him for His glory. We offer our bodies as a temple for His Holy Spirit.

When we delight in Him, these sacrifices of joy and thanksgiving in all circumstances become a blessed way to serve our gracious God.

Magnolia

THIS STAR MAGNOLIA GROWS at my parents' house and is filled with fragile white blossoms in early Spring. They are not known for their longevity, usually blooming for about a week or less. When I was growing up I loved cupping the blossoms in my hand and burying my nose into those petals to inhale their scent.

Just like the short, beautiful duration of the magnolia blossoms, our own lives are as fleeting as vapors that appear and then vanish (James 4:14). May our souls offer the sweet aroma of praise and spiritual sacrifice to the Lord while we are here.

Plants blossom as part of their death. As it is dying, the plant releases its seeds in the form of flowers. Yet those gorgeous displays of color and sweet scent attract pollinators to continue the next generation of flowers.

Death and life are forever connected. Never more so than the eternal life Jesus promises through His death on the cross to save whoever believes.

Delighting in What He Chooses for Us

"Yet they seek me daily, and delight to know my ways..."
(Isa. 58:2).

Psalm 37:5 tells us to commit our way to the Lord. We must be willing to accept and surrender to His way (which is always holy and righteous) and He promises to bring it to pass. I am not an expert, but if we focus on the first part of verses 4 and 5; delighting in the Lord, and committing our way to Him, then I don't think we need to worry about what the second two parts look like. God is faithful to His word.

Psalm 105:1-5 reflects a heart of worship. Our worship of the Lord can be so much sweeter after struggle and affliction. We are called to "Sing unto him," talk of His wondrous works, seek His face and strength, and glory in His name. We are called to remember, not the trial itself, but "...his marvellous works that he hath done; his wonders, and the judgments of his mouth: (vs. 5).

The Holy Spirit can help us celebrate the way He chooses to work. He is so good to us. "In the multitude of my thoughts within me thy comforts delight my soul" (Psalm 94:19).

Katsura Tree

ON THIS WALK I WAS TRYING TO TEACH my daughter about trees. I have this desire for her to love nature and I am trying to cultivate that. There is something wonderful about training our soul's eye to stop and notice the things God has made. He uses His creation to reveal His handiwork, existence, and inspire our delight in Him.

Down the path we encountered this spectacular Katsura tree. All its dancing branches swoop down to form a little protective space in which to marvel. The leaves grow all along the branches in little circles of varying scale. The bark looks like basket weaving. Best of all, the woody roots are trailing away from it in jungle-gym bumps and lumps. We climbed all over them.

The next time I saw that tree I had my youngest daughter with me. She woke up far too early in the morning and would not go back to sleep. God whispered that I could go for a walk, and she might even fall asleep on the drive or in the stroller.

I pushed the stroller down to that specific tree to admire it. As I stood under those swooping branches it occurred to me that this would have been a perfect opportunity to draw, but I was unprepared. I still had the opportunity to enjoy what He made.

The next time I tried to draw it she woke up and I had to put the sketchbook away. I really wanted to draw this tree but God was making me wait. He used it to teach me patience and priorities.

Was I delighting in God in each area of my life, or only when I could be outside drawing? We should be inspired by the Holy Spirit to delight in Him because of who He is. He is a delightful God! He promises the reward of giving us our heart's desire when we do (Psalm 37:4).

No illustration or description can accurately capture how it feels to sit under this tree. The word 'delightful' comes close. God designed for this tree to grow in that spot for decades long before I was born. He designed all those branches arcing around each other like coordinated dance moves, each of them going the way they need to go. He designed for the earth to slope there and the roots to raise up so that they form irregular steps.

And then He brought me to this tree in 2024 and introduced me to the wonderful thing He made. Yes, God! It is spectacular! And You made it! Our God is amazing!

When we delight in Him His blessings will flow like those leaves all the way down the branches to find us, waiting below, smiling up at our Father. We will see His goodness and faithfulness woven like that tree bark into all areas of our life.

We delight in the Lord by delighting in what pleases Him and who He is.

When We Delight in God

Do you struggle to delight in the Lord? Is there a way that He designed you to easily see Him at work and delight in Him? How might you learn to delight in Him in other areas of your life?

What Does God Delight in?

While we are told to delight in the Lord and in His word, we also have several verses mentioning what *God* finds delightful.

He delights in our obedience (1 Sam. 15:22). He delights in His righteous servants, their prayers (Pro. 15:8), and those that walk uprightly (Pro. 11:20). He delights in His children, and will correct them as His own (Pro. 3:12). Proverbs 11:1 says He delights in a just weight over a false balance. He is delighted by lips that speak truth (Pro. 12:22). He delights in showing mercy (Mic. 7:18).

From these verses we know that God delights in us when we exemplify His own character. May we allow the Holy Spirit to work righteousness and holiness in us so that the Lord may be delighted in His children. We know we are already pleasing to Him not because of our own works but because we have been washed of our sin by Jesus.

> When we obey God's commands we stay rooted in His love, and when we delight in doing so we are abundantly blessed. May the Holy Spirit help us take pleasure in Him and doing His will! What an incredible gift to have our own Lord and Savior pleased with us when we do not deserve it!

A Time and a Season

Sanctifying Seasons

> *"Every one of you should know how to possess his vessel in sanctification and honour." (1 The. 4:4)*
>
> *"And the very God of peace sanctify you wholly; and I pray God your whole spirit and soul and body be preserved blameless unto the coming of our Lord Jesus Christ." (1 The. 5:23)*

I struggled at first to accept that the challenges I faced would be a season for me. Time passed and instead of having a definitive end point I was still being carried through this time when things were changing everywhere. Nowhere more so than inside me.

For a while I kicked against the work God was trying to do in me. He wanted to use this season for my ultimate good and sanctification. I wanted to pretend that I was all set and nothing needed to change. How would we ever learn how to conduct ourselves with honor and holiness if we are not exercised through these sanctifying seasons (1 The. 4:4)?

He began to show me the peace of laying aside all that was not within God's plan for me. I could actually rest if I was no longer hoping in the wrong things, or in what God would do, but in God Himself. My flesh grew quieter and was no longer crying out against God's plan. Instead, I was curled up at His feet in surrender.

It was official: I was going through 'a season.' Whatever that meant.

God actually *helps us* become more holy and like Jesus throughout our life. What a great gift! He continues to teach me how to respond to sanctification with gratitude.

A Time for Sowing

Ecclesiastes 3:2 says there is "a time to plant, and a time to pluck up that which is planted;" The Bible has many references to sowing and reaping. To sow is to plant seeds, and to reap is to collect the yield from those seeds.

Galatians 6:9 says, "And let us not be weary in well doing: for in due season we shall reap, if we faint not." The "well-doing" refers to anything that pleases the Lord. We can think of it like planting seeds for harvest. We are told not to grow weary as we do the work He calls us to, with His character and love within us. It's easy to get weary.

When a seed is planted in ideal growing conditions it can germinate at the proper time for that species. Some seeds, however, can stay dormant for months, or even years before conditions are right to germinate (Kalman 10).

Maybe we aren't even sowing yet. Sometimes God is preparing the soil and it's not time to plant. We wait on Him. When it is time, we plant the very best way we can, as unto the Lord, because we want to give our seeds everything they need to grow well.

We may feel like desperate farmers. We are on our knees, covered in sweat, blood, and grime, agonizing over the bare dirt before us. Why isn't anything growing? Isn't this the dirt where we just planted seeds? Where are those green shoots?

There are seasons when the dirt remains empty. We forget what's happening in the soil out of sight. We forget that we are not the farmers at all. God is.

If you've been trying your hardest but it doesn't seem like you're getting anywhere, it is okay to rest in the full power of Christ and lay it all down at His feet. We are allowed to be imperfect; there is one Perfect Helper and that is the Lord. He will bless the efforts of labor that pleases Him.

The season of sowing is when we dig in and trust God's promises.

A Time for Reaping

In this blessed whirlwind of life, Galatians 6:9 helps us remember the reward of our labor. "…In due season we shall reap, if we faint not."

He has not told us the season of reaping, but rather asked for patience, reliance, and trust. If we knew the time of fruit, we might be tempted to choose our glory in getting there instead of His grace. He makes the choice that pleases Him easy, by making us rely on Him and His grace in the unknown.

Romans 2:7 uses a wonderful description for this season: "patient continuance in well doing." The reward mentioned is eternal life, along with honor, glory, and peace (vs. 10). But we also know God has promised there will be fruit to reap, so we will see it on this side of Heaven. The timeline, and the fruit itself may look different for each believer.

Maybe it is simply not yet time to reap.

When the apostles questioned Jesus about restoring the kingdom to Israel, He told them, "It is not for you to know the times or the seasons, which the Father hath put in his own power" (Acts 1:7). We are called to do the things He is setting before us without knowing the entirety of His plan. We honor and glorify Him through that faith.

Parenthood

A seed contains all of the information it needs to become a full-size tree. It gets planted, germinates, and grows into the same species it came from. Similarly our children, like us, are born with a sin nature (Rom. 5:12, Eph. 2:3, Psalm 51:5). They contain all the information they need to choose rebellion and sin.

They are born lacking the redemption that will save their soul. It is our job to train them up in the way they should go (Deu. 6:5-9, Prov. 22:6), to disciple them, and model the love of Jesus.

The season of parenthood is sanctifying. We are loaned these incredible little people to train up but they have their own ideas and intentions. Each day is an adventure. Sometimes I feel like a tree that's been hallowed out. God can use this season to hallow out our pride, impatience, disobedience, vanity, and selfishness in exchange for His character through the struggle.

At the end of some days I might only see the ways I failed and God reminds me I can't do it alone. He reminds me of grace. It is a blessed, yet weary season of emptying myself, having little control, and sowing for a harvest I may not reap for a long time.

In those moments when we feel we have no substance apart from parenthood, may we remember that raising children is a gift and God equips us for the work. God knows the state of each sparrow He has made (Matt. 10:29,31). Even the sparrow that is flying back and forth feeding her babies all day long.

As we plant, water and wait, may we labor for Him and His glory in this joyful and worthy calling as parents!

Mother Tree

THIS AUSTRIAN PINE TREE looked like a seasoned mom with sturdy branches for sitting on, and prickly needles to protect her kids.

In the tree world, there is a concept of "Mother Trees," which are the oldest in the area. They sustain the younger saplings as they grow. These mother trees are "the central hub that the saplings and seedlings nested around, with threads of different fungal species, of different colors and weights, linking them, layer upon layer, in a strong, complex web" (Simard 228).

"…these little seedlings were linked into the network of the old trees, receiving enough water to get them through the driest days of Summer" (Simard 227). Older trees can also help the younger seedlings through root grafts: roots from different trees that graft together into a single root to transport water (Simard 48).

When we share our faith with our kids we are like theses mother trees. Our roots entwine with theirs. We are rooted in God's love through Jesus, and our kids have access to His love first by our example.

When we teach our children the commandments of the Lord and communicate the great blessing of grace by teaching, correcting, and living it out, we are flooding them with the knowledge of life. We too, like Israel, are called to diligently teach His ways and commands to the following generations that come (Deu. 6:7).

We are also called to teach them the fear of the Lord (Psalm 34:11). Teaching them the holy fear and awe of the Lord shows them true wisdom, and sets them up for a good understanding (Psalm 111:10).

Through the Holy Spirit in us, we are teaching them the beginning of truth; a truth which ultimately leads to eternal life. When and if our children accept the Lord, the Holy Spirit will enter them and lead them in fearing the Lord, learning, growing, and doing His will.

Ultimately it is God that will do the work in their life, calling them to His purposes, but we do them a disservice if we don't teach them the gospel while they are in our care. And even if we fail as their parents, because we are imperfect, God can redeem that in their lives.

May we demonstrate faith in truth and action for our beloved little witnesses on their faith journey. Even if, instead of raising children, we are discipling others in their faith, our root system is sharing spiritual nutrients with theirs.

Do you remember the Christ-like counselors, mentors, or anyone who helped shape your faith as you grew up? If you're a newer believer, can you think of someone who seemed to model true faith in their life? Take the time to thank them for that example.

Transforming Change

"But we all, with open face beholding as in a glass the glory of the Lord, are changed into the same image from glory to glory, even as by the Spirit of the Lord." (2 Cor. 3:18)

When I became a mom I forgot who I was before. Any mother can tell you, especially in those early child years, that you wrestle with losing yourself. It can feel like you don't exist anymore. That your own wants and needs don't matter. That no one sees you.

It felt like I was living two different lives; when my daughter was asleep, I felt like myself. When she was awake, I was her mom. Why couldn't it feel like the same life and the same person? But through it, God changed me into who He wants me to be now.

If He hadn't grown and changed me through it then I wouldn't learn how to become a better mom. Change is a necessary part of God working holiness in us, and preparing us for what's next.

As we experience change we will see the Lord work in wonderful ways. "And he changeth the times and the seasons:" (Dan. 2:21). God is in control of every season, literal and figurative, and teaches us so much through them.

Saved Through Each Season

Ecclesiastes 3:1-8 tells us there is a time and season for everything. Listed examples include planting and harvesting, birth and death, laughing and crying, speaking and silence.

There is even a time to die. God decides the time. Our souls go to Heaven when we believe, but our bodies share the same fate as all other living creatures. This reminder keeps us humble (and thankful for salvation!). We remember the end of all things, regardless of the seasons in life. "All go unto one place; all are of the dust, and all turn to dust again" (Ecc. 3:20).

What does Jesus' death on the cross mean for you during this season of your life? The truth of His death, burial, and resurrection does not change, but we might focus on different aspects of it depending on what is going on in our lives.

Perhaps after a season of laying aside a sin that held us, God shows us the truth of His grace that is greater than our sin. Or maybe after a falling out with a brother or sister, God shows us the unity and reconciliation that the cross brings in order to restore that relationship.

Our salvation in Christ is a wondrous miracle! Salvation is living hope within us. We are redeemed and live free in the Lord's grace and mercy. It is a truth strengthened in each season He brings us through.

When we seek the Lord He will direct our paths and show us the right time and season for each thing (Prov. 3:5-6).

Wound Waterfall

I WAS FLOODED WITH EXCITEMENT at the sight of this tree. My dad, a fellow tree nerd, joined me at the park for conversation and tree admiring. We sat side by side in our camping chairs while I drew, and talked about family, faith, and life.

The wound in this tree flows all the way down one of its large limbs, cascading right through the center of it and spilling onto the ground. It reminded me how sometimes we have seasons of aching and waiting. I was there. I did not want to feel the way I felt.

But God showed me so many glimpses of His goodness during that time. He was there wrapping me in light, the same way this mortally wounded tree was encircled with golden green haloes of leaves. It was in the middle of a slow transformation.

Imagine this tree as a believer is their moment of death: the vessel cracked open; the soul arriving Home. In the Bible, God says that all creation is groaning together, waiting for the adoption and the redemption of our bodies (Rom. 8:22-23). We are all in a season of waiting on the Lord. Someday His children will be with Him in glory when our mortal vessels die and the redemption of our very bodies takes place. He has already redeemed our souls.

For now, we sojourn in the redemption of His blood, knowing we have been saved from our sins. We too are in the middle of a life-long transformation of the heart.

Waiting for Change

In our part of the country we look forward to any hint of Spring coming at the end of Winter. Little bits of green poking through the brush and buds forming on trees and shrubs. It is the continuation; life is proceeding.

But then…it snows again. Winter and Spring do this grappling match at the point of change. We are reminded that Spring is not a sudden event. But God has promised us that each season will continue changing (Gen. 8:22).

It's easy to remember how good He is when we are wrapped in warm sunshine and fresh air, but what about those cold months in between? God is good in the Winter too and there are blessings in every season. Winter is part of the plan He set in motion, therefore it is good. This predicted change is a blessing, no matter what season is coming next.

After a snowfall, the snow encircling the trunks of dark, deciduous trees melts first. It can leave a thaw circle around the base of the trunk because the heat absorbed by the dark bark gets released outward, melting the snow (Laskow, 2024).

Snow is listed along with trees in Psalm 148:8-9 as a part of God's creation that praises Him. Every unique snowflake is a work of art crying out in praise of our Creator. And each of them will melt as part of the cycle of nature, set in order by God.

God has a plan for the snow too! It comes down from the heavens and waters the earth, making things grow and yielding seed. God compares His word to the precipitation listed; it will not return void but accomplish His work in the place that He sends it (Isa. 55:10-11).

Sometimes we are tired of where we are at now. If you're growing weary of waiting on change, may God help you embrace where He has you, knowing His blessings are there too.

Leaves Changing Color

LAST FALL, WHEN OUR PLANE WAS LANDING in our home city, we soared over scores of deciduous trees all aflame with color. They were catching sunlight in a blaze of beauty. It reminded me of the wonder that still exists here in this often gray and rainy place we call home.

This tree was a beacon on the hill. Everything around it looked washed out in comparison. When trees prepare to Winter over, the chlorophyll that made them green in the growing season disappears. The yellow and orange that always existed in the leaf are now visible because the green has disappeared (Smithsonian Science Education Center, 2024).

God has a plan for change. Change upsets our peace and balance. It exposes the other colors inside us that were always present but are now visible. We learn about ourselves through change.

Broad-leaf, deciduous trees drop their leaves prior to Winter, and thereby lose a lot of surface area to better withstand wind (Wohlleben 139). All that foliage is like a giant wind sail. What gave the tree life in Summer would actually be detrimental in Winter. Shedding those leaves is necessary for survival.

Change is sometimes necessary for survival too. If we are unwilling to make a needed change, God is good to change it for us. Despite how we react to it at the time.

Maple Tree

SUMMER IS ONE OF GOD'S PROMISES (Gen. 8:22). What a glorious time of catching every last ray of sun and being outside as often as possible. We know it won't last, but it sure seems to wipe away our memory of every other season. It feels like a season when God has turned our "mourning into dancing" in a sense (Psalm 30:11).

When we trust God we can learn to find joy in each season (Psalm 5:11).

Red Maples can develop what's called a 'girdle root' that grows around the base of the trunk (Girdling Roots, Jan. 2024). You can see it at the bottom of the drawing. A root that's supposed to be engaged in life-giving actually wraps around the very thing it's trying to keep alive. It slowly begins to squeeze as it grows.

When we are resistant to change we may feel similarly strangled. Sometimes love means letting go.

A girdle root can be properly removed so it doesn't harm the tree. If there is a circumstance, event, or person in your life seeming to press in on you, perhaps it is necessary to make a healthy change. Examine whether you are acting as the girdle root for someone else. Pray for wisdom in how to handle those situations with grace, care, and love.

Accepting Change Gracefully

"For I am the Lord, I change not; therefore ye sons of Jacob are not consumed." (Mal. 3:6)

"So that we may boldly say, The Lord is my helper, and I will not fear what man shall do unto me." (Heb. 13:6)

When I visit a park I occasionally check up on the trees I've drawn there. The path naturally takes me past these old friends. I reflect on what God has done since then. From one season to the next, the landscape changes, and the trees change with it.

Change is an essential, inevitable part of life and yet we as a society are reluctant to accept it. Even good change.

What are some ways we can accept change more gracefully? Perhaps we can take comfort in the fact that although the circumstances around us change, God does not. He is constant and enduring through the ages, as well as the short span of life He gives us. "For

I am the Lord, I change not;" (Mal. 3:6). The doctrine of Jesus as our Redeemer will not change either (Heb. 13:8).

Our own words and opinions change often, but God's words do not. "Heaven and earth shall pass away, but my words shall not pass away" (Matt. 24:35). Psalm 119:89 says His word is settled in heaven. His truth endures for all generations (Psalm 100:5).

Praise the Lord that His character and His word do not change! God's character – this patient, loving, merciful, almighty Father who keeps watch over our souls does not change. Seasons of life come and go, and He is faithful through them all (Psalm 119:90). Winter, Spring, Summer and Fall all contain His goodness.

God's change in our life sets His purposes in motion.

When change is directed by God we know He will walk through it with us. We can take our reluctance, doubt and confusion to the Lord and ask Him to guide us in the necessary change. He can also grant us peace that passes understanding in the midst of change (Phil. 4:6-7).

For a Season

It can be difficult to accept the end of a season in our life. We mourn for that friendship or job that ended, our kids moving away from our protection or not needing us anymore. We grieve the people we have lost, the need to leave a place we once belonged, the delight of that season in our marriage when things seemed so easy.

As new seasons unfold before us we see we are still enveloped in God's presence and haven't left His love behind. His goodness is not tethered to any specific season. Time does not change the promises of God.

God will decide how and when the seasons begin and end.

Jesus came into His disciples' lives for a season. When Jesus was explaining to His disciples that He would be ascending into Heaven it meant He was going to leave them. Again. This was Jesus, their Savior and friend! They had served alongside one another, witnessed His miracles, mourned His death, and celebrated His life! He departed into Heaven in front of their eyes (Luke 24:51, Acts 1:9).

How could it be over now?

"…While they looked stedfastly toward heaven as he went up, behold, two men stood by them in white apparel; (Acts 1:10)" and told them Jesus would come again. Jesus had told them to continue His work here on earth until they saw Him again in Heaven.

Jesus left them with instructions. He commanded them to go into all nations and teach them, baptizing them in His name (Matt. 28:19). Jesus had finished the faith (John 19:30, Heb. 12:2, 1 Pet. 1:9) but He used His disciples to do great works on earth (John 14:12) and help establish the church.

When Jesus ascended He did not leave them comfortless either. While the disciples were sorrowful to hear that Jesus would be leaving them, Jesus tells them that He will send the Comforter to them (John 16:6-7). He gave them the Holy Spirit to guide, direct, and comfort them (John 14:26).

"The Spirit replaces sorrow with joy" (Ortlund 123). It is "…the continuation of the heart of Christ for his people after the departure of Jesus to heaven." When we feed the Spirit by nurturing our relationship with the Lord, He blesses us with joy.

Even when God calls our loved ones elsewhere, His blessings and goodness are always enough, and He is always with us. Others may come and go for a season, but God will not leave us. In this season, when He revealed upcoming aspects of my journey, I asked Him, "Stay with me, God. Stay with me." And He did. He will stay with you too.

Accepting Your Season

It can be difficult to accept when it is not your season for something you want to do. God may have planted a desire in your heart but it is not yet time in His great plan. Continue to wait on Him and seek His direction.

Say you want to start a ministry or begin a big project. Or perhaps you see everyone around you making an impact on the world for God or succeeding in their vocation. You look around you and see your limitations. Know that if it is truly God's will for you to do something, He will help you do it in His time. If you try to force it at the wrong time then you will miss seeing God work with you to make a way.

What is God asking you to do in *this* season? Do it well, faithfully, as unto the Lord. Seek God's will for your life right now. Pray that He would help you be thankful there and see His blessings. "But godliness with contentment is great gain" (1 Tim. 6:6). Through Christ we can learn to love where He has planted us.

He will bring the opportunities in His timing, and if He doesn't then perhaps He is asking something else of you instead. May we be willing to do the work He has laid for us. May we be willing to do it joyfully, with His help.

Greeting and Parting

I CAME UPON THESE TWO TREES one day while exploring. The trunks grow independently but they join together about six feet up in the air. At some point one slender trunk leaned back toward its neighbor until they collided. The bark rubbed away and the sapwood joined in a phenomenon called Inosculation. It occurs over a duration of time (Abreu, June 2024).

We may seem inseparable with friends or loved ones for a season before God calls us elsewhere. A few of our close friends have moved out of state over the years. There is great joy, however, in knowing we are all walking with the Lord and living in His will for our lives. We are unified across the distance because of the same Holy Spirit living within each of us (Eph. 4:3-5).

You've likely heard the old cliché that people come into our life for a season and then leave. While the saying is designed to help us cope with loss, in reality we often mourn first. Because that person who is gone was a part of us.

Or perhaps we are the one leaving. We see everything we are leaving behind and we are tempted to stay. How do we know when to stay, and when to leave? We should seek the Lord diligently through studying His word and praying (Prov. 3:6).

It is often easier to say hello than goodbye. What happens in the middle is a wonderful gift which the Lord directs. What we might choose for ourselves and others may not be in God's good plan. We might choose for someone to stay. We might choose to stay. But if God has a better plan then we must submit to it.

Sometimes God gives us a friend to walk beside us through a hard season. We might be that person for someone else. If it feels like they don't need us any more afterward, or have cast us aside, we still fulfilled God's purpose in coming alongside them for a season. It does not diminish the love He showed through us.

Can you think of a season when you were resisting change? When you were desperate to hold onto something you felt God taking away? When you look back now, do you understand it better?

When we are saved, God's Spirit enters into our heart and we become His. Unlike these trees, which continue independently away from the join, we have the amazing blessing of becoming inseparably reconciled to the Lord.

> God holds our roots steady throughout any changes in our environment and circumstances so that we remain grounded in Him. We weather the seasons with Him and remain rooted in His goodness and love.

The Comfort of Fellowship

Finding Community

> *"And let us consider one another to provoke unto love and to good works: Not forsaking the assembling of ourselves together, as the manner of some is; but exhorting one another: and so much the more, as ye see the day approaching." (Heb. 10:24-25)*

Just being together can breathe life into us. As we run this marathon, God's word demonstrates the importance of having a friend come alongside us – especially a fellow believer. We are told not to forsake gathering together (Heb. 10:25), that two are better than one (Ecc. 4:9), to bear one another's burdens (Gal. 6:2), and to love one another (1 John 4:11).

Trees have learned to connect and share, seeming to prefer thriving together for the benefit of all. Trees without community have little awareness of the world around them. They are not in communication with other trees because they are not rooted into the network of fungi connecting all the trees in the soil. They miss warnings about insect invasions and are excluded from the exchange of nutrients (Wohlleben 11).

May we find God-honoring connection with others. Doing life with others can be challenging, yes. It can also be beautiful.

Jesus calls us His friends (John 15:14). We are friends with the Lord God almighty when we believe and follow His commands. He is a friend that always sees us, always welcomes us. He is the friend that WANTS us.

Not only did Jesus consider you worth dying for, but He thought you were worth saving. Everyone around us is loved by the Lord too. May we learn to be less focused on ourselves and prioritize care and love for others. We may serve the Lord by loving one another.

Jesus said, "For whosoever shall do the will of God, the same is my brother, and my sister, and mother" (Mark 3:35). Look for brothers and sisters in Christ who will magnify the Lord with you, speak truth, and live their faith genuinely. Serve the Lord alongside one another as you do life together.

Being a Good Neighbor

Luke 10:29-37 tells us that a good neighbor is one who shows mercy on another. In this parable the Samaritan man has compassion on the one suffering. Our neighbor is any other person on whom we may show the love and kindness of Christ.

Kindness and mercy break down our walls and brings us together. Mercy can look like undeserved kindness, or withholding some consequence we deserve. God is the origin of mercy, and His tender mercies are over all His works (Psalm 145:9).

Copper Beech Tree

IF I WANTED TO DRAW other people's trees, I would eventually need to speak to them. It's so easy for us to hide in our own world, in our house where everything is familiar and safe. But that hides the gospel away too.

I had the pleasure of drawing the oldest tree in Spencerport, recommended by a family we know from our church. I was going to a stranger's yard…to sit and draw their tree. Yes I had permission, but I still showed up feeling like the whole neighborhood was watching some lady draw a tree at 5:30 in the morning.

I thanked the woman for letting me draw her tree and greeted her dog. I completely forgot to introduce myself to her.

The Comfort of Fellowship

Loving others can be uncomfortable. It stretches us. When we remember we are on a mission to show love and shine light for the Lord then it becomes less about us and more about impacting a soul. Even if it's through small acts of kindness.

This tree was not a pristine, mint-condition specimen. It has a big wound hidden from the watchful eye of the street. We too hide our weakness and faults. But God's word says, "Confess your faults one to another, and pray one for another, that ye may be healed. The effectual fervent prayer of a righteous man availeth much" (James 5:16).

This command also implies compassion. By trying to be perfect, we isolate ourselves and estrange others. No, God's word reminds us that we ALL have sinned. We ALL fall short of the glory of God (Rom. 3:23). This common ground of needing Christ is our greatest unifying strength.

Mimosa Tree

THIS IS A SILK TREE, but we always referred to it the way Grammy does, as a mimosa tree. I had never seen another tree like it. It has these tiny, delicate leaves connected in rows to form larger leaf clusters. They look like homes in a housing track lined up on straight streets.

What does it mean to love your neighbor as yourself (Gal. 5:14)? How many of us actually know our neighbors at all? These days we draw our blinds and hope no one sees us getting the mail in our pajamas. We might nod a head to a passing stranger on a walk around the neighborhood, but do we know their name?

Galatians 5:14 is a challenge to love another as we do our own flesh; to help nourish and care for others. We are already tempted to love our own selves. May we never be too busy to show God's love to others.

This tree's blossoms are unique. Instead of petals unfurling, it showcases wispy pink strands. They are like outstretched arms, reaching to help, or to intercede with prayer to the Father. Or perhaps a group bowed close in prayer, so that they all become part of the whole. We know that when we pray together, God is with us (Matthew 18:20).

Loving Those Around You

My young daughter joyfully told me how everyone loves God. God has been convicting me to explain to her that no, not everyone loves God. *It is God who loves everyone.* There are those who don't love God and have not accepted Him into their heart. They do not yet know how loved they are!

The love of Christ fills us up and overflows into loving others. It starts with Him.

We move toward God, fellowshipping with other believers in truth, and away from any fellowship with darkness (Phil. 3:17-20, Eph. 5:11). We may not follow the path of unbelievers. If they are not for God then they are considered His enemies (Jam. 4:4).

Although we are instructed not to have fellowship with unbelievers, we must love and pray for them. We must share the gospel of Jesus with them since He is the way to eternal life. Yet Paul also warns to be vigilant, so that believers would not be led astray by lies, false teachers, and the enemies of Christ (Acts: 20:29-31, Phil. 3:18-19).

If we want to truly understand how to love others, knowing God's love is a great place to begin. His word says that having hate for a brother means we cannot truly love God (1 John 4:20).

God loves us despite our sin. We are challenged to do the same for others. Because even when we see a whole lot of mess in someone else, we should recognize the mess in ourselves. "And such were some of you: but ye are washed, but ye are sanctified, but ye are justified in the name of the Lord Jesus, and by the Spirit of our God" (1 Cor. 6:11).

Loving others means choosing to see with God's eyes and serve as His hands and feet to do His work on earth.

We have the ability to do life with others. What varies is how intentional we are about that life and loving others in it. I had my own intentions for the love I wanted to share with those around me, but God directed me instead to simply love who He put in front of me at that time. Would I love the soul(s) He had given me to love?

We can pray for opportunities to show the love of Christ to those around us.

Waving Tree

I PULLED UP TO A DARK LOT and stared upward at the lightening dawn of streaked cotton-candy ripples. God was out early too, and He was painting. I found this waving tree-hand by the shore.

When someone waves to you, it means they see you. They acknowledge you. It is a very simple kindness – this greeting. Depending on

The Comfort of Fellowship

your mood, it might go deeper than that. This greeting can communicate that you matter enough to say hello to. A reminder that you exist.

Trees were some of my earliest friends. I grew from a painfully shy child into a slightly-less-shy adult. When I was growing up, nature never laughed at me. It never excluded me. I was always welcome to come and sit. To watch and listen. The same is true of our Lord. I am always welcome in His embrace.

God finds ways to 'wave' at each of us. He looks for ways to speak to us and show us we are seen and loved by Him. Thank You, God!

Sometimes it seems easier to keep our head down and go on our way, doing our own thing. Been there. My fear of awkwardness, confrontation, and unacceptance has often kept me from opening my mouth to speak love to others. But we are called to greet each other (3 John 1:14). May love and kindness overpower our fear. It can when we let the Holy Spirit drive it.

The Hug at the Top of the Hill

AS I WAS SCANNING THE PARK FOR TREES to draw, one curving branch down to the ground on a rise caught my eye. Basically, any gnarly branches just call to me (tree nerd). I climbed the hill and smiled at these two branches reaching out like arms in need of something to hug. Someone to hold.

I've been that person, just needing to be held. I've also experienced the blessing of being the one to wrap my arms around a friend – giving them a hug from God. We might feel like we're climbing high hills in our life. The brothers and sisters who've already climbed that hill are at the top reaching down to pull us up and embrace us.

What if what you've been through could encourage someone else walking through the same thing?

We live in a world where love can be more difficult than hate. Yet God reminds us that His disciples (that's you and me when we have Jesus in our hearts) are known by our love for one another (John 13:35). What example are we setting of Christ's love?

The Encouragement of Fellowship

The baobab tree in Africa is formed by the fusion of multiple stems over time (Brittanica, Baobab | Description, Species, Distribution, & Importance, 2024). The trunk of the baobab tree stores water to sustain it in the hot and arid climate it calls home.

When we do life with other Christians we are like the stems of the baobab tree, fused in unity and holding the living water of Christ together. For Christians, comfort, community, and friendship are grown through struggle and a shared belief in our Savior. In the book of Acts the "brethren" meet together to encourage and exhort each other as they do God's work. They write letters to each other. These fellow believers come alongside each other to find strength in the unity of the Spirit and the joint mission of sharing the gospel.

"For as the sufferings of Christ abound in us, so our consolation also aboundeth by Christ." For everything He allows in our life, He moves to meet us there as "the Father of mercies, and the God of all comfort." It is a beautiful gift to comfort one another, just as we are comforted by the Holy Spirit (2 Cor. 1:3-5).

The Comfort of Fellowship

We have each other as a blessing from the Lord. As we commune together, we become a picture of the social nature of God – Himself existing in three parts joined as one: The Father, Son, and Holy Spirit. We are "knit together in love" (Col. 2:2).

Our community might change throughout our life depending on the season, the support we seek, and the way God wants to use us in the lives of others. If you find you are lacking Christian community, I encourage you to seek out fellowship and pray for the Lord to guide you into the right friendships.

Even when you feel alone, as a believer you always have fellowship with the Lord because He dwells within you.

Holding Up My Arms

"...Aaron and Hur stayed up his hands, the one on the one side, and the other on the other side; and his hands were steady until the going down of the sun." (Exo. 17:12)

The banyan tree of India is known for its massive sprawling canopy, and God designed a unique way to hold up its arms. The tree drops special limbs down from the branches that act as spare trunks once they root in the soil (Brittanica, Banyan | Description and Facts, 2024).

This network of trunks supports the gigantic canopy overhead. Endless scaffolding and reinforcements. Even if the original trunk dies, the remaining trunks can maintain the tree. In our fellowship too, God can use us as support for others in critical points of their life. When we don't have the strength to do it alone, God can send help and encouragement in earthly vessels – our friends, family, and other believers!

When our faith is being tested we have the privilege of sharing amongst each other the stories of what God has done in our lives. I poured over every story of God answering a brother or sister's prayer during this season. Every story of Him working something out for good in their lives. Each story encouraged me in my faith as I celebrated and praised God with them.

May we share those stories together and encourage each other in the faith.

Bearing Your Burdens Together

Having a friend walk through a trial with you can share the weight of your burden. We are called to bear each other's burdens, which fulfills the law of Christ (Gal. 6:2). The heaviness and trouble we face becomes lighter when the weight is distributed among others.

For a long time I believed I had to go through my struggles alone in this season. My arms grew so weary trying to carry it all myself. Eventually I trusted a few close Christian friends, family members, and mentors to counsel me. I am extremely grateful for the help they provided in praying, surrounding me with love and scripture, and encouraging me to keep fighting the good fight of faith.

The enemy will try to isolate us in our sorrow, sin and troubles. Pray over direction for who may bear your burdens with you. God is always there providing help and relief, and can raise up others to be His hands and feet carrying you in love while you are here.

Menorah Tree

THIS TREE ON THE BEACH had massive limbs raised skyward, looking like some sort of candelabra. They were like multiple arms raised toward Heaven, prevailing against the enemy as they worshipped.

Exodus 17:10-12 is a moving section of scripture. When Moses' arms were heavy, his friends came alongside him to support his hands. "…and his hands were steady until the going down of the sun" (Exo. 17:12). This allowed Israel to prevail against their enemy.

These men, Moses, Aaron, and Hur, did not defeat Amalek alone. God did that through His immense power and strength. This picture of weariness is for our benefit. We are reminded of the benefit of living life with others, and relying on God.

The Comfort of Fellowship

We lift up our brothers and sisters in Christ, holding their arms up when necessary. We weep with them and celebrate with them (Rom. 12:15). The Holy Spirit that exists in all of us is a powerful, living connection to the one true God. If we have the same Spirit, we have the same goals. We work together for His kingdom.

When you have Jesus in your heart you are part of a Heavenly family, connected forever to Him and other believers through His Spirit.

Growing together

Having a fellow believer do life alongside you can sharpen you (Prov. 27:17), challenge you to become more like Christ, and stir you up to good works for the Lord (Heb. 10:24).

I have been sharpened by godly women in different seasons of life, whom God used to directly minister to me when I needed it. I have asked for prayer many times from a few treasured and trusted friends who gave me godly counsel. They have helped water my soul.

My Sister's Birch Tree

THESE BIRCH TRUNKS WERE OUTLINED IN GOLD and looked like friends gathering together in celebration. Their leaves are in constant motion, fluttering like a halo of golden confetti. We too will someday share in the golden glory of Christ, rejoicing in the day we join Him in Heaven; the day when our faith is made sight.

The yellow leaves and trunk of this birch remind me of the aspen tree. The world's largest living organism (by mass) is a grove of aspen trees growing in Utah (Katz, 2024). It covers over 100 acres of land

The Comfort of Fellowship

and shares a single root system. This root system sends up shoots that become trunks above ground: tree clones to fill its forest.

Imagine if we did life this way – with no one but ourselves around. For ministry, it might be easier if you never had contrary opinions to work with. But all of your own faults and weaknesses would be magnified. Any gifts and talents you lack - you would lack forever.

One of the wonderful things about serving alongside other Christians is an expanded body of Christ with multiple functions, gifts, strengths and weaknesses (Rom. 12:4-8). To all be identical would make a useless body consisting of only arms. This body could wave to you very well but it would never hear, speak or walk.

If we were all the same, where would our reproof come from? Who would sharpen us? Who would comfort us (Prov. 17:17)? Our brothers and sisters in Christ help us in so many ways. Our differences help us glorify the Lord. We are all wonderfully made (Psalm 139:14).

If we think of the root structure of the Aspen forest like the Bible, then our faith should all emerge and grow from the same word of God. We are instructed to be unified in our Bible-based beliefs with the same Holy Spirit working in all Christians. "…by the name of our Lord Jesus Christ, that ye all speak the same thing, and that there be no divisions among you; but that ye be perfectly joined together in the same mind and in the same judgment" (1 Cor. 1:10).

Can you remember a time you disagreed with a fellow believer? Were you able to handle the conflict in a gracious way that glorified the Lord?

> *The love we draw in from God flows up and out of us. When we are rooted and grounded in the love of God we have the privilege of enjoying His blessings and provision in a stand amongst other trees, fellow believers laboring onward for God's glory.*

The Joy We Don't Expect

Reaping in Joy

> *"But let all those that put their trust in thee rejoice: let them ever shout for joy, because thou defendest them: let them also that love thy name be joyful in thee." (Psalm 5:11)*

> *"And my soul shall be joyful in the Lord: it shall rejoice in his salvation." (Psalm 35:9)*

God can give us incredible hope and peace in the midst of utter devastation. Only God can bring good things out of a hard season. The joy that God gives us after enduring hardship glows brighter because of the sorrow that came before it.

Tears turned to joy; mourning turned to dancing; a crown of righteousness for enduring trials faithfully.

Don't forget that we already have so much cause to celebrate as believers. We have been saved through the blood of Jesus Christ our Lord. "Restore unto me the joy of thy salvation; and uphold me with thy free spirit" (Psalm 51:12).

At the beginning of this book I quoted Psalm 126:5, "They that sow in tears shall reap in joy." He answers His children's sadness with joy and peace.

Embrace the Joy You Weren't Expecting

Sometimes we hesitate to embrace the joy that comes after a difficult season. We don't trust it. It doesn't seem to belong to us, and it could vanish anytime.

When God relocates our joy from the world to Himself, we remember how good He is. We wonder how God could possibly be so good to us! We are not promised happiness in this life, but we find contentment, joy and peace when we do life with the Lord.

There have been times of indescribable joy since enduring that difficult season. I have no explanation for it other than God is good. Joy can take the form of gratitude.

Even if we feel we do not deserve the joy God has granted us, may we accept it as a gracious blessing from our Lord. "For the eyes of the Lord run to and fro throughout the whole earth, to shew himself strong in the behalf of them whose heart is perfect toward him" (2 Chr. 16:9).

A gift from God is good even if it is unexpected. We may learn to embrace what He has given us and find joy in Him through it. Even if the way He chose to answer our prayer is different than the exact way we wanted, we can learn to embrace His answer with gratitude.

Why We Sow in Tears

While we are not always thankful for what we are presently going through, we may look back years later and know we were transformed through it as God worked it out for good in our lives. It's hard to enjoy the process until we begin to feel better and see fruit. Then we know God was with us.

Friend, He was there before the sorrow, holds you during it, and will be with you after.

God is the best place to take our pain because He can do something about it. Remember that as a believer you have the ability to boldly approach the throne of grace for mercy and help in times of trouble (Heb. 4:16). "God is our refuge and strength, a very present help in trouble" (Psalm 46:1).

There are many resources out there on healing. I encourage you to find one that is biblically sound. God can provide us with additional resources for help and healing – tools and wisdom that are a blessing - but remember to seek Him for direction.

When we experience sorrow we have a small understanding of how Jesus endured great heaviness on the cross. "Surely he hath borne our griefs, and carried our sorrows:" (Isa. 53:4). He did it for us. And as God teaches us to be like Him, we will experience sorrow as well. The sorrow has an end.

Our sorrow has the benefit of reminding us not to love this life too much. We must not forget Who we are waiting for, and where we are going. Our treasure is in Heaven and we look forward to going there as a reward and relief from the strife in this life (only when He calls us Home).

When you are sowing in tears, remember you will reap in joy. Remember that while weeping lasts for a time, the joy is coming (Psalm 30:5). Recommit to the Lord as you struggle and endure, knowing He is with you, has a good plan for you, and is worthy of your trust.

He cares about our pain and bears it with us. In Heaven, "…God shall wipe away all tears from their eyes; and there shall be no more death, neither sorrow, nor crying, neither shall there be any more pain: for the former things are passed away" (Rev. 21:4).

Think about how intimate and touching it is for God to wipe away the tears from our eyes. I wipe my baby girls' tears to let them know I care because my heart hurts when theirs do. God does this for His children too.

We sow in tears because God wants to bring our hearts back to Him: the source of our joy. Most of what I went through in this season was actually between me and God. He had a lot to teach me through it.

Whatever the cause of our sorrow (our own sin, or simply for our ultimate good and God's glory), may it always lead us into God's loving arms! May His Spirit help us praise Him as we endure, as we repent, as we return to Him.

You are seen by the One who made you, known by the One who formed you, and loved by the One who saved you. You are His beloved child and He is holding you. He has a good plan for you and your story isn't over yet.

His Ways, Not Ours

In Isaiah 55:8-9, God tells us the simple truth which baffles us: His ways and thoughts are not the same as ours. They are higher. May we arrive at peace with this. He does things His way, in His time.

After those two verses, the Lord explains how He sends rain and snow down from the heavens to water the earth. It trickles into the dirt and waters the harvest for the one planting seeds, and grows grain for bread to eat. His word goes out likewise, it does not return void but accomplishes the purpose for which He sent it (vs. 10-11).

The things He allows in our life are intricately connected in His sovereign plan with His complex, all-knowing purposes. Each event leads to the next and affects us and others far beyond what we can see, experience and comprehend. His living word speaks and it echoes.

We may not understand how He works but we are not necessarily supposed to. Occasionally He may allow us to trace different events and interactions in our life and see His grand orchestration in it. For His glory! He tells us all throughout scripture how much He loves us. If nothing else, may we understand how loved we are by God. We will be loved through it all.

God Has a Reason

In Genesis 37:24, Joseph is cast into a pit by his own envious, angry brothers. In that pit, betrayed by his own family and unsure of his future, it is easy to imagine his despair. Then he is sold as a servant, and later accused of adultery and imprisoned. He endures all

The Joy We Don't Expect

this with the Lord, and eventually God elevates him to be second in all the kingdom of Egypt.

After many years and famine, his brothers come to him asking his forgiveness. He says, "ye thought evil against me; but God meant it unto good, to bring to pass, as it is this day, to save much people alive" (Gen. 50:20). God had a plan for Joseph to get to Egypt and used him to save many lives during the famine (Psalm 105:16-17).

If Joseph had lain down in that pit and given up on life he would have missed God's good plan for him.

Daniel in the lion pit. The three boys in the fiery furnace. God is with His children in our circumstances. Do we accept our afflictions with the resignation that makes them our grave? Or are we allowing God to work through us and the places He has us (if He has chosen to allow it in His will)?

Gravedigger

THIS MAGNOLIA TREE LOOKS LIKE it just buckled down into the mud. The branch is trying to lift itself out but it is struggling under the weight of its own sorrow.

Was there ever a time when you wanted to give up? It's tempting. Sometimes, in our dark moments, we are tempted to stay in the dirt. We are tempted to lie down in that cool, dark place and stay there.

Don't dig your own grave; we do not get to end our story. It is tempting to become frustrated with how slowly healing goes. It can feel crummy for a long time. But please know that where you are at in any given point is not where you will stay forever. God is there with you. He "raiseth up all those that be bowed down" (Psalm 145:14).

David describes his struggle as being smitten down to the ground. His enemy has made him "to dwell in darkness, as those that have been long dead" (Psalm 143:3). He feels he was put in a grave.

When we feel, in our temporal afflictions, that the graves are ready for us (Job 17:1), may we remember God's reviving healing power. "And ye shall know that I am the Lord, when I have opened your graves, O my people, and brought you up out of your graves, And shall put my spirit in you, and ye shall live…" (Eze. 37:13-14).

"O Lord my God, I cried unto thee, and thou hast healed me. O Lord, thou hast brought up my soul from the grave: thou hast kept me alive, that I should not go down to the pit" (Psalm 30:2-3). God is a great healer, lifting us out of any pit we may feel trapped in, whether it be a grave of sin or sorrow, or some kind of stronghold apart from Him.

The Holy Spirit can remind us how good God is. He is much more powerful than our enemies and holds the victory over sin and death. "Death is swallowed up in victory" (1 Cor. 15:54-55). David remembers God's wondrous works in his life and stretches out his hands to the Lord who is able to help (Psalm 143:5-6). May we do likewise.

Healing in Layers

"O Lord my God, I cried unto thee, and thou hast healed me."
(Psalm 30:2)

THE JOY WE DON'T EXPECT

"He sent his word, and healed them, and delivered them from their destructions." (Psalm 107:20)

Drawing with pens requires patience. You can achieve a wide range of values by varying the lines to build layers. Through spiritual patience we can learn to trust God as He heals and teaches us in layers.

God has a plan for our healing, and for the way in which He heals us. Just look at the greatest example: He designed for a Savior to come at an appointed time and save us from sin, from the moment that sin first entered the world (Isa. 53:5-6, 10-11, Rom. 5:19). A broken relationship restored.

Our healing is part of His plan! A good plan that does not end with the trial but the redemption of it.

We come to Him broken and aching with need and He heals us. While we seek Him and pray to Him, He blesses us with His perfect peace. "And the peace of God, which passeth all understanding, shall keep your hearts and minds through Christ Jesus" (Phil. 4:7). May He bind your wounds with peace.

Seek the Lord through your sadness. Bring it to Him and worship Him.

I thought healing would look like courage, strength, and the absence of pain. If that were true, who would get the glory? How long would I remember God's goodness if I never experienced hardship again? If I thought I had healed myself?

Think about your own experiences for a moment, and reflect on a time you felt God healing you. What did His healing look like for you? God works in each situation specifically, giving grace, mercy and strength to His children.

Spiritual, emotional, and physical wellness are all connected, and prayerfully pursuing healing in each area is helpful. The healing of one wound, and the end of one trial, is not the end of all wounds. We return to our great Healer often in this life, and praise God for that!

A State of Need

It is amazing how emotional pain can feel like physical pain. Both have a healing process. Both take patience and grace. When we are in need of healing we have a compassionate Father ready to scoop us up and bind our wounds.

Isaiah 40:28-29 reminds us of God's power. He is our everlasting Lord, the Creator of the whole earth. He never gets tired or weary, and has unfathomable understanding. His power is given, not to the strong, but to the weak. Verse 31 offers the comfort that those who wait upon the Lord will renew their strength.

"Broken" and "healed" are opposites. Surely they cancel each other out, right? But the process includes both. God is there in our needing, and in our fulfillment. The apostle Paul said, "every where and in all things I am instructed…both to abound and to suffer need" (Phil. 4:12). Could our perpetual state of need for the Lord be part of His healing?

Throughout our life we are continually brought back into a state of dependency on the Lord. We are always in need of Him but we forget. What a wondrous thing to be reminded how we need Him! May God grow our faith every time we come to Him in need.

Suffering and trials are part of everyone's life on this side of Heaven, including Christians. James 1:12 promises a crown of life to all that love the Lord, who have endured temptation. When we endure affliction and temptation, we know that the world is watching us. May they behold our good works of faith and glorify God (1 Pet. 2:12).

The world does not need to see us handling our trials exceptionally well. They need to see the healing, grace, and strength of God on display in our weakness, for His glory. We are a witness for Him simply because we need Him.

The Joy We Don't Expect

In Need

THERE'S SOMETHING FASCINATING about the simultaneous chaos and stillness of splintered wood, cracked trunks and snapped branches. I was looking at the innards of this tree, with wooden shards sticking up every which way. I don't think of tree death as violent, but this scene was a little gruesome for the tree...at one point in time.

I discovered this tree with absolutely no initial context. Did it fall recently? But no, the trunk extending out over the creek was covered in blooming honeysuckle vines. The splinters of wood were dark and wet with rot. The green shoots coming off it seemed oriented upward, with the leaves facing the sun above. They had been growing that way for a while. It did not fall recently.

The vines growing over it are like decorative garland that creeped up in need of a structure on which to rest. The lime-golden-green moss growing on it is breaking down the substrata (non-living material where living material grows) to release nutrients for other plant life (Brittanica, Moss | Definition, Characteristics, Species, Types, & Facts, 2024). There is so much texture in a range of hues and values.

It is a decomposing, slowly changing state of brokenness-made-beautiful. A gift for those around it.

"The sacrifices of God are a broken spirit: a broken and a contrite heart, O God, thou wilt not despise" (Psalm 51:17). When God asked for sacrifice in the Old Testament as an atonement for sin, it needed to be a clean, spotless animal (Exo. 12:5, 29:1, Lev. 4:3). The best that one had to offer. By this logic, wouldn't God want a happy, perfect and sinless heart? The fact that David is communicating God's desire for a sacrifice that is "broken" and "contrite" seems counterintuitive.

While it is true that only a perfect, sinless soul can enter Heaven, Jesus already paid for our sin on the cross. We can and will enter Heaven when we believe, confess our sins, and repent.

The broken heart of a believer is of great value to the Lord because a repentive, humble heart is one ready to heal, and God delights in our healing and restoration. When we come to Him in our sadness and despair we communicate our trust and reliance on Him.

When He Hasn't Healed Us Yet

There were many times when I thought, 'God's word says that He heals the broken hearted and binds up their wounds (Psalm 147:3), but He hasn't done that for me (yet) so it must not be true, so is any of it true, and is He really good if none of this is true?'

Satan will try and deconstruct fundamental truths to weaken our faith. The word of God becomes the truth we cling to as the storms rage around us (and in us). God's word says He will heal us, but it looks different for everyone in their walk with Him. He has already healed our sin through our salvation in Jesus.

The four gospels are full of examples where Jesus heals people. Often Jesus will ask the person if they believe He is able before He heals them, and rewards their faith with healing. Sometimes we fall

The Joy We Don't Expect

into the trap of thinking if we just have enough faith then God will heal us, and if He doesn't, it means we don't have enough faith.

In 2 Corinthians 12:5-10, Paul is recounting His plea for healing that God did not grant. I don't think anyone can make the argument that Paul didn't have enough faith.

In verse 5, Paul declares that he will gladly glory in his infirmities. It is remarkable that he bears his infirmities gladly, and that he is rejoicing in them at all. What follows are his reasons why.

His infirmities keep him humble, and ensure that no one will think more highly of him than they should (vs. 6). To prevent himself from being "exalted above measure" he was given a thorn in the flesh (vs. 7). God's answer to Paul's affliction is, "My grace is sufficient for thee: for my strength is made perfect in weakness" (vs. 9).

God does not remove the thorn from his flesh, and that is difficult for us humans to swallow. However, He gives Him grace to handle it, promising strength where Paul is weak. He does the same for us.

We may not know God's reasons for what He does and doesn't do in our life until we get to Heaven. If He has already healed you, He has a reason. If He hasn't healed you yet, He has a reason. May the Holy Spirit help us trust our loving and merciful God.

Does Paul bemoan the fact that God chose not to heal him? We know he asked at least three times before he received that answer (vs. 8). That indicates a serious desire for relief. We do not have a record of Paul complaining after this answer from the Lord. Instead we see a resolve in the rest of verses 9 and 10.

Jesus has made it clear that this "thorn" is part of His will for Paul's life. Therefore it gives Paul the faith, confidence, and acceptance-born freedom to glorify the Lord in it. "Therefore I take pleasure in infirmities, in reproaches, in necessities, in persecutions, in distresses for Christ's sake: for when I am weak, then am I strong" (vs. 10).

Can you think of a time in your life that you prayed for healing in a specific area and did not experience the Lord moving to answer that prayer? How did that make you feel? It can understandably feel, in our flesh, like the Lord has abandoned us.

We suffer because of the curse of sin on the world, and God chooses what to allow in our lives, though evil never originates from Him. He is always, only good.

Even if God does not remove a 'thorn' from our flesh, He will give us grace and strength to bear it. That grace is sufficient for us, and our weakness glorifies Him. We can take comfort knowing we are never walking through our trials alone when we have put our faith and trust in Jesus.

Paul was given an ongoing opportunity to praise the Lord and lift up His name in a way where it is ONLY God who shines, not him.

I don't know what your own healing will look like, friend. But I know when you trust and believe in Jesus, you will have an almighty, tender-loving, forever friend to help bear those burdens for you. He has good thoughts toward you and promises to use it for good in your life somehow.

Healing Wounds

I THINK THE HEALED WOUND on this pine tree is absolutely beautiful. The bark layers are well defined, radiating outward from the center.

When a tree is wounded, new tissues are exposed which attract insects hoping to feed on them (Purdue University, Tree Wounds and Healing, 2024). Fungal spores can enter and decompose the wood, and the tree is more susceptible to pathogens and disease.

The wound weakens the tree. Therefore the tree will try to repair itself by regenerating tissue to close the wound. Callus tissue forms at the edges of a wound to reconnect vascular tissues across the exposed area (Karunarathne, Sachinthani I., et al., 2024).

If it is a large wound that takes a while to heal, then woundwood can form because the callus tissue has lignified into wood. Woundwood looks like a bulged woody area around the wound. The formation of woundwood is a defense mechanism of the tree. It seals and compartmentalizes the wounded area.

The Joy We Don't Expect

Unhealthy trees struggle to close wounds because they lack sufficient resources or energy to heal. It is similar to when our flesh and spirit are warring inside us. If we only feed our flesh, our relationship with the Holy Spirit weakens; we then struggle to heal when we encounter hardships in life. If our faith is strong, and our relationship with the Holy Spirit is fully fed on God's word, then those hardships affect us in a gentler way.

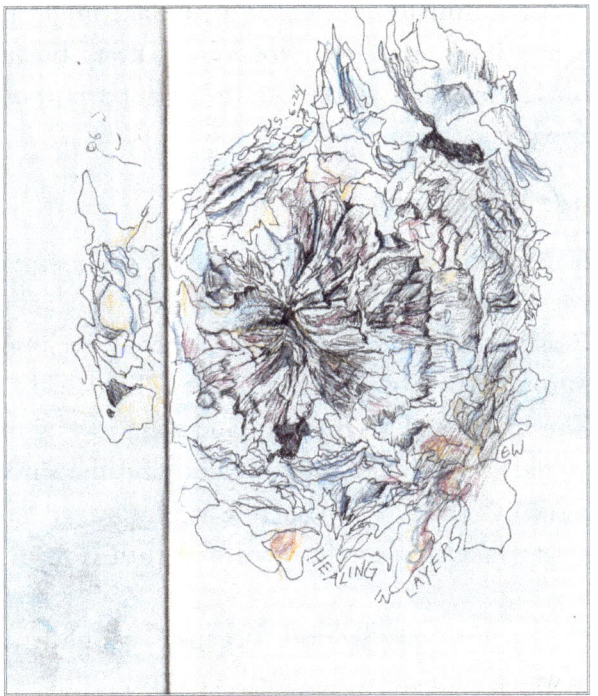

Since the healing of tree wounds is an active process, the tree continues to grow in diameter and may 'push' the wound inside the bark and sapwood (Tree Care Industry, 2024). Woundwood then shows up in cross sections as a dark area of wood, sometimes surrounding a scar-like mark.

Are you clinging to your old pain, even though you don't want to? Are you purposefully harboring unpleasant memories to atone for past sin? Why is it so important for you to remember? Instead of pushing your own heart wounds inside you, take them to God for healing.

Even God Himself does not look at us and see our sin. When we are saved God says our transgressions are blotted out (Isa. 44:22). Let us move past any sin and regrets we have in our past and live life in the freedom of Christ; in the gift of grace.

I pray that God's goodness and faithfulness would completely eclipse your trials. Initially, every breath you take might just feel like one the enemy didn't steal from you. Then, every breath you take becomes inhaled love and grace. God has a good purpose and plan for you. Keep going.

Laying Aside What Hinders Healing

We discussed in a previous chapter how God does not ask us to heal ourselves before He will help us. However, there are times when God might ask us to take an active role in our healing. I remember being surprised by how much it seemed that I had to do. I had expected Him to do it all for me, but God was growing me.

We are told to "lay aside every weight, and the sin which doth so easily beset us" (Heb. 12:1). When we know we struggle with something, let's take that to the Lord and turn from it so we can heal properly.

I kept re-opening my wounds because I wouldn't change my actions in a way that pleased the Lord. God is binding up our heart wounds but we can actually hinder the process. It is as if He is sewing sutures to close up the wound and we are taking a seam-ripper to them.

Why would we sabotage our own healing? How many times will we return to bondage? We can be so self-destructive when left to our own devices.

Sometimes God might choose to allow a wound to reopen to reveal that it has not healed properly. It is His way of making sure we don't seal the wound with rot inside. Then we realize how greatly we still struggle with a particular weak spot.

The Joy We Don't Expect

God can use our struggles for His glory, and work good through it. He is a greater and more powerful physician than we can fathom.

Chestnut Tree

THIS MEMORABLE TREE sits in my parents' yard near their trampoline. It bears cone-like clusters of white blossoms. These large flower stalks are a grand sight when they fill the tree and I admired them whenever I bounced on the trampoline next to it.

In Summer, however, came the fruit. Those large, barbed nut capsules were like little unchained flail balls. I would run outside barefoot, full speed, and remember too late that the chestnut tree had dropped its fruit. Then I would skid to a halt, hopping around to pry the prickly balls from my flesh.

In the Bible we read about this concept of a 'stumblingblock.' Leviticus 19:14 warns not to put a stumblingblock before the blind – for the obvious reason that they would trip and fall over it. It poses a physical danger, as well as a spiritual danger. Spiritually, a stumblingblock is anything that causes our faith to falter, or hinders our walk with the Lord.

Romans 14:13 says, "…that no man put a stumblingblock or an occasion to fall in his brother's way." If an action of ours causes a sister or brother in Christ to stumble, it is an offense against the Lord. Yes, everyone must answer for their own sin and choices, but purposefully doing something to 'injure' someone's faith, cause them to stumble spiritually, or tempt them toward a sin – that is very serious to the Lord. It would be like tossing a handful of those barbed balls at their feet.

Perhaps we realize later, as the Holy Spirit convicts us, that something we did or said became a stumblingblock for someone. Let's pray and seek opportunities to mend that. Instead of tripping each other, we are called to build each other up spiritually and encourage one other to walk uprightly.

Ezekiel 14:1-5 warns us not to put our own stumblingblock in front of our face – in other words, we should not set our temptations before us because it would invite sin. Oh, if we could spot those stumblingblocks, remove them from the path and toss them away!

Can you think of a time when you seemed to be healing from something, only to find a stumblingblock in your way? May we be *for* our own healing, avoid stumblingblocks, and support the healing of others as well.

Ready to Move Forward

Getting to the point where we are ready to ask for and accept help is a great start to healing. Oh the things we would never have learned if God hadn't brought us to a place where we were ready to hear them! Thank You, God!

Satan will try to keep us stuck in our own ways. He will make it seem like those ways are always about to give us everything we want. We might end up thinking something like, 'it was almost right that time, next time will be better.' But if those are our own plans and ways, they consistently fall short of the lasting fulfillment God offers.

The beauty of letting go is that it can happen over time. I never thought I'd get there. God chose my healing in His particular way for His glory and my good. God allowed a series of uncomfortable things to eventually help me let go. The injustice that felt so personal, the pain I couldn't let go of, memories on repeat…God worked with me over and over until I let go. It happened over years. Sometimes I still struggle. But God is always good and never leaves us.

If we are capable of doing so, and if part of the suffering is a result of our own choices, He may ask us to take steps toward Him first. Then He blesses those steps. It is His way of asking us whether we trust Him, and whether we are willing to do it a better way…His way.

We come to God finally ready to heal and accept the process in its entirety. We are ready to surrender our soul to the Physician and see Him work! We might be surprised to find God has been healing us already.

There may be times where you are physically or emotionally incapable of taking any steps yourself. Pray and speak up. We do not need to endure alone. Do not hide your suffering when you are in great need. There is always hope.

I encourage you to seek counseling if it is right for you. It can be extremely helpful to find a trained and trusted individual to enter into your predicament and walk with you. I have been in counseling and found it very helpful for a season. If you need help, turn to the Lord and also ask Him to direct your steps in any additional tools and services to aid you on the journey.

You are not a failure if you need extra help. It does not make you a 'bad Christian.'

Recognizing Growth

"But grow in grace, and in the knowledge of our Lord and Saviour Jesus Christ. To him be glory both now and for ever. Amen." (2 Pet. 3:18)

"...but be ye transformed by the renewing of your mind, that ye may prove what is that good, and acceptable, and perfect, will of God." (Rom. 12:2)

Trees know about stillness. No one sits down to watch a tree grow. It's an impractical way to measure growth. Trees grow slowly, by human standards. For trees, youth includes an age of one hundred years! It is when you come back to the tree later that you can see the growth. That's when you see it's been growing all along. You see it in the change.

During this season it was hard to focus on anything besides how far I had to go, how much I did not like the process, and did not like who I was.

God carried me. He planted me down in new soil, watered me, shined His light in me, and my roots began to grow in His love again. I began to understand who He is and how loved I am. You too are so dearly loved by God.

I used to think I understood exactly what my own healing would look like. Of course it must mean that the things which used to hurt wouldn't affect me anymore. It meant that my heart would be strong. I'd be emotionally, spiritually, and physically fit, living on my metaphoric mountain top. I'd be brave.

I don't think it's that simple anymore. It is not one mountain, but a mountain range. It is not a single patch, but layers. It means you can occasionally reflect on a painful experience or season without entering into it. Without feeling like you are still there. Without reliving it.

Healing means you don't dwell on the trial itself anymore, but God's goodness in it. Your memory of His faithfulness and how He brought you through it all becomes much bigger than the details of your pain and trauma.

Healing can look like finally making the choices you need to make instead of the same ones that kept you stuck. There were actual times when I had to walk in a different direction than the one I was tempted to walk, and God was there leading me. It might look like not chasing after. Not pursuing. Staying with God instead.

He has taught me about His grace and drawn me into a closer walk with Him. He has proven Himself faithful over and over. He grows us as He heals us.

When we are firmly rooted we are dwelling richly in the love and presence of the Lord with all His help, strength, and sustenance. But firm rooting needs maintenance. We must remember to assess those roots often and pray for God to keep us grounded in Him.

Measuring Progress

Deciduous trees prepare to emerge from dormancy after they have measured the duration of daylight, and the temperature and its longevity. Now it is warmer and their waiting ends. God calls them forward and they resume growing.

Remember, the waiting for trees is active. There are still metabolic processes happening within the tree during Winter. The waiting for us is active too. God has still been growing us there.

One section of verses that God keeps bringing me back to is Philippians 3:13-14. Whenever I start to spiral back into memories of things I did or said in the season that launched this tree-drawing adventure, or am flooded with memories of what others did or said to me, God reminds me of those verses. I see redemption in them.

May we forget what is behind and reach for what is ahead, pressing toward the mark "for the prize of the high calling of God in Christ Jesus" (vs. 14). When your past or heart grapples for your attention, set your eyes on the Lord and seek His kingdom.

Don't try and measure your progress too early; you'll get discouraged if you only see the ways you aren't yet where you want to be.

Trust that God is doing a good work and will continue to keep your soul as you endure.

I kept wondering why God was allowing certain things to remain in my heart when I believed He could so easily remedy them. Psalm 30 ends with this redemption for mourning, "To the end that my glory may sing praise to thee, and not be silent" (vs. 12). I would not be writing this book for His glory if He had spared me all the heartache this season brought.

In our trials He has given us a song to sing, a reason to praise and glorify Him, and teaches us to be thankful through all He does and allows. Only with His help.

Make a list of the ways you struggle in this present season, or a previous one. Pray over the list as you go. Try to be specific. As you grow and heal over time, go back to each item on that list and check to see where you are now. Write in any positive changes you see next to the old list items.

I did that for myself and was thankful for each reminder of the progress God was making in my heart, even small ways that things had changed for the better.

A Blade of Grass

One blade of grass growing upward has an extremely limited view. It is looking skyward at one small circle of blue in the distance. Green walls surround it. When it is grown it can see the whole sky. And the sky is much bigger.

I may have been looking at God in this season but I had a very narrow focus on what He was and wasn't doing in one area of my life. I wrestled with God's answer to my prayer so often over the past few years. With His guidance and help He liberates our minds to think beyond ourselves and what we are going through. There are so many other blades of grass and God is so big.

There is so much more to life and living as His children than what we are going through today. Give it to Him.

The Joy We Don't Expect

Cedar Tree

I STILL REMEMBER WALKING toward this tree from a great distance. It towers over the valley, dominating the basin where it stands; solemn, massive, and regal.

My dad, walking next to me, exclaimed how it would be a great one to draw. I thought to myself, 'It's much too healthy looking. There's nothing wrong with it.' It was too unlike all my other trees. But as we approached I admired the shape of it and agreed that I would probably draw it. Eventually.

Here's the thing: I'm still tempted to dwell on the story. The chaos and brokenness. The wound. The pain. Somehow holding onto pain keeps us safely tethered to the thing we don't want to let go. The decaying, lopsided, gnarly and broken trees will always be of great interest to me. There's a difference though, between dwelling on the pain, and sharing the testimony of God's work.

There was something wonderful about the idea of drawing a healthy, powerful tree. At least one.

The reason redemption and healing seem so connected is because they are. We have been restored to a right relationship with God, our sins have been forgiven, and we wear the righteousness of Christ. Restoration, redemption, salvation, and healing are all woven together. There is so much mercy in redemption!

All the Greens

THIS TREE LOOKS LIKE SOMEONE HIT PAUSE on a pivotal moment; the right side falls through the air indefinitely while its adversary stands with fists still raised. It reminds me of the moment when it is all happening to us, and we know we are in the middle of something significant.

The Joy We Don't Expect

Sometimes we hit pause on the fall because we don't want to go through the process of landing and getting back up.

It is occasionally necessary to return to a specific event or lie from our past that never ended for us. We hit pause and walked away from it, leaving it unresolved. In chapter one we discussed letting go of the need to finish something. This is different. Some things need to be confronted in order to heal properly.

In 2 Kings 6:3-7, the prophet Elisha and his company go to fell some trees by the water in order to build a larger dwelling place. As they are cutting, one of the borrowed axheads falls into the water and sinks. Elisha instructs the man to identify where it fell, and lifts it out of the water.

My uncle once compared this scripture to a past event we may need to revisit to identify the root cause of an issue. If you can identify where an issue began, you can understand and address it properly.

What axe heads are still in the water of your life? Is something unresolved in your past, affecting your present? Did you bury something that didn't stay dead? Pray for God to reveal where a tenacious struggle first began so you can remove it from the water and continue the good work He has for you.

If it still causes you pain, pray for God to allow you a healthy way to address it. When we try to heal by ourselves we may feel like we are perpetually falling; when we allow God to heal us and surrender to His process for it, we land safely in His hands.

A New Perspective

It is an exquisite blessing to look back at the valley you walked through from the hill on the other side.

Occasionally God allows me to reflect on moments or encounters that affected me greatly during the season of rending in my heart. When similar moments happen now He is reminding me how far He has brought me since then. Because of the difference. In this way He has allowed me to experience a moment being rewritten in time.

Maybe He chooses to reveal just enough that you can thank Him for doing it His way…enough to thank Him for His 'no' along with His 'yes.'

What if, in those moments where we wrestle with regret, confusion, or intense sadness, we could listen to the Holy Spirit's encouragement that God is going to work this out for good someday, somehow, in His great plan. We just can't see it yet.

Remember His blessings are everywhere. "I had fainted, unless I had believed to see the goodness of the Lord in the land of the living" (Psalm 27:13).

Sycamore Row in Spring

I SAT ON A HILL DRAWING THIS VIEW of the park, absolutely stunned by all the flowers in bloom. Watching everything come to life in Spring reminds me how God opens His hand and satisfies "the desire of every living thing" (Psalm 145:16). It is a season of seeing

His goodness and fruit after persevering through the cold, frozen ice of Winter.

Sometimes God allows us to see the landscape as a whole, from up high, to show us what He did. We couldn't see it when we were in it because He wanted our eyes on Him alone. God can change our vantage point, and thereby breathe new understanding into our circumstances. He shows us the good He was doing while we were busy wondering 'why,' or 'why not.' What a gift and encouragement to keep going.

This view from the hill top is similar to how God sees everything. From above, in its entirety. He sees this vast picture, yet He is intimately invested in every detail. His understanding is infinite (Psalm 147:5) and the wondrous works that He has done cannot be numbered (Psalm 40:5).

He Deals with Us Bountifully

We should love God for who He is, but we often love Him when He does what we want. In His great goodness and wisdom He knows this about us, and desires to bless us and show us His goodness. It should not puff us up to know that God desires to be good to us, but rather inspire the praise and worship of a good Father who chooses to bless us.

When our mind is renewed and we return to a right understanding of the Lord (and ourselves), we remember how good God has been to us. Only God can offer the perfect, selfless love that doesn't condemn (John 3:17), but loves in spite of (Rom. 5:8).

God brings us through some very difficult things. At the beginning of this season I just wanted to die and be in Heaven. Now I am thankful He allowed me to live and feel incredibly thankful for all He did in my life and heart. "I shall not die, but live, and declare the works of the Lord" (Psalm 118:17).

In this season of my life I had a reason to run straight into God's arms every hour of the day. What an intimate way of experiencing His very core – who He is and His great love – in how He heals us.

The journey we don't expect can lead to the joy we don't expect, because God is good and faithful.

> *A tree that is firmly rooted is difficult to yank out of the ground. Even as we endure hardship, our tree may recover and its wounds heal when we are rooted with the Lord. When we are rooted in His love we are grounded in grace, mercy and forgiveness.*

Leaving a Legacy

Walking with God

> *"In all things shewing thyself a pattern of good works: in doctrine shewing uncorruptness, gravity, sincerity, Sound speech, that cannot be condemned; that he that is of the contrary part may be ashamed, having no evil thing to say of you."* (Tit. 2:7-8)

> *"…be diligent that ye may be found of him in peace, without spot, and blameless"* (2 Pet. 3:14)

When we go to a funeral it can be moving to hear how the recently deceased is remembered. Whether we knew the person well or not, we hear a testimony of the life they lived from the people they mattered to.

What will our loved ones say about us when we are gone? What will they remember, for a time?

Within a tree, the part called "heartwood" is dead, inner wood that provides structure to the tree. Heartwood does not decay while the outer layers are intact (USDA, Anatomy of a Tree, 2024). Similarly, our memory is alive for a time if we are 'survived' by the ones we leave behind.

When our faith is strong in each area of life, like those outer layers, our heart is well protected to leave a legacy of walking with God. If you're reading this, you are still here. What is God asking you to do while you are here? To love, to keep His commandments, to be ambassadors for His kingdom, to give Him glory...Are you doing that?

Jesus endured the cross and sat down at the right hand of the throne of God (Heb. 12:2). As we mentioned in the chapter on obedience, He did it with joy because He knew the reconciliation and salvation that would come because of His sacrifice. May we too endure suffering with joy, if it is His will, knowing the eternal reward of our endurance waits in Heaven with God.

Looking Back

At the end, will you define your life by its challenges, or by how God was faithful in them? What a reason to rejoice if, through the testimony of our faithful suffering in God's will, someone may be inspired to grow in their faith, or come to trust Jesus!

Leaving a legacy of Christ-like character begins with living it out in truth now through the power of the Holy Spirit. May the Holy Spirit direct each one of us to find contentment in doing this life with Jesus in our heart and glorify Him all the while!

If you look back at your life, you might find things you would change or do differently. All of those events and choices brought you to where you are today. Can you learn to find joy where you are today? All things work together for good, in God's mercy and sovereign plan.

A Living Wake

Several years ago now we had a living wake for a beloved member of our church who was dying. I did not know him well but I had spoken to him a few times. His legacy spoke volumes. Those around him stood and gave accounts of his life and how it impacted them. He got to hear them.

We knew that the man was dying, but God still loved him and had a plan for him right then in that room. He had a plan for everyone in that room to hear what was said. Being surrounded by sorrow and kindness was moving. Hearing those stories made me want to be a better person.

Knowing Jesus makes me want to be a better person too. His Holy Spirit is in us, inspiring us to do His good work and love others. The world is watching us. Let us live and love as His ambassadors here on earth. We never know how we might be used in someone's life.

We sang a song based on Psalm 23 and I cried in a room full of strangers and some friends. That psalm is often read at funerals, but it gives such hope in life as well. We learn that God is with us, leading us and taking care of us all our life. And we will be with Him in the green pastures of Heaven as well. "Surely goodness and mercy shall follow me all the days of my life: and I will dwell in the house of the Lord for ever" (Psalm 23:6).

Praise Him Continually

Even if all I leave behind are temporary echoes of the life I lived, I pray those echoes are praising God.

Will we still be found praising God when we are full of days? Worship is not reserved for the young and energetic. God calls all the earth to worship and sing to Him (Psalm 66:4). That means whatever age you are, in whatever season you are in, you are directed to praise Him.

At the end of our life our faith should not be waning, our praise growing weak and tired. "But I will hope continually, and will yet praise thee more and more" (Psalm 71:14). As the days and years go by we are to increase our praise for the Lord. We see more of His goodness as He continues His work in our heart (vs. 17). We have more to sing about.

It is impossible to know how many days we have left (Psalm 71:15). May we be found faithful and obedient when the Lord returns! Our age does not diminish our value to God. Nor does our quantity of life dilute the power of Jesus' blood for our salvation. Our abilities change as we grow but they were never the thing to boast in. It is God at work in us to accomplish anything He helps us do.

Perhaps you're reading this thinking, 'My time has passed.' 'I just don't have the energy anymore.' 'I'm stuck right here, what can I do?' You can work on your relationship with God and seek His face. You can bask in His love for you. You can choose to praise Him "more and more." You can show His love to anyone you meet, and tell them about your Savior Jesus. You can pray for others in need.

We are God's children regardless of our physical age. Aged men and women are still part of the body of Christ. You still have a purpose. You matter.

Retired Organ

THIS TREE LOOKS LIKE AN OLD ORGAN with branches for pipes. It is not a tender sapling but a gigantic elder. It sings for the Lord because He made it. As an 'organ,' maybe it plays no longer, having retired years ago.

As children of the living God we do not retire from singing the songs of His goodness. He gave them to us to sing. Just as our prayers should not cease, neither should our praise!

The limbs that would have angled outward above the recesses were cut like severed pipes. All you see is the beginning of the song they stopped singing. What song are you singing now in your life? Who are you singing to?

There are a few elderly women at our church and I just love hearing them praise the Lord. I witness them praising God, singing through pain, emotional turmoil, overwhelming circumstances, and great upheaval in seasons I have yet to encounter. The older you get, the more God has walked you through, and the more pipes you have to carry your song.

What song will you hand to the next generation? We draw in the breath He gives us and send it up through our pipes to make melody for Him. Don't retire your faith; turn it into an organ of praise for the Lord.

Growing Up

> "But speaking the truth in love, may grow up into him in all things, which is the head, even Christ." (Eph. 4:15)

We cannot understand the design and map for how a child grows in a mother's womb. The way the bones come together is a mystery (Ecc. 11:5). He fashions us in our mother's womb and has a plan for us even before we are born (Psalm 139). He made our souls and put them in these bodies.

Who we are seems first rooted in our home life and environment. It is forever a part of our story. As we move out from under our parents, we transition from one faith environment to another.

Even trees undergo multiple tenants. Animals, insects, and fungi end up working together to make spaces that become homes within the same tree. Woodpeckers can open holes in trees that get widened after fungi moves in to further decay the wood in that opening

(Wohlleben 126). Eventually larger animals may move in and make it their own.

Whatever faith environment you stepped into or out of, you have your own choice to make and you will answer for it. It is necessary for our faith to become our own; we must actively choose the Lord while He draws us.

Our parents cannot save us (try as they might). Each of us must make our own choice to trust the Lord and believe in His death, burial, and resurrection. Our faith becomes real or it falls apart. Which is true for you?

In 1 Peter 2:2, the word of God is equated to life-giving milk for a newborn baby. It is all we want as new believers, and it contains everything we need to grow and thrive.

When we are spiritually young in the faith, Ephesians 4:14 warns us that we can be "tossed to and fro" by all the different lies and deceit in life. When our faith matures we become firmly rooted in the truth. We "grow up into him in all things" (Eph. 4:15).

Maturing spiritually means we become more skilled in the word of righteousness (Heb. 5:13). We move beyond milk and thrive also on meat, having honed discernment by studying the word. "But strong meat belongeth to them that are of full age, even those who by reason of use have their senses exercised to discern both good and evil" (Heb. 5:14).

Feed your soul the truth of God's word and you will grow strong in your faith.

The Next Generation

I once watched a mom in church holding her baby. He was so new and small in her arms. Babies are easy to love because no one has any idea who or what they will grow to be. "Can a woman forget her sucking child, that she should not have compassion on the son of her womb? yea, they may forget, yet will I not forget thee" (Isa: 49:15). Only God knows our complete story and only God can love us for the entirety of it.

The Old Testament records a seemingly endless cycle of righteous kings and evil kings for Judah. One king would do so much good in his reign, tearing down false idols, and altars to other gods. The next generation raised them up again.

It seems disheartening, but God still used those righteous kings to do His good work in their generation. When a leader follows God, it is a powerful testimony for the Lord.

"One generation shall praise thy works to another, and shall declare thy mighty acts" (Psalm 145:4). You are a voice for your own generation, and that voice matters for the next. Those unrighteous kings led many of their people astray. The righteous kings set an example of godly obedience and reverence. However, even good works fall short unless there is true faith behind them.

May we praise the Lord and serve Him faithfully with His help. In 2 Timothy 1:5, Paul mentions two generations of godly women who helped shape Timothy's faith. His "unfeigned faith" began with his grandmother and mother. Our faith too can help shape the next generation.

If we are spiritually mature, let us encourage, exhort, and teach the next generation of believers. Let's live our faith in truth. If we are new believers, may we subject ourselves to the godly teaching and sound counsel of those more mature believers than ourselves, while always turning to the word of God as ultimate truth.

In this finite life, we have the incredible chance to share the story of God's goodness with other generations, whether they be our kids, neighbors, or others. "Come and hear, all ye that fear God, and I will declare what he hath done for my soul" (Psa. 66:16). God's truth, and your testimony of His work in you are two gifts you can praise Him for and give to others.

Adulthood

RECENTLY MY TODDLER TOLD ME that she wanted to be a grown-up. I had a million thoughts about that. Right now she plays and learns. How could I explain to her the complexity of being an adult? All the worrying, caring, loving…she couldn't yet understand the weight of responsibility over so many things.

Right now her job is to ask questions, and my job is to answer if I can. God's word is there to help me. It reminds us *both* of truth. She reminds me to have child-like faith in the word of God, trusting and believing my Heavenly Father.

A tree grows from a seed to a seedling that then becomes a sapling. The sapling resembles a smaller version of the parent tree (Kalman 12). We, however, are not identical to our parents. They have a shaping influence over us, but God has unique and individual plans for each of us. This is true even of siblings who grow up in the same household but have different experiences.

LEAVING A LEGACY

God has good work for us to do in each season of our lives. We are always being born, growing old, and dying (sometimes before we grow old). Even trees eventually stop growing vertically as it becomes more difficult to direct water and nutrients to the uppermost branches. The exertion is too much for the tree (Wohlleben 65).

We might stop growing physically too, but we are forever learning and growing on the inside as the Lord works on us.

Backyard Looking In

I'VE GROWN FOND OF THIS PARTICULAR VIEW of my house, looking in from the backyard.

Looking in at my home from the outside is sobering. Lord, show me how to stay. What do I want our life to look like? What does *God* want it to look like? How can we pray to better serve our families? How can we model the love and grace of Jesus to them?

"…but as for me and my house, we will serve the Lord" (Jos. 24:15). We cannot effectively raise children for Christ if we don't put in the work to teach them the details. We must give them scripture and love in truth, each day. Even if you are not a parent, your example of faith will speak to the generations around you and the people God puts in your path.

Sometimes I think about the houses around me and the people living in them. They are all around us, out of sight. Doing life within their walls and occasionally outside them. What are they going through right now? When I drive by those houses at night and see a light on, I wonder if they are, at the end of their day, in a quiet place where they feel warm and loved.

God's love is not bound by the walls we do life in. It bleeds into all the backyards across the world.

Looking at Eternity

> *"And this is life eternal, that they might know thee the only true God, and Jesus Christ, whom thou hast sent." (John 17:3)*

> *"Who will render to every man according to his deeds: To them who by patient continuance in well doing seek for glory and honour and immortality, eternal life." (Rom. 2:6-7)*

Death is everywhere; it is anytime. For believers we spend eternity in glory with the Lord. When His breath leaves us our bodies become dust again (Gen. 3:19) but our soul goes Home to Heaven. It is a joy to go Home.

But He has a good plan for us while we are here.

What are we doing with the time He gives us? "For we must all appear before the judgment seat of Christ; that every one may receive the things done in his body, according to that he hath done, whether it be good or bad" (2 Cor. 5:10).

Someday we as believers will celebrate and partake of His glory for what we did in this life through His Spirit. He sees it all and He will reward our labor for His name and kingdom.

Furthermore, God knows us by name as believers. Our names are written in His book of life (Phil. 4:3, Rev. 3:5)! Those that don't believe will not be able to enter the gates of Heaven. If they should come questioning why they cannot enter in, the Bible says that Jesus will say the chilling words, "I know you not...depart from me..."

Revelation 20:15 says that anyone whose name is not in the book of life will be cast into hell fire. However, those that have accepted Him into their hearts through true belief by faith, of them Jesus says, "I will not blot out his name out of the book of life, but I will confess his name before my Father" (Rev. 3:5). Jesus will commend us to God, and absolve us of any sin judgement because we are covered by His blood and counted righteous.

We are warned not to entangle ourselves with the affairs of this world (2 Tim. 2:4). If we become too invested in the world we will forget who we are as Christians, and why we are here. It will be difficult to follow the Lord if we get tangled up in every net of the world along the way. May we stay mission-minded for the cause of Christ, as pilgrims here, forsaking any lust that wars against our soul (1 Pet. 2:11).

When the world walks away from the Lord, and if even those close to us walk away from the Lord, may we stay with God, knowing He holds the words of eternal life. "Then Simon Peter answered him, Lord, to whom shall we go? thou hast the words of eternal life" (John 6:68). No one else can save your soul.

Jesus has gone to prepare a place for us. "And if I go and prepare a place for you, I will come again, and receive you unto myself; that where I am, there ye may be also" (John 14:3). What a beautiful promise! Heaven is the best Home and Jesus is the way to get there (vs. 6).

Jesus is returning. May we be found faithful when He returns.

The Graves Opened

When Jesus died, one of the supernatural events listed in Matthew 27 is the dead rising from their graves and walking among the living.

Verses 52 and 53 say the bodies of the saints which slept arose and went into the holy city, being seen by many people.

Can you imagine seeing this with your own eyes? It would be evident that something otherworldly just happened. That wasn't just any old person they crucified. Verse 54 says the Centurion and those with him knew Jesus was the Son of God because of those events.

It also functions as a foretelling of His coming resurrection. With the dead rising from the grave, God was proving that His Son Jesus had abolished death. That while a body may die and be buried, the soul of a believer enters Heaven with everlasting life. He was claiming His power over life and death, and the salvation of souls.

When the women sought Jesus at His tomb, they were asked, "Why seek ye the living among the dead?" (Luke 24:5). Jesus is risen and our hope is alive in Him.

Jesus gave His life and chose the moment of His death. Matthew 27:50 speaks of Jesus taking an action, dying with intention. Jesus "yielded up the ghost." No one could take His life without His permission. No one had power over Him. He chose to surrender His life so we might live.

Cemetery Tree

GOING TO THE CEMETERY is such an odd experience. It does not feel natural to walk amongst tombs. This tree was wriggling up between the tombstones. As believers we are like the living walking among the dead – those who have not yet accepted Jesus.

When you walk among the graves you have the peculiar, prickling sensation of company. The bones of someone who used to be alive are decomposing beneath your feet. Empty, hallow bones. A broken vessel now; no Spirit to inhabit it. Someday, you'll join them.

Wherever our body may lay in death, a soul that believes will be in Heaven with our Savior. You will wake up in His presence and see His face!

Leaving a Legacy

Being reminded of death teaches us so much of life. "It is better to go to the house of mourning, than to go to the house of feasting: for that is the end of all men; and the living will lay it to his heart" (Ecc. 7:2). At funerals we remember the end of all things and why we are here. We become thankful we still have breath in our lungs to praise the Lord. We are reminded to be about His work, doing His will and serving Him on this side of Heaven.

Funerals are a reminder that when the world is looking down at graves, we are looking skyward to the Lord, finding hope amidst the sorrow of death. The tomb He rose from is also the grave He calls us out of.

Paul knew there was a crown of righteousness waiting for him in Heaven (2 Tim. 4:6-8), and all who love the Lord shall have one too.

We too can take Revelation 3:11 to heart that our crown is in Heaven, and we should hold fast to the Lord and His commands. May we go about the work of the Lord, knowing we are not laboring in vain. May our faith not merely be for white-washed appearances of tombs which disguise dead bones, like that of the Pharisees (Matt. 23:27), but alive and true.

Did You Leave Something Behind?

We are driven to discover our purpose, and then leave something meaningful behind to remember us. We don't want to be forgotten. The purpose we are searching for is not found within us but within Christ and the works He will do through us. "For we are his workmanship, created in Christ Jesus unto good works," (Eph. 2:10).

What does a life-well lived look like? Is it enough to impact a single person? Is it enough to love like Christ, to encourage unseen, to serve faithfully without witness? God is our witness (Job 16:19). Must there be a record of us here somewhere, to know we mattered? We have a record right now in Heaven.

Is it okay to be forgotten? Knowing we still lived and loved for the Lord, that He saw all of it, and that He is pleased? Consider again; what are you working toward? "For what shall it profit a man, if he shall gain the whole world, and lose his own soul?" (Mark 8:36).

What Remains

HAVE YOU EVER WATCHED A CHILD spend time building a tower, only to topple it over seconds after it is finished? This tree seems to be a reminder that we are in the middle; leaning toward death, and clinging to life. "For whether we live, we live unto the Lord; and whether we die, we die unto the Lord:" (Rom. 14:8).

We adults build and keep, preserve and savor. Maybe we can take a lesson not to hold on too dearly to the things we build. "For we brought nothing into this world, and it is certain we can carry nothing out" (1 Tim. 6:7).

What will remain behind us on this earth when we die? We can't take our success, our status, our popularity, 401(k) accounts, trophies or achievements with us when we die. It all gets left behind.

Leaving a Legacy

2 Peter 3:10-12 reminds us that the Lord is returning, and to have an eternal mindset. Are we prepared to meet our Savior face to face? What is it that really matters as we breathe the breaths He gives us on this side of Heaven? This earth will dissolve away, along with everything in it, but our choices now matter. "…what manner of persons ought ye to be" (2 Pet. 3:11)?

Titus 2:12-13 reminds us to live soberly and righteously in this life, with our eyes looking to Heaven for our ultimate hope, our Savior Jesus.

Leave a Message

THIS MAGNOLIA TREE WAS DELIGHTFUL to draw! All the meandering branches carried messages carved by others.

When you write your name on something it becomes a record that you 'were here.' You stood in that spot. You share that moment with whoever reads those words after you. But for those who come after you, your message will never hold the meaning it did for you when you wrote it.

They'll read those words without knowing who you are. Your heart and initials will tell them that someone was loved. Your life's mantra carved into bark will inspire thought for a moment, maybe. What could you say now, to impact the people you meet in person? What would you say to someone walking through the things you walked through in your life? What do you wish someone had told you?

If you write something unpleasant as the message you leave behind, then you're saying that unpleasant thing to everyone who comes to the tree, wall, or stall after you. "Let your speech be alway with grace, seasoned with salt, that ye may know how ye ought to answer every man" (Col. 4:6). "And be ye kind one to another, tenderhearted…" (Eph. 4:32).

Words are powerful and they tend to stay with us, whether we want them to or not. Every one of us has said words we wish we could take back. Each of us has heard words that wounded us. Let's speak compassionately, knowing even our words can show the love of Christ.

Here or There? Wheat or Tare?

Matthew 13:24-30 compares the kingdom of heaven to a field where good seed of wheat is sown. The enemy sneaks in to plant his own bad seed, or 'tares,' in with the good. "But when the blade was sprung up, and brought forth fruit, then appeared the tares also" (vs. 26).

The farmer's solution is to let the wheat and tares grow together until the day of harvest. The tares are those who reject Christ and never accept Him into their heart. At the end of their life, fire awaits them. The wheat are those who put their faith and trust in Jesus. They will be saved, and gathered into Heaven instead.

We all have a choice to make, whether to accept Christ or reject Him. At the time of harvest, we will be removed from the field and leave this earth. God is merciful to allow us to grow until that time. He is not willing that any should perish, but only true believers will be with Him in Heaven – those that walked with God and had a real relationship with Him.

Keep praying for the unsaved to accept the Lord. Live your faith as a witness to them.

Keep Speaking Truth

In John 9 we see Jesus miraculously heal a blind man. He suffered this blindness so the works of God could be manifested in Him. And Jesus healing him right then was that work of God on display. God may be building a testimony in you to shine Him to others, through what He is allowing you to experience now.

We follow the healed man's next moments as he undergoes an investigation of this miracle, and just who is responsible for it. It is a powerful testimony of God's power.

First, the healed man is questioned by his neighbors. Then the Pharisees. After that the man's parents are called in and questioned. It's still not enough. They continue to ask the young man what happened because this miracle confounds the Pharisees. Finally the man tells them that Jesus must be of God because there is no other way He would have the power to restore his sight.

The beauty of it is that his story doesn't change. When this man is questioned, he tells the truth every time, staying faithful in his account of how Jesus healed Him.

Keep telling the truth of the gospel. Jesus tells the apostles to "preach the gospel to every creature" (Mark 16:15). We too are called to share the hope and love of Christ to a broken world. Even if the world doesn't like the story, it is true and the Lord has called us to share it. God decides if and when others will hear and accept it.

No More Years

When my daughter was three, she asked me one day, "What will happen when I have no more years left?"

My heart was moved with emotion at her words, but the Holy Spirit told me to tell her the truth. I said, "Then God will call you home with Him. You'll be in Heaven. But in order to go to Heaven with Him you have to believe in Jesus and accept Him as your Savior."

I wanted to force her to accept Him right then! To know her need for this Savior who died for her sins. I desperately want my precious baby girls to understand. But these are the conversations I pray we keep having…the questions I pray they keep asking.

What will happen when *you* have no more years left?

Let go of who you think you're supposed to be and what you think you're supposed to do and let God love through you, courageously, in whatever ways He chooses to use you. Keep running to

Him. Keep singing. Let's share the story of what He has done for us. You are so loved.

> *Stay rooted and grounded in God's great love! He decides how long we continue on this earth. He is the one growing us. Let us praise Him and continue to give Him the honor and glory He deserves (Psa. 145:5).*

THE END

Acknowledgments

Thank You, God, for being faithful during it all. You never left me, but surrounded me with love. You were gracious, merciful, and patient when I did not understand.

To my husband, Peter, for allowing me to pursue this passion. Although God has designed us differently, you have always tried to understand me. I'm grateful! Thank you for who you are in our lives, and for choosing to love me.

I am thankful for my two beautiful daughters, Jane and Aria, whose delight and curiosity in life is inspiring! You are both a great gift and answer to prayer. I'm so grateful to be your mama!

To my parents, Dan and Kerry, thank you so much for being there for me even when I had no idea how to let you be there for me. Love you both so much, and I am forever grateful to have been born into a family with such loving parents as you both. You have demonstrated God's love to me in countless ways.

Thanks to my sister, Becca, for giving me sound godly counsel and always being there for me. When I came to you overwhelmed you were there to bear the burden with me. You are a gift from the Lord for all the seasons we walk together!

Thank you to my in-laws, Mimi, Phil, Jen and Kate, for welcoming me and loving me as one of your own. Mimi, you are a constant source of encouragement and love in action. To my sisters-in-law: Jen Anderson, for helping me access research, and always encouraging me and others to learn and grow, and Kate Peck, for modeling love and acceptance.

I would like to thank my amazing test-readers and sisters in Christ, Lorie Pawley, Sara Pielaet, and Arlene Starke. Your time, review and encouragement in this process were such a blessing! I know God spoke to me through you many times and told me to keep going. I am thankful for your friendship and love.

Tabitha St.Denis, you pointed me to the Lord over and over, loving me and showing me grace through your listening ear and kind, God-seeking heart. More than a few of these trees reflect your love toward me in this season. I am thankful for you.

My grandparents, Marjorie, Randy, Ann and Fred, for sharing special moments of appreciating God's creation together. For tree walks, leaf-collecting, gardening, exploring, playing, and wondering together. Thank you for loving me.

Thank you to my dear friends who stayed by my side. Some of you I've known a long time, and others He brought me during this season specifically. I can't put into words how thankful I am for each of you, and how God used you in my life. I'm thankful God brought us together.

Jenn Mckee, thank you for walking with me for a time.

Thank you Tessa Emily Hall, for your valuable insight in the need to restructure and your encouragement in this project.

Thank you to Rachel Hall of Writely Divided Editing & More, for lending your knowledge and creative hand in the interior book layout design.

To all those who walked with me through this season, near or far, I am so thankful for your prayers, presence, heart, counsel, encouragement and kindness. May God bless you all your days.

WORKS CITED

Abreu, Kristine De. "Natural Wonders: When Trees Fuse and Flourish as One." *Explorersweb,* 19 Dec. 2023, https://explorersweb.com/trees-joined-to-each-other/. Accessed June 2024.

"Anatomy of a Tree." *U.S. Forest Service*, U.S. Department of Agriculture, https://www.fs.usda.gov/learn/trees/anatomy-of-tree#:~:text=E%3A%20Heartwood%20is%20the%20central,ways%20as%20strong%20as%20steel.

"Autumn Splendor: Why Do Leaves Change Color in the Fall?" *Smithsonian Science Education Center,* 8 Nov. 2017, https://ssec.si.edu/stemvisions-blog/autumn-splendor-why-do-leaves-change-color-fall.

"Banyan." *Britannica.* https://www.britannica.com/plant/banyan. Accessed 18 July 2024.

"Baobab." *Britannica.* 28 June 2024, https://www.britannica.com/plant/baobab-tree-genus.

Broschat, T.K. "Palm Morphology and Anatomy." *Ask IFAS - Powered by EDIS,* https://edis.ifas.ufl.edu/publication/EP473. Accessed 2024.

"Emerald Ash Borer (EAB)." Department of Environmental Conservation, New York State. https://dec.ny.gov/nature/animals-fish-plants/emerald-ash-borer-eab. Accessed 24 July 2024.

Evans, Julian. *God's Trees.* 1979. Second Edition, Biblica, 2018.

Franklin, Jerry F., et al. "Tree Death as an Ecological Process." *BioScience,* vol. 37, no. 8, 1987, pp. 550–56. JSTOR, https://doi.org/10.2307/1310665.

"Girdling Roots." *University of Maryland Extension*. https://extension.umd.edu/resource/girdling-roots. Accessed January 2024.

Kalman, Bobbie. *The Life Cycle of a Tree*. Crabtree Publishing Company, 2002.

Karunarathne, Sachinthani I., et al. "Trees Need Closure Too: Wound-Induced Secondary Vascular Tissue Regeneration." *Plant Science*, vol. 339, Feb. 2024, p. 111950. DOI.org (Crossref), https://doi.org/10.1016/j.plantsci.2023.111950.

Katz, Brigit. "Pando, One of the World's Largest Organisms, Is Dying." *Smithsonian Magazine*, https://www.smithsonianmag.com/smart-news/pano-one-worlds-largest-organisms-dying-180970579/. Accessed 18 July 2024.

Lanzara, Paola, et al. *Simon and Schuster's Guide to Trees: A Field Guide to Conifers, Palms, Broadleafs, Fruits, Flowering Trees, and Trees of Economic Importance*. Simon and Schuster, 1978.

Laskow, Sarah. "The Strange Magic of Forest Thaw Circles." *Atlas Obscura*, 3 Apr. 2018, http://www.atlasobscura.com/articles/why-does-snow-thaw-around-trees.

Luley, Christopher. "Diagnostics: Assessing Callus And Woundwood In Plant Health Care." *Tree Care Industry Magazine*, December 2018. http://digimag.tcia.org/publication/?i=547743&article_id=3254222&view=articleBrowser. Accessed January 2024.

Lüttge, Ulrich, and Brigitte Hertel. "Diurnal and Annual Rhythms in Trees." *Trees*, vol. 23, no. 4, Aug. 2009, pp. 683–700. *Springer Link*, https://doi.org/10.1007/s00468-009-0324-1.

"Making and Breaking Connections in the Brain." *UC Davis Center for Neuroscience*. 11 Sept. 2020, https://neuroscience.ucdavis.edu/news/making-and-breaking-connections-brain.

Merhaut, Donald J. "FOLLOW-UP: How Do Trees Carry Water from the Soil around Their Roots to the Leaves at the Top? Clearly, They Are Fighting Gravity--so How Do They Do It?" *Scientific American*, https://www.scientificamerican.com/article/follow-up-how-do-trees-ca/. Accessed 2024.

Works Cited

"Moss." *Britannica.* 5 July 2024, https://www.britannica.com/plant/moss-plant.

Nakada, Ryogo, and Eitaro Fukatsu. "Seasonal Variation of Heartwood Formation in Larix Kaempferi." *Tree Physiology*, vol. 32, no. 12, Nov. 2012, https://doi.org/10.1093/treephys/tps108.

NETN Species Spotlight - Paper Birch (U.S. National Park Service). https://www.nps.gov/articles/netn-species-spotlight-paper-birch.htm. Accessed February 2024.

Ortlund, Dane Calvin. *Gentle and Lowly: The Heart of Christ for Sinners and Sufferers.* Crossway, 2020.

Prendergast, Dan, and Erin Prendergast. *The Tree Doctor: A Guide to Tree Care and Maintenance.* 2nd edition, Updated and Expanded, Firefly Books Ltd, 2017.

"Rain Gauge." Wikipedia, April 2024. *Wikipedia,* https://en.wikipedia.org/w/index.php?title=Rain_gauge&oldid=1235340698.

Simard, S. *Finding the Mother Tree: Discovering the Wisdom of the Forest.* First edition, Alfred A. Knopf, 2021.

"The Survivor Tree." *Oklahoma City National Memorial & Museum,* https://memorialmuseum.com/experience/the-survivor-tree/. Accessed January 2024.

Tozer, A. W. "We Must Die If We Want to Live." *Impactus,* 31 Mar. 2021, https://www.impactus.org/daily-devotional/we-must-die-if-we-want-to-live/.

Tozer, A. W., and James L. Snyder. *Delighting in God.* Bethany House, a division of Baker Publishing Group, 2015.

"Tree Anatomy 101." *Natural Resource Stewardship,* Iowa State University Extension and Outreach. https://naturalresources.extension.iastate.edu/forestry/tree_biology/101.html. Accessed 2024.

"Tree Wounds and Healing." *Purdue Extension Forestry & Natural Resources,* 29 Sept. 2020, https://www.purdue.edu/fnr/extension/tree-wounds-and-healing/.

Tsioras, Petros A., et al. "The Impact of Body Posture on Heart Rate Strain during Tree Felling." *International Journal of Environmental Research and Public Health*, vol. 19, no. 18, Sept. 2022, p. 11198. PubMed, https://doi.org/10.3390/ijerph191811198.

"What Do Trees Do in the Winter?" *Purdue Extension Forestry & Natural Resources*, 4 Mar. 2021, https://www.purdue.edu/fnr/extension/what-do-trees-do-in-the-winter/.

Wohlleben, Peter. *The Hidden Life of Trees*. 2015. English Translation, Random House GmbH, 2016.

www.ingramcontent.com/pod-product-compliance
Lightning Source LLC
Chambersburg PA
CBHW070610030426
42337CB00020B/3740